D.2

P9-DCI-241

SACRED WORK

SACRED WORK

Planned Parenthood and
Its Clergy Alliances

TOM DAVIS

RUTGERS UNIVERSITY PRESS
NEW BRUNSWICK, NEW JERSEY, AND LONDON

Library of Congress Cataloging-in-Publication Data

Davis, Tom, 1934–
    Sacred work : Planned Parenthood and its clergy alliances / Tom Davis.
        p. cm.
    Includes bibliographical references and index.
    ISBN 0-8135-3493-3 (hardcover : alk. paper)
    1. Planned Parenthood Federation of America—History. 2. Clergy—United
States—Political activity. 3. Birth control—Religious aspects—Protestant churches.
4. Birth control—Religious aspects—Judaism. I. Title.
    HQ766.5.U5D38   2004
    261.8′36—dc22

                                                    2004008242

A British Cataloging-in-Publication record for this book is available from the
British Library

Excerpts from Martin Luther King's address to Planned Parenthood, 1966
reprinted by arrangement with the Estate of Martin Luther King Jr., c/o Writers
House as agent for the proprietor New York, NY. Copyright 1966, Dr. Martin
Luther King Jr., copyright renewed 1996 Coretta Scott King.

Copyright © 2005 by Tom Davis

All rights reserved

No part of this book may be reproduced or utilized in any form or by any means,
electronic or mechanical, or by any information storage and retrieval system,
without written permission from the publisher. Please contact Rutgers University
Press, 100 Joyce Kilmer Avenue, Piscataway, NJ 08854–8099. The only exception to
this prohibition is "fair use" as defined by U.S. copyright law.

Manufactured in the United States of America

FOR

The Reverend Betsy Davis

1928–2001

a woman of immeasurable courage and compassion
whose life was spent
securing for hundreds of women
both hope and faith

Contents

Foreword by the Reverend Carlton W. Veazey · ix

Acknowledgments · xiii

Introduction · 1

CHAPTER 1 The Concept of Sacred Work · 5

CHAPTER 2 Margaret Sanger Recruits the Clergy · 27

CHAPTER 3 Building Public Acceptance, 1935–1957 · 47

CHAPTER 4 The 1958 Battle over the New York City Hospitals · 72

CHAPTER 5 Sacred Work in Baltimore, 1961–1965 · 88

CHAPTER 6 Victories in the Sixties · 104

CHAPTER 7 Planned Parenthood and the Clergy Consultation Service on Abortion, 1967–1973 · 121

CHAPTER 8 The Post-*Roe* Era, 1973–1992 · 142

CHAPTER 9 Deadly Violence and the Renewal of
Clergy Support   170

CHAPTER 10 The Future of the Alliance   192

Timeline   205

Notes   211

Bibliography   229

Index   235

Foreword

In this remarkable story of faith in action, Tom Davis bears witness to one of the great social justice movements of our time: the struggle for reproductive rights. His is the unique perspective of a clergyperson who has been involved for many years with what some people think is the opposite of a religious institution, the Planned Parenthood Federation of America. Davis helps us understand why working for family planning and contraception, abortion services, and reproductive health care is sacred work, not opposed to biblical views of justice but fully consistent with the commandments to love God and to love one's neighbor as oneself. He helps us also to understand why we must stay strong against the rigid theologies that oppose women's reproductive rights and a host of related positions. As he writes, these theologies dry up the soul and close the door to the future.

Sacred work is specific work, involving real women and men, who are struggling to be faithful in the face of real dilemmas. This book is meaningful because it comes out of Tom Davis's complete immersion in the real world struggle, as a chaplain at Skidmore College in Saratoga Springs, New York, as an advocate who has countered repressive forces trying to close clinics and deny services, as chair of the Planned Parenthood Clergy Advisory Board, and as a member of the Religious Coalition for Reproductive Choice board of directors. His account of the involvement of Protestant ministers—including his late, beloved wife, the Reverend Betsy Davis—and Jewish rabbis in the Federation shatters the myth that clergy just don't care about the messy business of sexuality and pregnancy and babies. As he shows, many clergy have stood by women in need. Religious institutions, though at times reluctant and ambivalent, have been a force in the progress toward sexual and reproductive self-determination.

Sacred Work is important, and I urge all clergy and people of faith to read it. In this time of unprecedented and escalating attacks on reproductive rights, this book is more than a history. It is a guide to what clergy and people in the pews must do to keep reproductive rights safe and legal. Let us agree that we will never again return to the days when women came, crying, bleeding, fearing for their souls, to our congregational offices, asking, "What will I do? Where will I go? Will God hate me?"—and we had little to offer. This book also instructs us about the radical reversal in attitudes toward religious freedom and the separation of church and state, to the point where many Americans now believe that there should be a strong religious influence governing civic life, and that this influence should mirror their own faith tradition. We must also continue our struggle to secure freedom of conscience in the face of those who would impose their own religious beliefs on us all.

The battle for legal contraception and abortion services has not often been considered on par with other great modern struggles for justice such as the workers' rights and civil rights movements, yet there is good reason to consider it as such. In religious institutions, contraception and abortion have often been ignored or minimized as women's matters and not sufficiently important for serious consideration. Davis terms the refusal to consider women as full moral agents "religious sexism" and argues that the struggle for reproductive freedom is revolutionary because it has freed women and created new possibilities for human equality. It is for precisely those reasons that reproductive freedom has engendered such fierce opposition. Davis discusses the insistence of some religions, whether the Taliban, a fundamentalist megachurch, or a Jewish sect, on controlling women's lives because it is "traditional" to do so. The reality is that they fear their institutions would change drastically and male control would be greatly diminished if women were accorded real equality. That same fear of loss of power also explains why conservative religious leaders condemn Planned Parenthood, an organization that serves women in their most intimate needs.

There are many surprising anecdotes and insights in *Sacred Work*, because we know so little about the involvement of clergy in the struggle for reproductive rights, other than the Clergy Consultation Service on Abortion. The unusual "spiritual alliance" of Planned Parenthood, a secular humanist organization, and religious leaders has been effective in achieving respectability and acceptance for birth control and addressing religious and social barriers to women's access to full reproductive health care services, especially those put in place by the Roman Catholic hierarchy. Things did not always go smoothly, though. Some clergy were fearful. Some Planned Parenthood officials and affiliates were more interested in marketing and maintaining cordial relations than in fighting for social change and justice for women. But ultimately the alliance works, and we all are the better for it.

Davis's continuous involvement and leadership in the movement enables him to provide a rare historical perspective. Before legalizing abortion could even be considered, a long legacy of social attitudes had to be radically altered. Planned Parenthood itself had been primarily a provider of family planning and contraceptive services, and providing abortion services was a new undertaking for it. To understand what have come to be called the "abortion wars," it is important to remember that the roots of today's conflicts were present decades ago in Protestant/Catholic clashes over birth control for women. Davis recounts fascinating stories of clergy trying to work out these conflicts. His account of the 1958 battle over contraception in New York City public hospitals and the breakthrough made possible by Protestant and Jewish clergy belongs in general history books. One diabetic Protestant woman who needed birth control and was denied it by a publicly funded hospital made it clear how wrong it was—and is—to impose religious doctrine on a person who needs a medical device for health purposes and who has no religious objection to the device. Perhaps by remembering the long history of these divisions between Protestants and Catholics on contraception, we will gain some perspective on finding solutions to the abortion wars.

To the thousands of clergy who have served with Planned Parenthood affiliates throughout the country, Tom Davis has written a tribute. For those who have labored for social justice in other venues, this book is a reminder that we too have done the sacred work of securing hope and dignity for those who need it the most—and that our work is not done. As in the struggle for civil rights, we will not be moved until justice and equality for women are a reality.

The Reverend Carlton W. Veazey
President and CEO, Religious Coalition for Reproductive Choice

Acknowledgments

Caren Spruch and Rachel Strauber, of the Office of Special Projects of the Planned Parenthood Federation of America, are the two people most responsible for the development of the latest chapter in a creative relationship between Planned Parenthood and its supportive clergy. They are also the two people who have done the most to make this book possible. Tolerating the many vagaries and eccentricities of clergypeople and sifting through the maddening profusion of Protestant denominationalism, they provided the ideas, the hours, and the patience to forge a nationwide network of 1,600 clergy who admire and support this gallant, embattled organization. Without Spruch and Strauber there would not have been much to write about.

Other people within the world of Planned Parenthood also contributed invaluable support. Gloria Feldt, president of the Federation, supported the project with thoughtfulness and wry humor. Paul Drisgula of Hudson Mohawk Planned Parenthood and Carol Blowers and JoAnn Smith of the New York State Family Planning Advocates not only gave critical reading to key chapters but also shared freely their wide experience and extensive knowledge of the long struggle over reproductive freedom.

Francine Stein, vice-president of development at Planned Parenthood Federation offices in New York, was especially helpful in sharing her experience and knowledge of the struggle to bring legal abortion to New York State.

Thanks are also due to Bob Blomberg, director, Innovations Group, Planned Parenthood Federation, who made the Clergy Advisory Board a partner in the planning of the colloquium on new reproductive technologies,

"Beyond Abortion: Critical Bioethical Issues in Reproductive Health for the 21st Century" in Snowbird, Utah, in July 2003.

I am grateful to a number of Planned Parenthood CEOs who gave their support to this project and to clergy work in general: to John Nugent of the Maryland affiliate; Chris Charbonneau of Western Washington; Kay Scott of Georgia; Larry Rudick of Alabama; Mark Salo of San Diego; Dian Harrison of the Golden Gate affiliate; Vicki Cowart of the Rocky Mountains; Barry Raff of Hawaii; Jim Richardson of East Central Michigan; Paula Gianino of St. Louis; Phyllis Kinsler of Central New Jersey; Kathie Wunderlich of the Northern Adirondacks; Paul Drisgula and Margaret Roberts of Mohawk Hudson; Patricia McGeown of Upper Hudson; Bonnie Bolitho of Stark County, Ohio; Betsey Kaufman of Cleveland; Nancy Kachel of Arkansas and Eastern Oklahoma; Patricio Gonzales of Hidalgo County; David Nova and Janet McDowell of the Blue Ridge affiliate; and Mark Pawlowski of South Central Michigan.

Finding primary sources on the history of Planned Parenthood is not always easy. In some cities the press refused to print anything about the Federation. And preserving its history was not the highest priority for an organization so frequently in crisis. But librarians can redeem such situations. With their help one can still find more than enough primary materials to provide a history of the long alliance between the Federation and clergy. I am especially grateful to Jim Byrnes and Jennifer Johnsen, librarians of the Katherine Dexter McCormick Collection at the Planned Parenthood Federation of America offices in New York City, who guided me to every document I needed; to Sonya McDonald and William Fischetti of the Western Historical Manuscripts Collection at the Library of the University of Missouri in St. Louis; to Susan Boone of the Sophia Smith Collection of Planned Parenthood papers at Smith College; to Tom Saunders, for his history of Planned Parenthood of San Francisco and Alameda County; to Fred Bauman of the Manuscripts Division of the Library of Congress, who gave invaluable advice on copyright issues; and to Ann Lehman who tracked down elusive quotes with the skill of a Sherlock Holmes. The Library of Congress also provided abundant microfilm from the Margaret Sanger Papers.

Grateful thanks are also due to a number of volunteers who have devoted a good part of their lives to supporting Planned Parenthood, especially Nana Henderson and Laurie Zabin of the Baltimore affiliate and Dorothy Roudebush of the St. Louis affiliate.

I wish also to offer grateful appreciation to Adi Hovav, my editor at Rutgers University Press, who made the writing coherent and the process enjoyable.

I owe a particular debt of gratitude to the Reverend Seth Staples, my mentor and friend in ministry, who gave a close critical reading to this manuscript, and whose unsentimental yet deeply humanistic theology has taught me a great deal about the complexity of the issues covered in this book.

When there was a manuscript crisis due to my inexperience with computers, the situation was saved by Nancy Stiefel, a computer librarian in Vero Beach. Her skill was impressive and I could not have been more grateful.

And special thanks are due to Elizabeth Gilbert, who guided me through the arcane mysteries of final editing.

Acknowledgment must also be given to a host of clergy too numerous to mention individually who took the risks inherent in helping women when both they and the women were being harshly criticized by "respectable society."

Because of various circumstances in my life, some of the writing was done while on the road. I am grateful to Danny and Rose, who provided friendly companionship, excellent meals, and a spectacular view of the Atlantic at their Florida restaurant, the Seaside Grill. Far more than all that, they were invariably kind to my late wife, Betsy Davis, during the long years of her illness. Their kindness was often the high point of her day.

In the latter stages of this work, no one has mattered more than my wife, Linda. She brought to the project the critical insights of an excellent librarian, realistic encouragement, astonishing patience, and a generosity of spirit that would sustain any soul.

The reader should know that this study is neither sponsored nor endorsed by Planned Parenthood. As a minister and a professor of religion who has done a great deal of volunteer work for this organization, I am clearly not a disinterested party. In studying with the American theologian Reinhold Niebuhr, I learned how to fully appreciate the subtlety of self-interest that affects all human institutions and all human beings. But I also learned that those who would seek to live out a biblical faith should enter into the waters of social and political struggle. In my experience, the people of Planned Parenthood, whether religious or not, and the clergy who support them have not hesitated to enter those waters.

That said, I am not uncritical of either Planned Parenthood or the clergy (including myself). This study is as objective as I can make it.

Permission to quote brief passages in the text was sought and granted by the following copyright holders and is gratefully acknowledged: Anthony Hoeltzel, Beth McLemore, Ann Obey, Mark Pawlowski, Alexander Sanger,

Tom Saunders; Beach Press; Commonweal Foundation; Georgetown Law Journal; Judson Press (see also chapter 7, note 14); Justice and Witness Ministries of the United Church of Christ; Lippincott Williams & Wilkins; James Brynes for the Katherine Dexter McCormick Collection at the PPFA Library, New York; *New York Post*; *New York Times*; W. W. Norton and Company; Ohio State University Press; John Nugent for the archives of Planned Parenthood of Maryland; *Poughkeepsie New Yorker*; *The Reconstructionist*; *The Record*, Troy, N.Y.; Regents of the University of California; Religious Coalition for Reproductive Choice; *The Roanoke Times*; *The Saratogian*; Second Presbyterian Church, St. Louis, Missouri; Susan Boone for the Sophia Smith Collection at Smith College; University of Missouri-St. Louis; Western Historical Manuscript Collection; Westminster John Knox Press.

Bible selections are from the New Revised Standard Version of the Bible, copyright 1989 by the Division of Christian Education of the National Council of the Church of Christ in the USA. Used by permission. All rights reserved.

For the epigraph to chapter 2, the Estate of Martin Luther King Jr. and Writers House grant permission to use excerpts from Martin Luther King's address to Planned Parenthood, 1966. Reprinted by arrangement with the Estate of Martin Luther King Jr., c/o Writers House as agent for the proprietor, New York, N.Y. Copyright 1966, Dr. Martin Luther King Jr., copyright renewed 1996 Coretta Scott King.

Sacred Work

Introduction

AT THE BEGINNING OF THE twenty-first century, when we think of religion and religious figures in America in connection with women's rights, specifically reproductive rights, most of us reasonably assume that all religious institutions are opposed to abortion, since that is primarily what we see in the media. In the media, clergy supporters of choice are virtually invisible. But in fact, as many would probably be surprised to discover, clergy all over the country continue to play a major role in advancing women's rights, rebutting right-wing arguments, and helping to make (and keep) abortion legal nationwide.

In this era it is hard to appreciate all the reproductive health benefits that were denied to women in the recent past. The woman who today goes to a modern public hospital to obtain contraceptive pills or shots often has no idea that for decades religious opposition forced those same hospitals to refuse to offer such services. The teenager from a dysfunctional family who does not want her parents to know that she is sexually active and the single woman starting her career are unaware that up through the mid-1960s clinics would not provide contraceptive services for unmarried women. Younger generations are only vaguely aware that abortion has not always been legal, and that the fight to make it so was due in part to an alliance between clergy and key women's advocacy and health organizations, specifically the Planned Parenthood Federation of America. My own involvement in the pro-choice movement began when my late wife, the Reverend Betsy Davis, and I came to teach at Skidmore college in upstate New York in the mid-1960s. Both of us were United Church of Christ ministers who had been active in civil rights issues at the University of North Carolina in Chapel Hill before coming to New York. Early in my tenure as chaplain and associate professor of religion, a group of students came to my office seeking help.

A student in their dorm was pregnant. Unwilling to tell her family, she was planning to fly to Puerto Rico to see if she could find an abortionist. At first the students supported her by taking up a collection for her, but deciding that her plans might be dangerous, they came to tell me the situation. It was a humbling experience because I had not the slightest idea what to do.

Fortunately, the college had a remarkable woman physician in the infirmary. I called her for advice and we spoke to the student together. The young woman looked so frightened. The doctor reassured her that the college would not cast her out and then said something that I have never forgotten. She gently told the student, "We know that the lives of women are very complicated." For the first time, her simple empathy suddenly made me fully appreciate the impossible struggles that women faced and still face when it comes to controlling their bodies and their lives. It turned out that the student's family was willing to stand by her. Her parents arranged the abortion and the student returned to the college soon afterward. A few years later, on May 22, 1967, the Reverend Howard Moody and twenty-one other leading New York City clergy startled the nation when the *New York Times* ran a front-page story describing the formation of something called the Clergy Consultation Service on Abortion. The service would help women find safe abortions in a nation where the procedure was illegal. It quickly grew into a nationwide network of nearly 1,500 ministers and rabbis. Betsy and I became the clergy who handled referrals for the service in our county in upstate New York. My experience in the consultation service was a crash course in the reality of women's lives in a world hostile to a woman's autonomy, a course first begun several years before. I learned that women sought abortions for many complicated reasons and some would risk their lives to obtain one. I also learned that despite being illegal, abortion was everywhere. There were networks of people in many professions who could lead a woman to a name and a number. It was often unsafe, especially for poorer women. Shortly thereafter, with the *Roe v. Wade* decision handed down by the Supreme Court in 1973, the consultation disbanded, believing that it was no longer needed.

Looking back, I am struck by the lack of visible opposition to abortion when it was illegal. The Roman Catholic Diocese of Manhattan did not make any public statement in response to the formation of the Clergy Consultation in 1967, nor did the Southern Baptists or any of the other religious institutions that today vigorously oppose *Roe*. But by the mid-1980s the antiabortion movement we recognize today began to seriously undermine the laws that protect a woman's right to choose as well as well as access to information about abortions and contraceptives. State grants to Planned Parenthood were jeopardized by the religious opposition which demonized pro-choice organizations. The law allowing a woman's right to choose was suddenly not as infallible as those who supported it thought. Pro-choice clergy again began to organize and support their local Planned Parenthood affiliates This would eventually lead to the Planned Parenthood Clergy Advisory Board and its network of 1,600 clergy nationwide.

The Planned Parenthood Federation of America has some remarkable strengths—endurance, cohorts of deeply committed people, the grace to rise above setbacks, and a capacity for vision. But it sometimes displays a notable weakness, the failure to appreciate the powerful role of religion— for good and for evil—in this society. The Federation's founder, Margaret Sanger, though not religious herself, did not have that failing. Early in her career she moved heaven and earth to enlist the support of influential religious figures. In the decades from the twenties to the fifties the American Birth Control League and its successor, Planned Parenthood, persuaded virtually every mainline Protestant church and the National Council of Churches, as well as Reform and Conservative temples and synagogues, to endorse the practice of birth control as not only a matter of choice but a moral obligation. In doing my research I was astounded to discover that in that era there were literally thousands of clergy, including many of the most well known rabbis and ministers of the time, who publicly supported Planned Parenthood.

But as Planned Parenthood became a fixture in American life, receiving government funding and generous grants from foundations, it became much more secular in spirit as well as in character. This was true of the national body as well as many, but by no means all, of the local chapters (known as affiliates). Sensing there was no longer a need for them, many liberal clergy moved on to other issues. This development is particularly ironic, since the principal opponents of Planned Parenthood have always been, and continue to be, powerful religious institutions. Such institutions marshall the most powerful sacred symbols—scriptures, the cross, God—to attack the work of Planned Parenthood. In this society such opposition carries weight with many people. To let such claims go unanswered is both foolish and costly.

But in recent years Planned Parenthood has once again welcomed and received the support of clergy who recognize that its efforts to bring reproductive health care to needy people are to be not condemned but supported. Many rabbis and ministers recognize that the cruel injustice of sexism lies behind much of the opposition to Planned Parenthood and to a woman's right to have access to contraception and abortion. For most clergy, the imperative to stand against such sexism is no less urgent than the need to stand against racism. As an ally, clergy bring to their firm support of the work of Planned Parenthood a religiously profound basis for reproductive freedom, the divine demand for justice.

This book is an account of the mysterious way in which the secular culture of Planned Parenthood and the religious world of the clergy are drawn together. Neither group may ever fully understand the other. It's certainly understandable for an organization barraged with attacks and picketing and demonstrations from religious people to be skeptical of religious support. Nevertheless, Planned Parenthood as an organization has come to understand that clergy have the ability to advocate for it both in the world of churches and synagogues and in the public world of press and politics. There have been times when the Federation and the clergy went their separate ways. But they come back together, because each group at its best focuses on helping people whom society does not always want helped.

If the rich history described in this book helps to correct the mistaken impression that religious people in America are overwhelmingly hostile to women's reproductive rights in general and to Planned Parenthood in particular, it will have achieved much of its purpose.

CHAPTER 1

The Concept of Sacred Work

IN THE SPRING OF 1997 the Planned Parenthood affiliate in Washington, D.C., opened a clinic in a nearby church. Soon after, indicating how incongruous the situation seemed to be, the *Washington Post* ran an article under the headline "Unlikely Alliance for Planned Parenthood." The *Washington Post* may have thought it was merely reflecting the popular understanding that the work of Planned Parenthood is opposed by all religious institutions. But in fact the *Post* had it all wrong. An alliance between churches, synagogues, temples, and Planned Parenthood has existed for over seventy years. No one can argue that Planned Parenthood's dedication to women's reproductive rights has not drawn the intense opposition of religious individuals and institutions that sometimes embrace tradition at the cost of justice. But that same dedication has also cultivated a spiritual alliance with clergy who believe that all women should have access to the information and services that allow them autonomy over their own bodies. Since its beginnings as the American Birth Control League in the 1920s, Planned Parenthood has expanded to include an international arm, some nine hundred clinics across the United States, and affiliates in every state. To its admirers, Planned Parenthood is a cultural icon, and to its detractors a curse on the land. In the midst of these extremes and below the public radar, mainline Protestant and Jewish clergy, in their alliance with Planned Parenthood, have played a major role in achieving respectability for birth control in a nation where religious convictions always involve social and moral issues and never more so than when the subject at hand involves women's sexuality.

This book will explore both the religious and the historical dimensions of this alliance. After a brief look at the nature of sacred work in the Bible's prophetic demand for justice, I will describe the religious sexism that wars with the demand for social justice. Next will be an account of the nature of the lives of the clergy caught between these two pressures. Finally I will tell the story of how Planned Parenthood was able to establish its mission in city after city against the most intense religious opposition and with the indispensable help of the clergy who spoke out in support. Most important, readers will discover that this alliance was far from unlikely: it was inevitable.

The Nature of Sacred Work

I contend that Planned Parenthood is engaged in a form of sacred work, the work, that is, of securing reproductive justice for women. It's a claim that bothers many people. Secularists are made uncomfortable because they don't like religious language. Conservative religionists are appalled because they believe that what Planned Parenthood does is sinful or, worse, evil. So it is critically important to be precise in saying what is involved here.

I do not mean that Planned Parenthood is a religious organization. It is not. Its founder, Margaret Sanger, was an atheist who felt that religion was generally a reactionary force in society. And while many people who work for the organization are regular attendees at churches, synagogues, and mosques, Planned Parenthood Federation of America (PPFA) is thoroughly secular. But when it comes to the issue of sacred work, that doesn't matter. For scripture is clear about one thing: sacred work, the work of justice, is *sacred* no matter who does it.

What are the religious and historical roots of the concept of sacred work? Central to all religions is the concept of the holy, the sacred. Rudolph Otto described the sacred as "wholly other," that is, a reality so different from the ordinary world, known as the profane, that all other distinctions pale by comparison. Mircea Eliade saw the sacred as a powerful reality, a reality that presents itself to us and is able to evoke awe and respect among believers.[1] In different religions the sacred takes different forms. In the East, it takes the form of brahman (Hinduism) or nirvana (Buddhism). In the West, it takes the form of a biblical God who has a will for the created world and, especially, for human beings.

Each form of the sacred evokes a response from the respective believer. That response is sacred work. In the East, the human problem is a philosophical one: the believer does not realize that he/she is divine. Sacred work is the task of meditation, study, and/or devotion to come to the realization that one—in fact—is one with the universe. But in the West the separation between the divine and the human is not philosophical, it is ethical. In the myth of the Garden of Eden, the human has "fallen," been expelled from the Garden because of a refusal to trust and love God. Instead, fallen human beings seek autonomy and/or control over one another. In scripture, God pursues fallen human beings through the form of a covenant with Israel and the commandments that go with that covenant. Central to the covenant is the commandment to love God, the neighbor, and the self. In the biblical view, sacred work is love, and in practical social realities, sacred work is justice.

To be sure, there is a ritual dimension to the human response to the sacred. But in the Hebrew scriptures, rituals are without meaning, even offensive, if the ethical commandments are being broken. One can see how this reality is spelled out in the law codes of the scriptures. In the Holiness Code of Leviticus is the powerful imperative "You shall be holy, for I the Lord, your God, am holy" (Leviticus 19:2). God's demand for holiness is all-encompassing for the believer. But most significantly that demand is not only ritual but also ethical. Both ritual and ethical commands are woven together in the Torah. The ritual demand is seen in verses like Leviticus 19:5–7: "When you offer a sacrifice of well-being to the Lord, offer it in such a way that it is acceptable in your behalf. It shall be eaten on the same day you offer it, or on the next day; and anything left over until the third day shall be consumed in fire. If it is eaten at all on the third day, it is an abomination; it will not be acceptable." Or verse 19b: "you shall not sow your fields with two kinds of seed; nor shall you put on a garment made of two different materials."

But far more predominant in that central chapter are the ethical commands, a long line of imperatives, which cover not only individual but also social ethics.

You shall not strip your vineyard bare, or gather the fallen grapes of your
   vineyard; you shall leave them for the poor and the alien. (v. 10)
You shall not defraud your neighbor; you shall not steal; and you shall not
   keep for yourself the wages of a laborer until morning. (v. 13)
You shall not render an unjust judgment; you shall not be partial to the poor
   or defer to the great: with justice you shall judge your neighbor. (v. 15)
You shall not cheat in measuring length, weight, or quantity. You shall have
   honest balances, honest weights. (v. 35)

Above all is the verse that stands as a summary of all moral biblical commands,

> . . . but you shall love your neighbor as yourself: I am the Lord. (v. 18)

But who is the neighbor? Here the God of Israel is not impartial. This God has a special concern for certain groups: "You shall not wrong or oppress a resident alien, for you were aliens in the land of Egypt. You shall not abuse any widow or orphan" (Exodus 22:21–22).

Aliens, widows, and orphans. A striking choice of groups to whom to be partial. The God of Israel is unique in such a choice. In the great kingdoms of the time, the favorites of the gods were usually the reigning monarch and the established classes of society. Yet in Israel to fulfill the command to be holy one must offer love and justice to aliens, widows, and orphans. Providing justice for these particular neighbors, so despised and ignored by the world, is sacred work.

In the writings of the biblical prophets, especially Amos, Isaiah, and Jeremiah, this sacred work takes a more specific political form, condemning the bribery of judges, usurious lending practices, and the excessive spending of the rich. Then as now societies were usually governed by rulers who had minimal interest in justice for immigrants, widows, and orphans. For such rulers the prophets had nothing but condemnation.

But ironically the main obstacle to the witness of the prophets, even more than naked political power, was morally bankrupt religion. The prophets had to confront not only the king but also legions of false prophets who would say exactly what the king wanted to hear and shrine priests who would use the power of the state against the prophetic demand for justice. The scriptures make clear that the prophets faced such religious opposition with depressing regularity. Always there were religious leaders willing to give divine sanction to policies of exploitation and neglect.

At times such policies, under the protective guise of this distorted religion, became instead a national scandal. In the eighth century B.C.E., in the Northern Kingdom of Israel, the king Omri had established a sacred shrine at Bethel. Israel now had a commercial class, and it was fashionable for the wealthy and powerful of the kingdom to come to this shrine and carry out extensive sacrifices as acts of worship to the God they viewed as especially devoted to the welfare of Israel. At the same time they wallowed in sentimental and nationalistic worship, the elite also carried out policies of incredible cruelty to the poor. The prophet Amos described it in these words,

Thus says the Lord;
For three transgressions of Israel,
    and for four, I will not revoke the punishment;
because they sell the righteous for silver,
    and the needy for a pair of sandals—
they who trample the head of the poor into the dust of the earth,
    and push the afflicted out of the way. (Amos 2:6–7)

To the prophets, such religiosity could only be blasphemous. The divine comment on such religion is

I hate, I despise your festivals,
and I take no delight in your solemn assemblies.
Even though you offer me your burnt offerings and grain offerings,
I will not accept them . . .
I will not listen to the melody of your harps. (5:21–23)

And then the prophet states what is important to God:

But let justice roll down like waters,
    and righteousness like an ever-flowing stream. (5:24)

The prophetic demand for social justice is continued in the New Testament. Jesus quotes Leviticus 19:18, "You shall love your neighbor as yourself," no less than three times. He makes it clear that it is the central command of his message. In the famous judgment passage of Matthew 25, those who are saved are those who cared for the sick, the jailed, and the poor: "Truly I tell you, just as you did it to one of the least of these who are members of my family, you did it to me." But what is most striking about Jesus is his different attitude toward aliens, widows, and orphans, to a degree not seen even in any of the prophets. He socialized with Gentiles, was open to children, and not only included women in his company but also conversed with them freely, allowed himself to be instructed by them, and—as in the case of the woman taken in adultery—did not judge them.

More instructively, Jesus also demonstrated how the sacred work of justice applied to women. In the famous passage in Luke 10:38–42, Jesus visits Mary and Martha. Mary sits down and joins in the religious discussions with the disciples. Martha complains to Jesus and wants him to order Mary into the kitchen. But he refuses, saying, "Leave Mary alone, she has chosen the better way." Had Jesus said, "Mary, help your sister. Your place is in the kitchen," some male theologians would have made it a central text of the faith. It would have been put in stained-glass windows and carved over cathedral doorways. But because he supported Mary's right to participate equally with the men, his words have been ignored by theologians for centuries.

THE THREAT OF RELIGIOUS SEXISM

Jesus' example was ignored primarily because scripture also contains a tradition of sexism as well as an imperative for justice. One finds it in both testaments. Again in Leviticus, not far from the command to love the neighbor, one finds these words:

> When a woman has a discharge of blood that is her regular discharge from her body, she shall be in her impurity for seven days, and whoever touches her shall be unclean until the evening. Everything upon which she lies during her impurity shall be unclean; everything also upon which she sits shall be unclean. Whoever touches her bed shall wash his clothes, and bathe in water, and be unclean until the evening." (Leviticus 15:19–21)

To select a bodily function and declare it unclean is a fateful step. Had the priests selected urination or salivation, then we would all be unclean all the time. Instead they chose a bodily function confined to women, and thus disabled women, particularly in matters related to the sacred.[2] That, of course, was the intention. But why?

In the late 1950s the Protestant theologian Reinhold Niebuhr laid out a scenario in the Christian Ethics course he taught at Union Theological Seminary in New York City. He said that in the earliest origins of humanity, men regarded as sacred the power of women to bear children. Clearly such power was of great significance, and equally clearly men wanted it. Since they obviously could not literally have childbearing powers, they would acquire them symbolically. Religion became the vehicle to take the power away from women. In Niebuhr's phrase, "the priest became the enemy of the woman." While women could continue to have the children, it was the priest who would decide the conditions under which that process was moral or immoral, whether the woman was clean or unclean, whether the child was legitimate or illegitimate. Tragically, hostility toward women has continued to be a major strain of religion down to this day.

The advent of female biblical scholars and theologians has helped to uncover the sexism and, sometimes, to redeem major passages that have been distorted due to the dominance of male interpreters, both religious and scholarly. For example, Phyllis Trible, former professor of Hebrew scripture studies at Union Theological Seminary in New York City, has pointed out that the Garden of Eden myth counters popular understandings by arguing that this myth in fact contains very little sexism. Male interpreters used it in a way that confirmed a patriarchal hold over society.

Trible locates a powerful antisexist theme within the story. She argues that before the Fall, there is no indication that Adam has "headship" or dominion over Eve. It is quite legitimate to infer that they lived together in equality. Certainly there is no evidence of male dominance and female submission. For example, when the serpent tempts the woman, she does not ask her husband what to do. As Trible points out, she makes the decision on her own.[3] Nor does he reproach her for acting without consulting him. He just eats. The fruit of the tree of the knowledge of good and evil is presented as the one thing forbidden to them, a symbolic barrier separating the human from the divine. Yet each of them reaches out and smashes that barrier. Why this happens is the profound mystery of the myth.

But Trible points out that once the disobedience has occurred, the relations between the man and the woman change radically. Now the man has the power to name the woman.[4] And it is in this situation, not before the Fall, that the fateful words appear: "Your husband shall rule over you." God does not say this as a command. Rather it is the sad divine acknowledgment that since they no longer love or trust either God or each other, the one with the biggest muscles will rule the other. What the story really says is that a man ruling over a woman is the first sign of a fallen world. Sexism is the first form of original sin, religious sexism no less than any other type.

In the New Testament, the apostle Paul at first appears to provide a powerful theological base for equality and justice for women. In the ringing line from Galatians 3:28, he says, "There is no longer Jew or Greek, there is no longer slave or free, there is no longer male and female; for all of you are one in Christ Jesus." But the promise in this verse is negated by the fact that whenever Paul dealt with specific situations, he fell back into the religious sexism of the first-century Middle East. He prescribes head coverings for women and does not permit women to speak in church. In Ephesians he reemphasizes the point: "Wives, be subject to your husbands as you are to the Lord . . . wives ought to be, in everything, [subject] to their husbands" (5:22–24). Worst of all is the non-Pauline epistle I Timothy, where we are told, "Let a woman learn in silence with full submission. I permit no woman to teach or to have authority over a man" (2:11–12). The letter even goes so far as to say that women "will be saved through childbearing" (2:15).

Of these two themes—religious sexism and the sacred work of justice—the latter is the more profound and compelling mandate. One of the saddest aspects of modern American religion is that such a statement is not seen as obvious. Those theologians and biblical scholars who used to claim that there was a biblical mandate for racism, that whites were superior to African Americans because the latter were under the curse of Canaan, have long been discredited and forgotten. But religious claims of a biblical foundation for men ruling over women are treated with seriousness. Yet the central biblical imperative, to love and render justice to the neighbor, collides directly with a social system in which men decide the place of women. The claim that God has given one gender the authority to determine the destiny of the other with no reciprocity undermines even proximate arrangements of equality between men and women.

Sexism, like the human slavery of the period, belongs to the culture of the times, not to the divine plan for humanity. Modern Christians can easily recognize the time-bound nature of the Pauline command, "Slaves, obey your earthly masters" (Ephesians 6:5). But many present-day Christians—like the Southern Baptists and the Promise-Keepers—do not see that time-bound quality when Paul says, "Wives, be subject to your husbands" (Ephesians 5:22). They consign the slavery injunction to the garbage heap of history, but they exalt wifely obedience into a central tenet of what they see as an ideal Christian society.

Once headed down this road, centuries of Christian tradition greatly amplified and deepened this pattern of religious sexism. The church fathers were chief offenders. Tertullian (160–225 C.E.), a leading Christian thinker, called women the "devil's gateway" and said that it was because of them that Christ had to die.[5] Jerome (347–420 C.E.) and other church fathers exalted celibacy in the spirit of Jerome's famous line, "Marriage populates the earth, virginity populates heaven." Augustine, the bishop of Hippo (d. 430), freely confessed his feeling that women were primarily meant to have babies, because obviously there was nothing else they could do. He also believed that sex was dangerous because it brought men under the control of women. In these early centuries of Christian development, women were pushed out of any positions involving ministry as the priesthood became confined to celibate men.

This male-dominated church then defined the role of the family and women's role in it. Inherent in that process was the chief means of control over women—the regulation of their reproductive life. Since the time of Augustine the church harshly condemned contraception. It held that every act of sexual intercourse had to be open to the procreation of children. Any form of sex that was not open to it was condemned. Thus coitus interruptus, condoms, diaphragms, masturbation, and douching were all outlawed.[6] These prohibitions affected men's lives as well, but they fell most heavily on women because only women bore the dangers of pregnancy. In these early centuries such dangers were of course considerable.

When the Protestant Reformation came along in the sixteenth century, Martin Luther rejected celibacy because he saw no biblical basis for a vow of chastity. Furthermore he rejected the idea that the monk had a special call from God, a call that was superior, while ordinary Christians had a lesser call. For him, there was no special religious vocation. He believed that the call came to every Christian regardless of his or her station. So in his view there was no reason why clergy could not marry. He himself decided to marry primarily as a theological statement—to seal his martyrdom before God and to spite the Pope—and then discovered that it was wonderful. His marriage to Katherine Von Bora and their family of four children became the model for the restoration of the family (over the monastery and the convent) as the "school for character."[7] In Geneva, later in the century, John Calvin for similar reasons also rejected celibacy. With this change, marriage placed women in intimate relationships with clergy where they could exert their influence. This increased respect for the institution of marriage, and marginally, this helped women. However, Protestantism did not challenge the idea that procreation was the chief goal of marital sexual relations. The Protestant reformers also condemned birth control, and continued the idea that males should have the authority to define the role of women. Prior to the nineteenth century no major theologian ever suggested that a woman should be consulted as to what she thought or wanted.

The sexism of organized religion has diminished in America, but certainly has not disappeared. In the 1960s and 1970s most mainline Protestant denominations opened their ministries to women. In 1972 Reform Judaism ordained the first woman rabbi, and Conservative Judaism followed suit a few years later. But in the United States today, the two largest Christian denominations (Roman Catholic and Southern Baptist) plus another large and increasingly influential faith (the Mormon Church) all refuse to ordain women to the priesthood or ministry. Stripped of theological terminology, the brutal fact remains that such policies of religious sexism subvert the demand for social justice. Not only are thousands of women denied a vocation in religious institutions, but the men in these positions have no reason not to continue to practice sexist policies.

THE NATURE OF CLERGY LIVES

Such is the biblical and historical background that has shaped the American society in which clergy operate, but many Americans have little idea of the real life of a minister or rabbi. There is no serious image of contemporary clergy in modern American media. In the popular arts, clergy are either absent, grossly sentimentalized, or portrayed as vaguely clownish people with one basic trait—they are out of touch. Both television and print media do a good job of exposing corrupt clergy such as the televangelist Jim Bakker or clergy charged with child abuse and sexual harassment. Everyone likes to see hypocrisy exposed, but these folks are hardly typical clergy.

On one level there is no great mystery. Clergy vary as widely as do people of any profession. There are vast differences of character and temperament. Some are clearly unfit, some are sexually and/or emotionally abusive or, at a lesser level, neglect congregational needs while advancing their personal interests. Many retreat from social problems into the mysteries and particularities of liturgical life. Many others are co-opted by the conservatism of their affluent congregations, thinking few thoughts that differ from those of the church governing board. Rabbis and Unitarian ministers fare somewhat better, since their congregations tend to expect that their spiritual leaders should be witnesses for social justice.

But despite all of this, most clergy make a strong attempt to serve honorably. To understand clergy situations, one has to appreciate the curious and vulnerable position of those who serve a congregation. They are "called" by a congregation to come and do the task of interpreting, teaching, and preaching the biblical mandates that guide the lives of believers. This, of course, is the formal description. In reality congregations may be looking for someone who will add new members and build up the budget. The dependence of ministers and rabbis on their congregations is quite extensive, both financially and emotionally. In many situations the congregation is still their landlord, and often—like landlords—slow to repair the property and quick to criticize the tenant. Should the congregation become dissatisfied, clergy face unemployment or, at the least, the need to pull the kids out of their schools and move to a job in another town. Some churches are known as "clergy killers" because of their propensity to work their ministers into exhaustion, abuse them emotionally, and then drop them. This is hardly a situation that supports clergy in carrying out a prophetic concern for social justice. More than a few ministers have wondered how long the biblical prophets would have lasted if they had had to serve an American congregation.

But on another level, there are many sympathetic and supportive congregations. Churches such as the Riverside Church in New York City strongly support the biblical imperative to pursue social justice. In degrees varying with the particular denomination and the particular congregation, their prophetic part of the tradition creates a sphere of free clergy action, a realm in which the minister is allowed, and even expected, to take steps to—in its most generic form—make the world a better place.

Many clergy try to fulfill that goal by getting involved with important but noncontroversial programs such as feeding and clothing the homeless, summer programs for inner-city children, and so on. But some clergy are willing to venture into controversial areas such as gay rights and abortion rights. Here discretion is necessary. Should the minister seriously embarrass the congregation, he or she will be history. Most Protestant churches and Jewish temples are, after all, democratic institutions and clergy who are deemed too radical can be voted out.

But if ministers or rabbis are discreet, if they have kept key leaders apprised and informed of what they are doing, then they will be able to take on controversial social justice initiatives on their own. In such situations it is understood that they do not speak for the congregation, but that a large portion of the congregation supports what they are doing. This was the situation of many of the clergy who began supporting Planned Parenthood in the thirties and forties. It remains true for many liberal clergy today.

But what is somewhat different in contemporary America is that almost all mainline Protestant denominations are struggling with a membership that is both aging and declining. To some extent this is also true of clergy. In this computer age, many attractive careers beckon to the most able students. By comparison a career in ministry seems faintly antiquated, and the ministry attracts fewer top students. Compensating for this, in part, is the entrance of many bright women into ministry. There were few to none in earlier decades, but now a steadily increasing percentage of mainline Protestant clergy are female. They have changed the way many religious institutions operate. They have brought inclusive language to liturgical material and hymns. Women rabbis and ministers have been especially creative in developing ceremonies to address situations—miscarriages, divorce, and others—that have been ignored by churches and temples in earlier decades.

The largest issue roiling traditional mainline religion is the status of homosexual members. Can they be ordained? Can they marry? Although some denominations (United Church of Christ, Unitarian, Reform Judaism) have resolved these issues, they are literally tearing apart the Episcopal, Methodist, Presbyterian, Lutheran, and American Baptist churches, where the membership is evenly divided. Many liberal clergy expend great amounts of energy in these battles for gay rights. But this has not diminished their willingness to invest time and effort in the Planned Parenthood affiliates in their towns and cities.

Finally there is the issue of the changing diversity of our population. The old white Protestant America is gone. There are more Muslims in America today than Episcopalians, and the local clergy association often has members who are imams. Although a few of the new populations such as Koreans may be mainline Protestants, most of them have no such connection. Liberal clergy have learned to operate in a world in which they are have no automatic status in a community simply by virtue of their profession. They have to earn respect. Some cannot make the adjustment and retreat to pulpits in small towns where life is much more like the past. But most seem to welcome the new world.

The Distinctive Character of Planned Parenthood

If such is the world of clergy, what about the other partner in the alliance, Planned Parenthood? What is its unique character? It is an organization, often called simply the Federation by its members, which still has many traits of a movement, such as enthusiasm and high idealism. To some it is a cursed organization and to many others, a lifesaver as well as a cultural icon. It has both a checkered past and a vital presence in current American society. And there is nothing quite like it in our cultural history.

The simple facts of its structure can be easily set down. In 2003 Planned Parenthood had 125 local chapters, known as affiliates. These affiliates manage 875 health clinics in 49 states and the District of Columbia. There are national offices in New York, Chicago, and Washington, D.C. The organization is a nonprofit whose funding comes from third-party reimbursements, private donations, patient fees, and government grants. With its 21,000 volunteers and staff it serves almost 5 million people each year. It also supports an independent foundation, the Alan Guttmacher Institute, which carries out research and education in the field of human reproduction. The institute's reports are widely respected even by those who disagree with the mission of Planned Parenthood. Finally, its services are far more varied than the general public knows, including emergency contraception, tubal sterilization, male contraception, vasectomy, HIV testing, prenatal services, infertility services, colposcopy procedures, pregnancy tests, abortion, breast exams/breast care, adoption referrals, and, in some affiliates, primary care.[8]

Far more revealing are its history and its beliefs. Planned Parenthood has gone through three distinct historical phases. From 1916 through the mid-1930s, the movement, focused on making birth control available, was a combination of social action, civil disobedience, feminism, and conservative financial support. In the second phase, 1940 to 1960, the social conservatism of the supporters dominated. Female leaders, knowledgeable about birth control, were replaced by businessmen who knew little of the field.[9] During this time, Planned Parenthood shunned controversy and embarked on an ill-fated quest for respectability. At the end of the period there were fewer clinics than there were in 1940. The third phase, from the mid-1960s to the present, has coincided with the second wave of feminism. Challenged by the abortion issue, the organization slowly but eventually returned to an increased involvement in social action. The character of that involvement can be seen in the secular humanism expressed in its statement of beliefs:

> We believe in the right to sexual and reproductive self-determination that is non-coercive, non-exploitive, and responsible.
>
> We believe that the free and joyous expression of one's own sexuality is central to being fully human.
>
> We believe in trusting individuals and providing them with the information they need to make well-informed decisions about sexuality, family planning, and childbearing.
>
> We believe that women should have an equal place at life's table and be respected as moral decision makers.
>
> We believe that children flourish best in families and communities where they are nurtured, honored, and loved.
>
> We believe in passion for change, for justice, for easing the plight of others, for caring, for living our convictions, and for confronting inhumane acts.
>
> We believe in action—to make things happen and to improve people's lives and circumstances.
>
> We believe in inclusion and diversity—and the power and knowledge they confer.
>
> We believe that the future is global and that we are part of a global movement.

We believe in the urgency of creating a sustainable world and living in peace
     with our planet.
We believe in leadership based on collaboration rather than hierarchy. We
     believe in acting courageously, especially as allies of those who have little
     or no voice and little or no power.
We believe that every right is tied to responsibility and that the fulfillment of
     responsibility is itself a source of joy.[10]

In many respects, everything the Federation has become was there in its
origins. Although she tried for years to get it, Margaret Sanger must have
sensed from the beginning that there would be no government money for
birth control. She also realized—as she saw the frightened faces of the
immigrant women who were present in 1916 when her clinic was raided and
she was arrested—that her clients had neither political power nor money.
If she was to open clinics, she would have to turn to people with wealth
who could support the work. As she brought these upper-class women to
her side, she was, wittingly or unwittingly, also determining much of the
character of the organization that would arise. Margaret Sanger planted the
seeds of the affiliates that would later emerge, first as part of the American
Birth Control League and, by 1940, as the Planned Parenthood Federation
of America.

Throughout the organization's history there has always existed this curious amalgam of wealthy conservative supporters, middle-class supporters
and employees, physicians, and both middle-class and poor clients. Among
those clients today are huge contingents of young people, immigrant women,
and people who come in for many specialized services, including HIV testing. This amalgam has produced both the strengths and the weaknesses
of the organization. In the past, one of the weaknesses was the prejudices
of the Federation's wealthy supporters. In the 1920s the American Birth
Control League—far more than Margaret Sanger—supported policies of
eugenics. In some cases their decisions were clearly racist. (More on this in
chapter 2.) By contrast, Planned Parenthood today makes a determined
effort at diversity in its national board, local boards, and staff.

Another weakness of the past was the preference for philanthropy over
social justice. Although some of its wealthy supporters were certainly action
oriented, many were not interested in political struggle. They simply wanted
to help impoverished people get the means to control their reproductive
lives, with a little health care thrown in. Birth control clinics, which opened
in both San Francisco and Oakland in 1929, grew out of an effort to obtain

clean, safe milk for babies. In Baltimore, the director of the first clinic, Dr. Bessie Moses, was from a wealthy Jewish family and raised money for the clinic by asking her friends. There was nothing wrong with such philanthropic work, but it was no substitute for an organized effort at political change. It had more the character of charity than of justice. In Planned Parenthood today, the effort at social justice predominates, but there are parts of the organization that still prefer philanthropy and resist direct political involvement. It must be recognized that the philanthropic approach, despite its limitations, was also one of the early strengths of the movement. Having the funds to establish clinics meant that women could be helped and data obtained that would document how desperately some needed the services provided. And it was also true that these wealthy backers could have ignored the cause of birth control and supported dozens of noncontroversial charities, causes that would have won them praise instead of criticism. The philanthropic backers who were consistent supporters over many years made Planned Parenthood a real presence when no one else would do it.

Within the organization problems sometimes arise because of the wide variations between the cultures of smaller rural affiliates and those of the large metropolitan clinics, with their sophisticated public relations and programming. This leads to some tension, as do the seemingly inevitable conflicts between the interests of the local affiliates and the national Planned Parenthood Federation offices in Manhattan. Such conflicts impair the organization, because energy that could go into development or programs is wasted on battles over turf and rivalries over potential donors. This resembles nothing so much as the culture of every American religious denomination, where there is always some degree of mistrust between central and local units.

Nor is Planned Parenthood free of the danger of focusing more on structure and process than on the mission. Revising by-laws, re-doing the nomination process, reexamining the accreditation standards, and so on can consume enormous amounts of organizational energy and funds. Changes in policy can be agonizingly slow. It took years of debate before the Federation agreed to allow a local unit to endorse a local political candidate with its own money.

Beyond these flaws, past and present, is one remarkable virtue—the organization's constancy and faithfulness to one task, seeing that women have access to the services needed to control their own bodies. It accomplished this in the earliest days, when it was a crime to send birth control devices through the mail. It accomplished it in the worst days of the Depression.

Even in the terrible days of the sexist fifties, when it lost whatever feminism remained within it and lectured women on their proper role in the family, even then the clinics were still there, sometimes the only place in town where a woman could get the birth control she needed. And in recent decades, as the organization accepted the task of providing abortions, it has endured arson, violence, threats, and murder and continues to resist attempts to shut down the clinics entirely.

Nothing is more human than to take for granted social advances that were bought at a great price. Over the years hundreds of thousands of women have used Planned Parenthood services—and millions of others have benefited—with no idea of what battles had to be fought for the agency even to be there for them. Women whose churches denounce Planned Parenthood use its services in great numbers.[11] And every year a number of women who passionately protest its policies come to it when they themselves are in need of an abortion.[12] Its greatest strength is that—however dim the perception—it has always understood that without reproductive freedom, women have no effective control of their lives. It can be argued that, since the suffragists, no agency in American society has been so important to the lives and health of women.

Rueful Irony: Bringing Sacred Work into History

It is one thing to understand the biblical imperative to work for justice in the world; it is quite another to actually accomplish it in the face of the powerful currents of economic and social self-interest that dominate American society. Those young clergy who try to remove injustices from social institutions immediately confront one of the great ironies of religious ethics—those not infrequent occasions when the unbelievers care more about the sacred work of justice than do the believers. The very priests and ministers who are supposed to have the concern of the prophets—to care whether people have enough to eat, are not oppressed, are free of racist and sexist discrimination—who are, so to speak, to be "the right hand of God," at times retreat into forms of triumphalism and otherworldly theology. A wry old International Workers of the World ("Wobblies") song—appropriately enough a parody of a hymn—says it best:

> Longhaired preachers come out every night,
> try to tell you what's wrong and what's right,
> But when asked about something to eat,

they all answer in voices so sweet,
"You will eat by and by,
in that glorious land in the sky.
Work and pray, live on hay,
You'll have pie in the sky when you die."[13]

In their place it is the unbelievers who take on repressive social institutions and pay the price of ostracism, injury, jail, and even death. And in the
end, it is usually these same unbelievers who are often the ones who change
the world. This pattern of secular leadership in justice issues is so pervasive
that, with the exception of Martin Luther King and several other African-
American clergy, twentieth-century prophetic leaders in America generally
have not been from the world of religion. One possible biblical interpretation is to argue that when God uses secular leadership to bring about justice it is as though one were seeing "the left hand of God" moving through
history. The prophetic claims are that God will always be involved in seeking to bring justice within history, and if religious people will not bring
about justice, then God will use other people to secure that end.

These modern secular prophets, like the biblical prophets, are caught up
in a unique dynamic that describes the way sacred work makes its way into
history. It is a dynamic of suffering, described by the Protestant theologian
Walter Bruggemann in his study *Hope within History*. Bruggemann notes that
whether we look at biblical empires or modern states, there are two groups
who do not think about hope for the future. One group, made up of those
who are in charge of the establishment—people who control vast wealth
and the political leaders and managers who serve them—is essentially unin-
terested in such hope because its members want to preserve the status quo.
They have no vision of a more just society. They like things more or less the
way they are. The other group without hope is the poor, those being exploited, who have no expectations that anything will ever be better for them.

But when those who are suffering give voice to their suffering, they are
changed. And when they proclaim both their suffering and their hope publicly, dramatic social change becomes possible. As Bruggemann states it,
"Suffering brought to speech concerns hope, because such protest in prayer
and public life is a refusal to let things be this way when they are in fact
unbearable." Who hopes? "Those who enter their grief, suffering, and oppres-
sion, who publicly profess it and move through it and beyond. They are the
ones who are surprised to find again and again, that hope and new social
possibility come in the midst of such grief."[14]

Biblical prophets like Jeremiah were the ones who gave public voice to such suffering. The kings and the priestly establishment responded by suppressing dissent and seeking to silence those crying out. But despite their best efforts they could not maintain the status quo. Society changed, and changed in the direction indicated by the prophets.

This biblical dynamic is equally true of modern American society. We have gone through periods of little social change because those being exploited were silent. But each time the oppressed groups found their voice, hope became possible and society changed. In order to secure such change, each reform seemed to require two things: a prophetic figure to capture the imagination of the affected group, and an organization uniquely suited to bring about the desired change.

One justice movement, long overdue, was the organization of unions to deal with the appalling working conditions in American mines and mills in the thirties. Mainline Protestant churches might have seen this as a justice issue, but in most cases they were governed by boards made up of middle-class people who were not working in the mines and factories. As a result they did not speak out for workers in exploitive situations. Fundamentalist churches, whose members were in the mines and mills, tended to focus on otherworldly concerns and personal salvation. They too did not speak out.

In their place figures like Walter Reuther, a product of a strong family of German socialists, became labor leaders. In January 1937 he led a band of workers into Chevrolet plant number four of the General Motors Assembly Works in Flint, Michigan. They drove out those workers who were not in support, sealed the plant, and engaged in a "sit-down strike." It worked. They won union recognition by the company. The tactic spread across the country. In March 1937, nearly 200,000 workers had engaged in such strikes.[15] With such tactics and through skilled use of the National Labor Relations Law (1935), Reuther and other labor leaders such as John L. Lewis, Philip Murray, and Harry Bridges created the Congress of Industrial Organizations (CIO) to organize many American industries.[16] Such leaders were charismatic, their unions were creative, and a large measure of economic justice entered American society.

A similar pattern developed in twentieth-century American racial affairs. At the turn of the century across the South, blacks were denied all basic rights, especially the right to vote. Most worked as sharecroppers and were kept in harshly dependent poverty. But the most bitter fruit of their powerlessness was the violent crime of lynching. From 1882 to 1968, 3,446 African Americans were lynched.[17]

Here again, in theory, there was nothing to stop the white Christian churches from protesting such racial inhumanity. These were, after all, fellow Christians who were being lynched. But except for a few lone voices, neither clergy nor churches demonstrated any vigorous concern with the issue. In their place, a number of prophetic African-American voices emerged to challenge that whole pattern of racism and to give voice to the suffering of millions of African Americans. In February 1909 Ida Wells-Barnett, Mary White Ovington, Oswald Garrison Villiard, Henry Moscowitz, William English Walling, and W.E.B. DuBois founded the NAACP. Although they never succeeded in passing a federal antilynching law, they became the force that tore down the legal basis of segregation in the 9 to 0 Supreme Court *Brown v. Board of Education* decision of 1954. In those lonely decades when white society had little interest in racial justice, the NAACP was the perfectly crafted organization to wrest the first small measures of integration from an indifferent legal system. Those achievements of the NAACP became the basis for a measure of long overdue racial justice. On that moral and legal foundation the Reverend Martin Luther King was able to carry forward the great civil rights movement of the sixties.

But the third great achievement of justice in America in the twentieth century has never been acknowledged as clearly as have the work of the unions and the NAACP. That achievement was women's successful fight for the right to birth control. Nowhere was injustice more clearly present than in the twentieth-century battle over contraception. Here was an issue that challenged the very heart of religious sexism. If women were able to determine their reproductive life, then the control over their lives by male-dominated political institutions would be threatened. At least one denomination, the Missouri Lutheran Synod, was explicit in its concern that the traditional relationship between the sexes would be changed.[18] A husband's authority over his wife might be diminished and women would be able to engage in improper sexual relations without the fear of pregnancy. Birth control was feared as a radical business indeed.

Consciously or unconsciously, the male establishment had created powerful barriers to any form of self-determination by women. In 1870 Congress passed the Comstock laws, which prohibited sending information on contraception and abortion through the mail. Such materials were defined as "obscene." In addition most state legislatures passed "baby Comstock" laws, which went even further in passing sanctions against contraception. Some of these laws established penalties for not only the senders but also the recipients of the information. The state of Connecticut went so far as to make even the practice of birth control a crime. A large number of physicians agreed with these laws.

In the 1870s physicians went further and mounted a highly organized "doctor's campaign" against abortion, led by Dr. Horatio Storer.[19] In large part it was motivated by an attempt to drive out competition by midwives, but it was also propelled by a contempt for native-born middle-class married women, who were not having as many children as immigrant women. In subsequent decades, the doctors succeeded in passing antiabortion legislation in most states, tried unsuccessfully to suppress abortions performed by physicians, and drove the practice deeper into the hands of nonphysician practitioners. These laws were a reflection of the fact that large parts of the political, religious, educational, and media worlds spent great energy in defining the role of women. The intent of all of this activity was control.

Because of these developments, American women in the early twentieth century were far more ignorant about contraception than their foremothers were in 1850.[20] The pain and suffering caused by this was staggering. Women had baby after baby, or resorted to dangerous illegal abortions that took the lives of many.[21] The presence of too many children destroyed numerous families, or at the least ruined the quality of familial life. In innumerable families the birth of an additional child caused, not joy, but bitter sadness.[22] But the leadership of the social and religious institutions of the time had little female presence, so this widespread suffering was, in practical terms, invisible.

One group, however, was inconspicuously absent from this phalanx of overt male opposition—Protestant and Jewish clergy. There had always been a few Protestant pulpits opposed to birth control. But most Protestant clergy were silent on the subject. On those few occasions when a resolution against birth control came before a denominational governing body, it was almost always voted down. One reason was that the whole subject was simply too sexual for public discussion. But there was a more compelling reason for this silence. Unlike Roman Catholic priests and bishops, Protestant ministers and Jewish rabbis had wives and families. This meant they had direct personal experience with the need for birth control. Wives spoke to their husbands about what they needed and wanted in family life. Those husbands felt the suffering and pain when no help was forthcoming. Many of these clergy families certainly used whatever forms of pregnancy prevention they had available. Even in a conservative church such as the Missouri Lutheran Synod, the clergy birth rate fell almost exactly the same percentage as that of the laity. In the 1890s these Lutheran pastors averaged 6.5 children. By

1920 the figure had dropped below 4.[23] From that vantage point most of them were not prepared to see contraception as an evil. They would not be hypocrites. But neither would they speak out in favor nor did they challenge the pro-natalist sentimentality that saw women only as mothers.

In the second decade of the twentieth century no person and no organization had emerged to give voice to that suffering. And this whole dismal arrangement was left unchallenged until a young nurse, Margaret Sanger, took it all on. Despite her faults, some of which were considerable, she changed the world. She was a brilliant organizer, an excellent fund-raiser, and, usually, a gifted tactician. But she was not religious.

American women had already shown great organizational skills in the campaign for suffrage and prohibition. Margaret Sanger built on those skills and began the American Birth Control League, which later evolved into the Planned Parenthood Federation of America. She and the movement she began changed medical practice, public opinion, and the laws of the nation. Just like the NAACP and the unions, her movement functioned in every respect as a secular force, which carried out the sacred work of justice when the religious world not only refused to act but even stood in opposition.

A key part of Sanger's efforts involved getting the religious world on her side, particularly Protestant and Jewish clergy who had been silent on the issue of birth control. After she spent years courting them and persuading them of the urgency of the need, they dropped their silence and began to make public statements in favor of birth control, first as individuals and then in the 1930s as denominations. And in the end these clergy made a decisive change in the way the public came to understand and accept the morality of legal contraception and legal abortion.

CONCLUSION

These issues are anything but resolved. We are in a curious time when the public, unaware of this history, tends to assume that most clergy want to set limits to contraception and make abortion illegal again. Nothing is further from the truth. But it is true that even among sympathetic clergy there is a tendency to overlook women's issues. Churches and synagogues have a comfortable theoretical consensus against racism that is not there when it comes to sexism. Not enough clergy have fully accepted the feminist warning that without reproductive rights, none of women's other rights may mean much.

In practical terms it is the organization called Planned Parenthood that has borne the burden of providing not only advocacy but also actual services to women in need. Like the unions and the NAACP, it emerged as the right instrument to promote justice for a group whose pain was being ignored. And while Planned Parenthood, like any human institution, has its faults and weaknesses, the very ferocity of the attack upon it—the clinic bombings, the arson and acid attacks, the anthrax scares, and the murders of those who work in its clinics—is perhaps the most powerful indication that its work is in the prophetic tradition of social justice, that it is helping women that many do not want helped. The prophets, the unions, and the NAACP were attacked in the same way. People of good will may disagree strongly with the work done by Planned Parenthood, but it is an inescapable fact that several generations of clergy, both ministers and rabbis, have believed that it is doing the sacred work of justice and have committed themselves to its support.

This book is an account of where, how, when, and especially why they have done this and why they continue to do it. At their worst, clergy are inclined to tell people how they are to live. At their best clergy listen to what suffering people are saying. Often what they hear strips away their naïveté, makes them face the brutal facts of modern society, and also confronts them with their hidden prejudices. Whatever spiritual power clergy have is a gift born of a willingness to stand not only with congregants but also with all those who face the hardest realities of life. And since spiritual realities cannot be separated from social and political life, the pursuit of the sacred work of justice takes clergy into the public arena. The realm of justice is a realm of hard, sometimes tragic choices. As Planned Parenthood and clergy each tried to stand with women making those hard choices, a bond was formed. This is the story of that bond.

Margaret Sanger
Recruits the Clergy

In our struggle for equality, we were confronted with the reality that many millions of people were essentially ignorant of our conditions or refused to face unpleasant truth. . . . The millions who were blind to our plight had to be compelled to face the social evil their indifference permitted to flourish. . . .

There is a striking kinship between our movement and Margaret Sanger's early efforts. She, like we, saw the horrifying conditions of ghetto life. . . . Like we, she was a direct actionist—a non-violent resister. She was willing to accept scorn and abuse until the truth she saw was revealed to the millions.

Margaret Sanger had to commit what was then called a crime in order to enrich humanity, and today we honor her courage and vision; for without them there would have been no beginning. Our sure beginning in the struggle for equality by non-violent direct action may not have been so resolute without the tradition established by Margaret Sanger and people like her.

—The Reverend Dr. Martin Luther King, "Family Planning: A Special and Urgent Concern," remarks prepared for the Planned Parenthood Federation of America, May 5, 1966.

IN THIS TRIBUTE TO THE life and work of Margaret Sanger, it is perhaps no accident that it was a clergyperson, the Reverend Dr. Martin Luther King, who recognized the vital connection between the civil rights movement and the reproductive rights movement. As a young minister in his first parish in Montgomery, Alabama, Martin Luther King joined a Planned Parenthood committee that gave out literature on unwanted pregnancies.[1] Dr. King recognized the prophetic elements of Margaret Sanger's movement. Each leader dealt with a situation in which there was a solution to a painful social problem, but not the willingness to pursue it. Each movement in its time tried to force the American people to face unpleasant truths. Each included cohorts of clergy. Though Sanger preceded King by four decades, he saw her as a model of a social reformer. What exactly did he see?

THE MUFFLED SOCIETY

It is difficult to take in how absolutely shut down was turn-of-the-century American society on the subject of sex. In one of the finest blooms of Victorianism, post–Civil War America had developed a "social purity" movement. People in this cause lumped together obscenity and contraception, because the latter was closely associated with prostitution and because there seemed to be no way one could discuss birth control without sexual references. Spearheading the movement was the New York Young Men's Christian Association's Committee for the Suppression of Vice. The result of their efforts was the Comstock laws, which defined birth control and abortion as "obscenity." Though often ignored, these laws were not paper tigers, but statutes that were enforced with some vigor. More than a few people went to jail for giving out contraceptive devices or even for writing about the subject.[2] The effect was so chilling that not only was there no organized protest against the laws, but people censored themselves. In 1915 Dr. William Robinson (1867–1936) published a medical book called *Fewer and Better Babies.* Two of his chapters were entitled "The Best Safest and Most Harmless Means for the Prevention of Conception" and "Means for the Prevention of Conception Which are Disagreeable, Uncertain or Injurious." These chapters consisted of nothing but blank pages. In this dramatic way he made it clear that Comstock censorship prevented him from teaching contraception even to medical students.

Some physicians wondered whether they were breaking the law when they discussed the subject among themselves. Ironically, even the feminists of the time did not resist the laws, because they didn't like contraception. They believed it conflicted with their demands for "voluntary motherhood."[3]

Despite this intimidating climate there were people who spoke out against the blackout. Emma Goldman, a leading figure in American socialism, and Mary Ware Dennett, a leading suffragist, both advocated for birth control. But the person who came to embody the birth control movement was Margaret Sanger. Sanger came from a large family in Corning, New York. Although the family was Roman Catholic, her father was a stonemason whose real religion was social radicalism. Margaret Sanger claimed that one of her strongest memories was of a visit by the noted social radical, Robert Ingersoll, a prominent agnostic and a supporter of women's rights and even of artificial contraception. She particularly remembered the fact that church members threw vegetables at him and denied him the use of the Town Hall. But something that may have been far more impressive to young Margaret

was her awareness that her mother had eighteen pregnancies, eleven children, and died at the age of forty-nine.

Sanger herself worked as a maternity nurse on the Lower East Side of
Manhattan, delivering the babies of immigrant women. It was in this setting that she saw the horrific consequences of decades of the suppression of
sexual information and social denial of unpleasant truths. She saw women
having frequent illegal abortions, women overwhelmed by poverty and too
many children, women dying because they had no knowledge of how to
prevent one pregnancy after another.

In 1913, hoping to find some birth control information that would be of
help to the poor women she treated, Sanger went on a six-month search in
some of the finest American libraries, including the Library of Congress. She
could find virtually nothing. She marveled at how completely this information was suppressed. In effect, there was no practical knowledge of birth
control available in America.[4]

She went to Europe and traveled around in search of what she couldn't
find in the United States. There French women shared with her their family
recipes for contraceptive douches, suppositories, and tampons. She also
learned about the uses of diaphragms. Returning to America in 1914, she
began to publish a small magazine entitled *The Woman Rebel.* The motto
on the masthead, "No Gods, No Masters," was a perfect expression of her
spirit. Seeking a confrontation with Anthony Comstock, she published an
issue that contained an article defending several anarchists and an article
by Herbert Thorpe in defense of assassination. These articles were so provocative that she was indicted by the federal government and charged with two
counts of publishing lewd and indecent articles and one count of inciting
to murder and riot.

She fled to Canada and then to Europe, traveling under a false pass-
port. After another extended stay during which she did more research, she
returned to America in 1915 to face her trial. But public opinion was turn-
ing. A picture of her and her three young children appeared in the papers.
It generated support, and the federal prosecutor decided to drop the charges.
Victorious, she embarked on a cross-country tour lasting three and a half
months.

She moved westward from New York, beginning with Pittsburgh and
Cleveland. One of her Cleveland appearances was at the First Unitarian
Church, an early sign of the religious support to come from that denomination. She moved on to Chicago, where she had a hard time locating a
venue, but was finally successful. In Minneapolis she drew hundreds. Then

on to Indianapolis to address the National Social Workers' Conference, to Milwaukee and St. Paul. In all these cities she organized birth control leagues. The most infamous incident occurred in St. Louis, where a theater she had rented locked her out because of protests from Catholic priests and laypeople. In Portland, Oregon, she was arrested at her meeting for distributing copies of her pamphlet, "Family Limitation," a guide to the use of condoms, douches, and other contraceptive methods. Hundreds of outraged women who were there suddenly insisted that they be arrested too. After refusing bail and spending the night in jail, Sanger became a cause célèbre. People sent thousands of letters of support and requests for the pamphlet.[5]

When she finished the tour she had put in place the roots of a national movement. With an organizational skill not unlike that of Paul the apostle, she had started local birth control societies that were mostly self-directed. She would have found the comparison to Paul hilarious, but, in fact, she did what he did, begin vital organizations in widely scattered localities that would live on long after her.

Believing that simply advocating birth control was not enough, she opened the first American birth control clinic in Brooklyn. Flyers were printed in three languages, English, Yiddish, and Italian, and distributed throughout the poor immigrant neighborhoods. The flyers exhorted women not to have dangerous illegal abortions, but to come to the clinic for safe contraceptive information. Not only local women but women from as far away as Connecticut and Massachusetts came. After ten days, the police closed the clinic and arrested Margaret and her sister Ethel. The charge was that they had violated Section 1142 of the penal code, which made it a crime in the state of New York to give out birth control information. Ethel was tried first, found guilty, and went to Queens County Penitentiary, where she went on a hunger strike. In response, the authorities forcefed her and the process almost led to her death. On January 29, 1917, Margaret Sanger went on trial. A three-judge court found her guilty, but was willing to give her a suspended sentence if she would promise never to violate Section 1142 again. There was a pause as the court waited for her answer, but finally she said simply, "I cannot promise to obey a law I do not respect." She was sentenced to thirty days in the workhouse. Shouts of protest rang out in the courtroom. The sentence was also served at Queens County Penitentiary. Even in jail she defied the law by giving birth control information to the other women inmates.[6]

Upon her release she tried to take advantage of the support she had received and organize it into a coherent movement. Even at this early stage in her work, she embodied the basic principle of resistance in a muffled society, that is, if it is forbidden to talk about a certain subject, then one must shout it from the housetops. In her case, she never stopped talking and out of her speaking came a transformed society. But first there was much work to be done.

"THIS MEETING MUST BE CLOSED! : THE CONFLICT
BETWEEN THE BIRTH CONTROL ORGANIZATIONS AND
THE ROMAN CATHOLIC HIERARCHY

Social reform movements generally evolve—or devolve, according to one's point of view—into organizations. The first United States birth control organization was founded in 1921 by Margaret Sanger. Called the American Birth Control League (ABCL), it was immediately challenged by religious opponents who sought to silence it. The conflict between birth control proponents and the Roman Catholic hierarchy was to go on over the next four decades. Consciousness and, ultimately, acceptance of birth control entered American society largely as a by-product of this long battle. Both sides were determined. At the outset the contest looked grotesquely uneven, as the largest church in America faced a motley assemblage of social reformers. But in the end, the social reformers held the field.

As the conflict began, what exactly was the church's position? The church had long been on record as condemning contraception. In the early twentieth century the Roman Catholic Church in America became the chief opponent of birth control. It routinely made the argument that the practice was contrary to natural law and immoral because it separated sex from procreation. With the creation of the ABCL it made its opposition more intense and activist.

In 1916 the Reverend John Ryan, a well-known opponent of women's suffrage, published a seminal article, "Family Limitation," in the *Ecclesiastical Review*, a journal put out by the Catholic University of America. This article set forth the new emphases in American Catholic policy on birth control and, in capsule form, included almost all of the arguments the church used over the next five decades. First, he insisted that the ethical imperatives were absolutely clear. In his words, "there is no possibility of a legitimate difference of opinion on this subject among Catholics."[7] Second, he believed that American Catholics were not deliberately committing mortal sin, but rather that they were "obstinately unconvinced" that contraception was immoral. He set forth the Thomistic argument from natural law to convince them. Third, he attacked contraception because of its supposed deleterious consequences. "Such devices are debasing to those who employ them, inasmuch as they lead inevitably to loss of reverence for the marital relation, loss of respect for the conjugal partner, and loss of faith in the sacredness of the nuptial bond."[8] Finally, he pointed out that the church did allow regulation of births by abstinence from sexual relations by married persons. "It is just possible that many men have never thought seriously of adopting [abstinence in marriage] because they have never been encouraged to consider the possibility and the reasonableness of resigning the exercise of their marital rights."[9] While many might wonder how many men would consider it reasonable to give up sexual relations in marriage, these arguments nevertheless became the case against birth control put forth by the Catholic Church in America. It's noteworthy that at this date the church offered only abstinence. There was no mention of the "rhythm" method (or periodic abstinence) of birth control that would come later.

Official notice of this policy to American Catholics came in the form of a pastoral letter on the subject by the American bishops in 1919. They were brief and blunt, if not too theological. They said that birth control was selfish and an individual crime that would ultimately harm the nation. It was a "detestable thing."[10]

Furthermore the church believed that since contraception was in opposition not only to church law, but also to natural law, it was wrong for all citizens, Catholic or not. Therefore ecclestiastical authorities did not hesitate to use community pressure, political lobbying, and boycotts to suppress it wherever it appeared.

Even against this background it was startling to see in one event how far religious opponents might go to silence the proponents of contraception. In November 1921 Margaret Sanger had called together a major conference in New York City for the founding of the American Birth Control League. The list of sponsors was impressive, including Winston Churchill and the novelist Theodore Dreiser. Attending were many former suffragists, social scientists, wealthy supporters, and many others from both public and professional associations.[11]

The conference was to close with a large public meeting at Town Hall on the night of November 13. Among the earliest to arrive that night was Anne Kennedy, the editor of the *Birth Control Review*, a magazine that Margaret Sanger published. She found a group of police on stage who appeared to be following the directions of a Monsignor Dineen. She asked what was going on and the following dialogue ensued:

"This meeting must be closed."
"Why?"
"An indecent immoral subject is to be discussed. It cannot be held."
"On what authority? Are you from the police?"
"No. I'm Monsignor Dineen, Secretary to Archbishop Hayes."
"What right has he to interfere?"
"He has the right."[12]

When Sanger arrived, she found the hall ringed by police. Forcing her way in, she discovered a number of people looking confusedly toward the stage. The police, under the direction of a Captain Donohue, were announcing that the meeting was closed. Margaret Sanger went on stage to see what was happening. Anne Kennedy related her conversation with the monsignor. Margaret Sanger then repeatedly tried to speak. The police stopped her and eventually arrested her (which was her intention). Her principal speaker, Harold Cox, former member of Parliament and editor of the *Edinburgh Review,* also tried to speak and was also arrested by police. The audience began to sing, "My Country 'Tis of Thee." Sanger then refused to get in the paddy wagon and walked to the police station, followed by many of her wealthy supporters, some in their limousines.

At the station, as the authorities began to sense a public relations disaster, it seemed that suddenly no one was in charge. Much the same was true of the aftermath of the raid. There was much finger pointing and denial of responsibility. In the *New York Times* the next day, the headline was "Birth Control Raid Made by Police on Archbishop's Orders." The archbishop issued a statement saying that "decent and clean-minded people" would never talk about birth control in a public. setting.[13] Representatives of the American Civil Liberties Union joined with prominent financiers such as Henry Morgenthau, Paul Warburg, and Lewis Delafield to protest the infringement of free speech. The mayor convened an official inquiry that ultimately avoided the issue of church involvement and blamed the raid on the police.[14] But most newspapers supported Sanger, the public learned much more about this growing birth control movement, and the net result was beneficial to the cause.

If indeed the church had been behind the incident, the arrogance of it, the recklessness, was breathtaking. A leader of one church, admittedly the largest and most powerful in the city, was using police power to stop people of other religions—or no religion—from hearing a speaker in a public hall.[15] If true, it was a testament to both the determination and the myopia of the church on this issue.

CLINICS AND IDEOLOGY

Apart from dealing with religious opposition, the first two decades of the birth control movement through the twenties and thirties were a time of trying to win grudging support from the press, academic communities, and the medical establishment. It was a slow process of building alliances with other social reform groups, resolving internecine disputes, and above all, trying to get clinics open so that at least some women could gain control over their reproductive lives. Access to contraceptive means was extremely limited in those days. It was a time when the medical profession recognized no valid reason for contraception other than "the cure and prevention of disease." The medical profession saw birth control as dangerous to the morality of the community. Sanger had a far broader view. Believing every married woman had a right to contraception, she opened a clinic, the Clinical Research Bureau, which interpreted "the cure and prevention of disease" quite broadly. In these early years Margaret Sanger was the predominant reproductive rights advocate. But as the American Birth Control League matured, its approach to issues and organization began to diverge from Sanger's. Reflecting her disagreements with the type of women governing the American Birth Control League, she once wrote,

> I had always had a dread of [organizations]. I knew their weaknesses and the stifling effect they could have. They seemed heavy and ponderous, rigid, lifeless, and soulless, caught in their own mechanism to become dead wood, thus defeating the very purposes for which they had initially been established. Even the women who were able and clever at systematizing such bodies terrified me with their rule-and-rote minds, their weight and measure tactics; they appeared so sure, so positive that I felt I was in the way of a giant tractor which destroyed mercilessly as it went.[16]

Because of internal quarrels, the movement would sometimes produce two voices that did not agree.

Among the less wise alliances that were made was Margaret Sanger's and the birth control community's involvement with the eugenics movement. In

the twenties much of the intellectual community in America fell in love with
eugenics, the scientific attempt to improve the human race by encourag-
ing the reproduction of the fittest people and discouraging the reproduction of the unfit. From the perspective of a post-Nazi age, the idea of using
state power to determine which people were fit enough to reproduce seems
abominable. A political incorporation of eugenics was responsible for two
of the darker chapters in American history, compulsory state sterilization
laws and ethnically restrictive immigration laws. One indication of the general acceptance of the idea of eugenics was the fact that in the twenties 75
percent of American colleges offered courses on the subject.[17]

Margaret Sanger made overtures to eugenics advocates for two reasons.
First, they had made it socially acceptable to talk about sexual reproduction, and second, they were scientific authorities of a kind, respected and in
a position to bring some of that respectability to the birth control movement. Down to the present day, Sanger is attacked by antichoice writers as
a racist because of this part of her writings and work. Many scholars have
detailed her views.[18] But a careful reading of the material makes clear the
vital difference between the eugenicists, who wanted the state to use its
considerable powers to encourage the fittest people (often, but not always,
identified as people of North European stock) to reproduce while using
coercion to discourage the unfit from reproducing, and Margaret Sanger,
who opposed that. Sanger wrote: "Eugenicists imply or insist that a woman's
first duty is to the state; we contend that her duty to herself is her first duty
to the state. We maintain that a woman possessing an adequate knowledge
of her reproductive functions is the best judge of the time and conditions
under which her child shall be brought into the world. We further maintain that it is her right, regardless of all other considerations, to determine
whether she shall bear children or not."[19] She insisted that reproductive
decisions should always be in the hands of women. She believed in voluntary motherhood. And she was confident that humanity would improve
through the cumulative result of the decisions of individual women.

When it came to the specifics of some of the proposals, she accepted the
idea of immigration restrictions, but when the 1924 Immigration Act was
passed, limiting immigration from South European countries, she objected
to this ethnic and racial profiling.[20] She believed it was individuals, not
ethnic groups, that varied by ability.

Concerning compulsory sterilization, she supported the practice and
failed to see the dangers of abuse. It was a time when a Supreme Court
decision (*Buck v. Bell*, 1927) upheld Virginia's compulsory sterilization law.

The 8 to 1 majority opinion, written by the celebrated jurist Oliver Wendell Holmes, contained the stark line, "Three generations of imbeciles are enough." In the wake of that decision, over 12,000 Americans were ordered to be sterilized. Caught up in the movement of the times, Sanger made insensitive statements for which there is no defense.

But while Sanger was not too sure-footed in some of her ideological alliances, she was far more purposeful in her determination to get contraception into the hands of women. Sanger recognized the importance of a clinic that offered services and research opportunities. On January 2, 1923, she opened the Birth Control Clinical Research Bureau directly across from the offices of the American Birth Control League. The word "research" was anything but decorative. In addition to services for women, she wanted careful records kept so that she would have scientific data to demonstrate that birth control was efficacious.[21] Until the Depression, the Clinical Research Bureau and the early clinics of the American Birth Control League were almost the only places where married women could get access to contraception. For unmarried women there were no clinics.

The problems in opening such a clinic were formidable. Finding a physician looked impossible because of the opposition of the medical profession, but she persuaded a leading gynecologist of the time, Dr. Hannah Stone, to take on the challenge. When the state of New York would not issue a license for the clinic, Sanger went ahead without one. Finally, she enlisted the considerable resources of her businessman husband, Noah Slee, the president of the Three-in-One Oil Company. It was illegal to import the German diaphragms that were most effective, so they were shipped to Slee's factory in Montreal, where they were repackaged into drums that bore the label of his company. They were smuggled into New York in those containers.[22]

Over the next fifteen years, the Clinical Research Bureau had many homes, was disparaged by the medical community, and was raided by the police, but nevertheless served thousands of women and became the source of a wealth of acceptable data that led finally to the American Medical Association's endorsement of birth control in 1937.

REACHING CLERGY BY VOICING THE REALITY OF SUFFERING

Margaret Sanger had a unique ability to focus the attention of the public on the suffering of women in her time. Her special genius was to confront high-minded theological opponents with the brutal suffering of actual women's lives: "when I am confronted with arguments against Birth Control, arguments that are as a rule presented by learned theologians or indefatigable statisticians, the dim far off chorus of suffering and pain begins to resound anew in my ears. How academic, how anemically intellectual and how remote from throbbing, bleeding humanity all of these prejudiced arguments sound, when one has been brought face to face with the reality of suffering!"[23] This is the aspect of her work that began to resonate with clergy. Some would sympathize with her claim that such crises cry out for practical solutions, not theology or anemic intellectualism. A number of the clergy she corresponded with were famous, people like the Reverend Howard Melish, a prominent Episcopal leader in Brooklyn; Dr. Harry Emerson Fosdick of the Riverside Church; the celebrated Unitarian leader the Reverend John Haynes Holmes; and the Reverend E. McNeill Poteat of the Southern Baptist Convention. But she also began to get sympathetic letters from lesser-known clergy who believed in her cause. Typical was a letter from the Reverend James Oesterling, superintendent of the Inner Mission Society of the Evangelical Lutheran Society of Baltimore, who wrote to her to offer his support, to ask for some free literature, and to complain about his colleagues "who practice but do not preach birth control." He closed by calling for God's blessing on her efforts to pass a national law for the dissemination of birth control information "in spite of the Pope."[24]

She was seen by women of all classes as one who could express the particular suffering of those who had no means to control their reproductive lives, women who were enduring the consequences of a society whose face was set adamantly against the contraception that would ease their pain. She saw with perfect clarity the injustice of the simple fact that the only means of contraception available to most married couples—withdrawal and condoms—were both in the control of men. There were no contraceptive means in the hands of women.

Some biographers have noted that Sanger exaggerated her own importance in bringing birth control to America while ignoring the fact that American physicians knew about contraception.[25] But such criticism misses the point. That doctors had some knowledge of contraception meant little or nothing to masses of women unless they could get it. Margaret Sanger made birth control accessible. She opened clinics, she went to jail. She advocated, and she took on the critics of birth control. With the exception of a few courageous physicians, doctors had not done these things. Women appreciated the difference. If one is going to do the sacred work of justice, one must take action. She did.

The Reverend John Haynes Holmes, a famous New York Unitarian minister of the time, recognized her extraordinary prophetic qualities and abilities as early as 1916. Listening to her speak at a rally at Carnegie Hall to support her sister Ethel who was on a hunger strike while in jail, he said this: "Margaret took the audience and lifted it up. . . . She had it—the power of a saint combined with the mind of a statesman. I realized that night that she was one of the great women of our time."[26]

She challenged the sentimentality of those who championed the birth of children regardless of circumstances. After the Town Hall raid in 1921, she rented the Park Center Hall on Columbus Circle in New York City to stage a debate. She invited those who disagreed with her to come and set out their point of view. Every one of them advocated abstinence as the only allowable means for married people to prevent birth. In only two sentences she demolished their argument: "The law requires a married woman to give of herself to her husband or forego his support. This makes self-control by women impractical, if not impossible."[27] Throughout her life, while she sometimes made strategically flawed decisions, she never forgot her feminist roots. She remained centered on women and the critical importance of their being able to control their own lives. Her most remembered statement typifies her thought: "No woman can call herself free who does not own and control her body. No woman can call herself free until she can choose consciously whether she will or will not be a mother." That focus on women was central to her success.

It is true that Margaret Sanger espoused other reforms besides birth control. In January 1912, ten thousand textile workers from many countries went on strike in Lawrence, Massachusetts. Mostly immigrants, the strikers did not get the backing of traditional labor unions like the AFL, which focused on native-born male workers. But women played a central role in this strike as they dramatized the effect of low wages on the lives of children and their families. Sanger picketed at the strike scene. She also editorialized in favor of socialism and far more radical economic changes. But she never lost sight of the reality that even should real economic justice come for the working class, it would do nothing to bring reproductive freedom to women. Even those who saw clearly the link between poverty and the inability to prevent the birth of too many children tended to focus exclusively on ending the poverty. In fact, as she was well aware, reformers from Teddy Roosevelt, the trust-buster, all the way over to the Marxists were opposed to birth control. Then, as now, women were urged by activists to work for general economic reforms.[28] But Margaret Sanger realized that the same "liberal" men who were advocating economic reforms were quite capable of controlling and dominating their own wives at home. She fully appreciated the injustice of such behavior, the all-too-human phenomenon of being liberal in areas where one has no control, but conservative and controlling when one has power. Ironically, she recognized the trait because she had the same fault herself.[29]

She won the allegiance, or at least the serious attention, of all sorts of women: women from Vermont farms who gathered to hear her, rural southern women, wealthy society women, and poor women. Even if the audiences sometimes gave no visible sign that they agreed with her, her speaking of birth control had nevertheless forever broken the power of a muffled society over them. Her words had now put the subject on the table. Women who were fearful of raising the subject themselves could now refer to what Margaret Sanger had said. They could talk to each other about it.

Through this process, women began to speak and find their own voice. By 1928 fifty thousand letters had come to her asking for help. That year she published a representative sample of them in a volume entitled *Motherhood in Bondage*. Here was an ocean of suffering, most of it quite unnecessary. She had no difficulty understanding the world from which these letters came. As a young nurse, she had gone home to take care of her mother, whose life was shortened by constant childbearing. Here is a sample letter from a child mother whose body was not ready for the constant pregnancies:

> I was married when only fourteen years old. My first baby came, died at birth. I was torn so badly. In eleven months another baby came. Then the third one came. I went to the hospital to have the laceration repaired. This was three months after the baby came. Then I got that way again so when baby came these parts had not got strong so it was torn again. The baby died. All my babies are instrument cases. Then I had another baby and since then I was that way again but had a miscarriage. I was not strong enough to carry it. The doctor told me I could not have living babies so I let him open the womb and he had done it four or five times but I would rather not have to again, but I want to get well. You know I cannot keep on having abortions.[30]

There were dozens of letters about the helplessness and heartlessness of doctors, many of whom seemed to have only one or two children in their own families:

> I have been married twelve years and in that time I have been pregnant nine times, bearing five living children and two born dead and two miscarriages at about two or three months, and my third child was too weak to stand this

world and left us at seven months. . . . I have been home from the hospital
only a week and the two doctors that took care of me told my husband 'One
more child and I won't answer for her life.' I asked them what we should
do to prevent conception and they said, 'You must be very careful.' that is all
they would say. My husband is very much worried. We are very dear to one
another.[31]

And finally there were many letters from mothers raised in ignorance and
desperate for knowledge that was denied them even by their own mothers:

I have told you things that I have never breathed to any human before, and if
you do not tell me what to do, it is really a crime to withhold this knowledge
from a woman, and if ever a woman begged for knowledge it is certainly I.
My mother had only two children, myself and a sister younger. Whether there
would have been more I do not know, for she didn't believe in telling these
things and don't to this day, so we were brought up in absolute ignorance of
such matters, and that it was an unpardonable sin to be caught talking or even
thinking about such things, and now I and my sister, who is less fortunate than
I, are paying the price.[32]

By 1938 there were 374 birth control clinics all across the country.[33]

RECLAIMING THE SACRED

America is a religious nation. True, Americans have prized separation of
church and state, but that should not blind the perceptive observer from
appreciating how large and pervasive are American religious sensitivities.
Almost from the beginning of the nation, waves of religious revival spread
westward, fostering religious enthusiasms and a faith that was both warmly
emotional and, often, anti-intellectual. Such faith formed—and still forms—
a public that takes matters of religion seriously. This means that if a particular cause can be shown to be offensive to the sensibilities of religious
people, it will have a difficult time of it. If birth control's religious opponents could portray it as something that was dangerous to, or destructive
of, traditional religious values, then it might be possible to stop it before
it could obtain public acceptance. Sanger was aware that to have all of the
sacred symbols arrayed against her movement was a major problem that
had to be faced. She learned that she could not counter the moral claims of
the Catholic Church as a lone secular person. The fight was too uneven—

one woman and a fledgling movement against a historic worldwide church. So she made a tactical decision. She recognized that Roman Catholicism was not the only historic faith in America, nor was it as large as Protestantism. Sacred power and sacred symbols might be found elsewhere. Therefore she turned to Protestant ministers and Jewish rabbis.

She began by corresponding with individual clergy such as John Haynes Holmes and the equally well known Rabbi Stephen Wise. She was especially grateful to the Commission on Social Justice of the Central Conference of American Rabbis when it included support of birth control as part of its 1930 "Message of Social Justice." Commission members said, "Where the intelligent regulation of birth can avert suffering and degradation, the voice of mercy speaks. That voice should not go unheeded. . . . Again, without love for humanity, love toward God is an empty phrase."[34]

In a letter to Rabbi Edward Israel Sanger expressed her thanks: "I think it is a beautiful statement and a courageous one. . . . You have dared to point out many of the glaring defects in our present day system, and have, with temperance and vision, made definite recommendations toward sane and humane solutions."[35]

Then she sought opportunities to speak to religious assemblages. One of her biographers said that she would travel hundreds of miles for only five minutes on the platform of a denominational meeting.[36] She saw to it that birth control literature was distributed at church conventions and lobbied church leaders with innumerable letters.[37] Years of this effort plus the growing public awareness of birth control began to have an effect on Protestant churches.

The first "establishment" religious body to show signs of limited approval of contraception was the prominent Episcopal bulwark, the Anglican bishops of the Lambeth Conference. Composed of all the Anglican bishops in the world, the Lambeth Conference met every three to five years. Prior to the late 1920s the bishops had already delivered themselves of several opinions on birth control—all of them negative.

In 1908 that august body had said that contraception "cannot be spoken of without repugnance."[38] Presumably, one could hardly exaggerate the evil which would come in its wake. But in the next twenty-two years, the increasing discussion of contraception, the growing birth control movement (which was being supported by Episcopal women's groups) and the subject's shift from unmentionable to controversial changed the climate within many parts of the Episcopal Church. So in 1930 the Lambeth bishops changed their position. They gave tentative acceptance to marital contraception with these cautious words, "Where there is a clearly felt moral obligation to limit or avoid parenthood, the method must be decided on Christian principles."[39] This Lambeth decision, however modest to modern ears, was a bombshell to Roman Catholics. They were outraged. The Catholic magazine *Commonweal* said that the endorsement of birth control by the Episcopal Church "is a sad proof of how not merely disunity alone, but palpable abandonment of Christian principles, has affected the churches separated from the Rock of Peter."[40]

Those in disagreement could comfort themselves with the thought that at least no American church body had accepted birth control. But in 1931, one did. The step was taken by the Committee on Marriage and the Home of the Federal Council of Churches of Christ in America, the large ecumenical organization of mainline Protestantism that was later to become the National Council of Churches. Chaired by the theologian Reinhold Niebuhr, the committee issued a report that favored birth control on economic and medical grounds, arguing that contraception could help prevent overpopulation and relieve poverty (claims that are still made on United Nations Web sites). But it also stressed birth control's benefits for the health of women and children. It then proclaimed something that was for the times quite radical. It said that birth control was a benefit because it promoted a "sex union between husbands and wives as an expression of mutual affection."[41] At the time, this was the first favorable word about marital sex—apart from procreation—that had come from a church body.

This was too much for the American churches of 1931. A storm of disapproval broke over the heads of the Federal Council. Southern Presbyterians and some Lutherans were going to withdraw. Northern Baptists were irate. At the latter's convention in 1933 a committee censured the Federal Council by releasing a statement saying that the council certainly did not speak for it.[42] Although it was not publicly known, Margaret Sanger's collected papers reveal that she worked closely with members of the Federal Council. And when the funding for the Committee on Marriage and the Home was imperiled by so much opposition, Sanger worked quietly to raise money to replace the lost funds.[43]

But even among the as yet unpersuaded denominations, there were signs of change. In February 1936, a Baptist Youth Conference at Calvary Baptist church in Omaha, Nebraska, passed a recommendation favoring the dissemination of birth control information.[44] And in November of that same year, five hundred members of the convention of the Western New York Baptist Young People unanimously recommended an expanded program for birth control education.[45] Coming from the future church leaders, these actions were signs that change would eventually come.

In 1931 the General Council of the Congregational Christian Church had endorsed birth control by calling for "voluntary parenthood." And in May 1930 the Unitarian Church had vowed to support "all reasonable efforts in their communities for the promotion of the birth control movement." But these two groups were the most liberal denominations. The larger denominations were still silent on the subject.

The next big breakthrough came from the American Episcopal bishops at their convention in 1934. At Atlantic City on October 20, they endorsed birth control information that had as its aim "a more wholesome family life, wherein parenthood may be undertaken with due respect for the health of mothers and the welfare of their children."[46] Before the convention Sanger had strategized with Guy Shipler, the editor of the influential Episcopal magazine *The Churchman*. In a letter she said, "It would be simply grand if you could carry an editorial as you suggest urging the matter [of birth control] for the attention of the General Convention. Any further information you can give us regarding the Deputies or Bishops will be welcomed."[47] Using the information she had, she lobbied the bishops heavily. The vote on the resolution was close—44 to 38—and Margaret Sanger was in the thick of it, sending excerpts from *Motherhood in Bondage* to wavering bishops. Her involvement made a difference. It was the practical working out of her conviction that such religious support was critical for her movement.

Now the remaining large Protestant denominations—Methodists, Presbyterians, and Lutherans—had to be persuaded. Among the Methodists, two of the larger Conferences—California and New England—endorsed contraception. By the end of the 1930s, the Methodist Church had officially endorsed birth control. At first the Presbyterians dithered, preferring not to touch this controversial topic. But in 1931 the Special Commission on Marriage, Divorce, and Remarriage of the Presbyterian Church also opened the door to acceptance by affirming that families might be limited not only by continence but also by contraception that respected Christian spiritual ideals.[48]

Presbyterian acceptance had a certain weight to it. If the Presbyterians (a wealthy denomination sometimes described as "the Republican Party at prayer") would accept birth control, then it could no longer be considered a radical idea. The Lutherans took much longer, not ratifying birth control until 1956, but here too sections of the denomination were supportive of contraception much earlier.

The culmination of this process was a neutralizing of the sacred power claimed by Sanger's opponents. A claim by the clergy of one church that they speak for God, for divine rules that can never be violated no matter how humane the circumstances, may be impressive so long as it is unchallenged. But when an equal number of other clergy say that the sacred power proclaims no such rules, then there exists something far less imposing than before; we now have a disagreement about what constitutes responsible morality. When that is the case, the layperson is, in effect, free to decide, free to make a choice as to which sacred power (if any) he or she accepts.

The clergy Margaret Sanger persuaded transformed a one-sided battle into a more equal contest. As the movement grew, more and more people with clergy collars were showing up at the annual Planned Parenthood dinners. They participated publicly in the opening of new services in various cities, and, more than their symbolic value, many of these clergy had earned the respect of their communities through years of service. When they added their presence and their prestige to the activities of each local affiliate, the public image of the organization was subtly enhanced. Through all these means, clergy brought a measure of sacredness to the movement that would come to be known as Planned Parenthood.

Conclusion

Margaret Sanger was not a person who lacked serious faults. She did not easily share power with others and, in modern terms, was hardly what one would call collegial. But she was one of those rare figures who alter history by the force of their personality and the cumulative result of years of pushing one particular issue. Though many would resist the comparison, and though she would be amused, she shared more than a few traits of biblical prophets, who, when convinced of injustice, were unrelenting in their attacks upon it.

Margaret Sanger demolished the principal defenses of the old cruel anathema against contraception. Those defenses were silence and the shame that flowed from religious disapproval and condemnation. She demolished the silence by speaking about it. Like a prophet she raised the subject everywhere, from lectures in major public halls to street corners where she faced hecklers. She took away the shame by being shameless. She said in a thousand forums that there was no shame in being responsible about one's ability to bear or not bear children. Even further, she said not only is there no shame in a husband and wife sharing sexual love for its own sake, it is in fact something which is sacred. A strange term for a woman known to be an atheist, yet ironically it was precisely on this subject that her language became most religious: "I contend that it is just as sacred and beautiful for two people to express their love when they have no intention of being parents. And I contend that they can go into that relationship with the same beauty and the same holiness with which they go into music or to prayer. I believe that it is the right understanding of our sexual power and of its creative energy that gives us spiritual illumination. I say that there is more than one use to make of it, and that is the higher use development of our soul. . . . and soul growth."[49]

Clergy could come to her support because they came to realize that in truth she was far closer to biblical morality than were her religious opponents. Both Jesus and the rabbis of the Talmud would have been horrified at religious rules that had to be obeyed no matter how much human misery they evoked among impoverished helpless people. Jesus stated it baldly in Mark 2:27: "The sabbath was made for humankind, and not humankind for the sabbath." The rabbis were famous for their use of humane casuistry to effectively nullify texts such as Deuteronomy 21:18–21, which commanded the execution of disobedient sons. The rabbinical spirit is expressed best in a famous saying of the sages, "Without love toward humanity, love toward God is an empty phrase." Sanger focused on remedying human suffering.

How to relieve that suffering, how to give people hope, is what many clergy believe biblical faith is all about. In this regard, Margaret Sanger had the same spirit as Harry Hopkins, the legendary high-level aide of President Franklin Roosevelt. In his first day in office in the depths of the Depression, Hopkins signed checks for millions of dollars dispensing desperately needed relief to the poor. When colleagues urged him to take his time in formulating plans that would work best "in the long run," Hopkins said, "People don't eat in the long run. They eat every day." Margaret Sanger had that same urgency. It is what made her great in religious as well as in secular terms.

To their credit, a number of clergy joined Sanger in her urgency for the freedom to choose contraception. From the 1930s on, clergy support for Planned Parenthood grew steadily. In city after city, affiliates found that some clergy were more than willing to speak out publicly in defense of the work of the clinics. By the 1960s it was precisely the religious and moral authority of these supportive clergy that changed public opinion about birth control. An example of the shift can be seen in the changed attitude of President Dwight Eisenhower. In the fifties he thought that population control (which everyone understood to mean birth control) was an "inappropriate area" for government action, but by 1963 he reversed his position.[50] The changing climate also provided cover for public officials reluctant to refer welfare clients to Planned Parenthood or to support expansion of birth control services to unmarried people on welfare. (See chapter 5.) It was hard for opponents to demonize Planned Parenthood when churches opened their church buildings to host affiliate clinics. It was even harder to maintain that a service housed in the most respectable Episcopal church in town was an evil thing.

By the end of the 1930s Margaret Sanger had brought about a partnership between clergy and Planned Parenthood. However reluctant clergy might have been at the beginning, they had caught some of her spirit. She had captured their consciences and, in many cases, their hearts. Now they would do what she could not do, bring the sanction of the sacred to the work of Planned Parenthood.

CHAPTER 3

Building Public Acceptance,
1935–1957

IN THE STRUGGLE TO MAKE contraception socially acceptable in America, the Planned Parenthood movement experienced certain great public victories. In 1958 both Planned Parenthood and supportive clergy persuaded the New York City hospital system to end a ban on birth control. In 1962 Planned Parenthood clergy in Baltimore persuaded the Maryland State Welfare Board to drop its ban on providing contraceptive services to people on welfare. In 1965 the *Griswold* decision established a constitutional right to contraception and in 1973 the *Roe v. Wade* ruling did the same for abortion. These are some of the great victories of the movement, and the clergy were a vital part of every one.

But before any of that could become possible, the very idea of contraception had to achieve a certain level of social acceptability. In the thirties, forties, and fifties, it was the distinctive role of the clergy to bring the sanction of the sacred to birth control and to the work of Planned Parenthood and to point to the fact that responsible use of contraception was not only moral but also had a spiritual dimension. In order to do that, writings had to be produced, public statements issued, and dozens of battles fought and, usually, won.

Margaret Sanger carried on the early fights with few allies, but in the 1930s she finally brought a number of mainline Protestant and Jewish denominations to her side. Now some of the leading clergy of those religious bodies were willing to add their voices to the cause. Theirs were voices, which—like the Roman Catholic hierarchy—presumed to speak for the sacred.

This was a kind of interregnum period, the time between the era when birth control was widely condemned and the time of full public acceptance. From 1930 to about the late 1950s, there were literally hundreds of local skirmishes between the opponents of birth control and Planned Parenthood and its clergy supporters. In this chapter we will look first at the religious context of the times and then give typical examples of the three main forms of clergy advocacy: public statements defending the morality of contraception, organizing a national network of clergy supporters, and clergy defense of physicians dismissed from Roman Catholic hospitals.

The Religious Context: Tensions between Catholic and Non-Catholic Communities

Protestant and Jewish clergy involvement on the side of birth control at first did little to change the implacable opposition of the Roman Catholic Church. In this pre–Vatican II era, relationships between Roman Catholic and non-Catholic clergy were nothing like the general cooperation and friendliness of current times. In those days the two groups had little contact. Much of the American Roman Catholic world was still living in a kind of "ghetto Catholicism," a defensive, sometimes belligerent suspicion of the non-Catholic realm. Some of this was understandable and certainly justified.

In its development in America, Roman Catholicism had faced considerable anti-Catholic bigotry. Father John Cogley has argued that anti-Catholicism is the oldest and most enduring prejudice in American life.[1] When large numbers of Irish and German Catholics began to arrive in America in the 1830s, the overwhelmingly Protestant nativists, as they were known, became violent toward them. In 1834 a Protestant mob, enraged by a fraudulent tell-all book about convent life and led by Congregationalist ministers, burned down the Ursaline convent in Charlestown, Massachusetts.[2] Other inflammatory tracts led to a wave of anti-Catholic riots in the big cities of the East. This poisonous climate gave rise to the "Know-Nothing" party, a force that rode to power on anti-Catholicism and anti-immigrant sentiment.

Another aspect of anti-Catholic prejudice was the Protestant attitude that the public schools belonged to them. Protestant foundations supervised the curricula that promoted Protestantism and included insulting references to Roman Catholics in those curricula. Roman Catholic leaders asked that the public schools remain secular and leave the religion to the churches. In

New York City and other places, their wishes were ignored.[3] In reaction to this intolerant climate, Catholics felt the need to have their own schools.

In the twentieth century, the most painful anti-Catholic episode was the defeat of the Democratic candidate, the Roman Catholic governor of New York, Al Smith, in his run for the presidency in 1928. Although most political observers then and now believe he would have lost anyway, Roman Catholics were outraged at the slanderous rumors that circulated freely— that Protestants would lose their citizenship, that the Pope would rule America, and so on. The Ku Klux Klan burned crosses at his campaign stops in the South. The blatant anti-Catholicism, which destroyed Smith's candidacy, confirmed the suspicions of Catholics who felt they were still treated unfairly by the Protestant majority. And in the wake of that rejection, one historian notes that the Catholic community carried out a "remarkable emotional withdrawal" from secular America. The church created a complete set of institutions to parallel those of the general society. There were Roman Catholic schools, youth centers, sports leagues, nursing homes, hospitals. Along with the *Reader's Digest*, there was a *Catholic Digest*, a Catholic Book Club, Catholic medical societies, Catholic bar associations, a Catholic Historical Association, and a Catholic Sociological Society.[4]

For its part, the American Catholic Church appeared to have little interest in the beliefs of other religious groups in America. All were categorized simply as "non-Catholics." In those years the defensiveness of the Roman Catholic Church was embodied in a whole host of church policies and practices. When Protestants or Jews married Roman Catholics, the non-Catholic partner generally had to sign an agreement that the children would be raised Catholic even if the Catholic parent died. In another example, Roman Catholic laypeople were not to enter Protestant churches for weddings or funerals without special permission.

Despite these practices, powerful connections were made with influential sectors of society. As the church established a welfare system that reached non-Catholics as well as Catholics, it encouraged the professionalization of its social workers. It also became a support for the public welfare system and an influence on its social workers (who as a consequence were very slow to endorse contraception).[5]

On the Protestant side there was a powerful concern about doctrinal positions taken by the Roman Catholic Church. In 1864 Pope Pius IX had issued a "Syllabus of Errors." This document condemned as "errors" two beliefs very dear to Protestant hearts. It condemned the belief in the separation of church and state and the belief that error had as much right to be expressed as truth.[6] Despite the fact that many American Catholics ignored such papal pronouncements, Protestant clergy and laypeople tended to take them at face value. Taking them seriously meant assuming that if Roman Catholics had political control of government, they would freely discriminate against those whose views were "errors." A famous book of the post–World War II period was *American Freedom and Catholic Power*, by Paul Blanshard.[7] Blanshard gave the most extreme interpretation possible to the church statements that fed those fears. Since the "Syllabus of Errors" was expressly repudiated by Vatican II in 1963, most people today would regard these suspicions as ridiculous, but in this immediate postwar period, there was as yet no John Kennedy in the White House to demonstrate that a Catholic president would not be governed by a church. So such fears were perhaps more understandable in the forties and fifties.

Aggravating the situation was the fact that many ministers also felt that priests had had a narrow and provincial seminary education. In matters such as birth control, numerous Protestant clergy saw the Catholic Church as socially backward and afraid of modern education and progress. Their bias was obvious, but there were some grounds for such a belief. In the nineteenth century Pope Pius IX had set his face against "modernism," and subsequent popes often spoke as though they too deplored much of the modern world. A big part of the problem was that the two groups simply didn't know each other. The almost complete lack of contact between Catholic and non-Catholic clergy meant that public expressions of opinion could have a sharp hostile tone. For example, in 1947 a Methodist bishop, speaking to a combined meeting of the Planned Parenthood Association and the Church Federation of Greater Chicago, characterized the religious leaders who attacked Planned Parenthood as people who were "as sincere as their forebears who tortured Galileo."[8] Such words were perhaps to be expected in a situation where two groups did not communicate and regarded each other with hostility.

The times were also much harder on the Jewish community in America. In the long years of the Depression and World War II, that community did not have the prestige and influence in society that it has at the present time. It had to struggle with the much stronger prejudice of anti-Semitism. Jews were barred from everything from country club memberships to corporate boards to children's summer camps. So-called Gentlemen's Agreements prevented Jewish citizens from buying homes in many neighborhoods. Nevertheless, despite the urgency of combating prejudice against their co-religionists, many rabbis were also willing to make a strong public commitment to the cause of birth control.

Reform rabbis were involved for a variety of reasons. For much of the nineteenth century and the early twentieth, with a few exceptions, rabbis did not speak out on prophetic social issues. In his study *A History of the Jews in America*, Howard Zachar notes that the Central Conference of American Rabbis made only two social pronouncements in its first eighteen years (1885–1903). Zachar argues that after the turn of the century, the group became much more activist because of the influence of liberal Protestantism's Social Gospel ideology, the idea that biblical theology requires that believers try to create more just social institutions in the world.[9] In the late teens and early twenties, the Central Conference began to make pronouncements favoring minimum wage, workmen's compensation, and the right of labor to organize and bargain. Given this climate of support for social reform, it was not surprising that some rabbis responded positively to Margaret Sanger's request for help. But they may also have been sympathetic because they were honoring the ancient Jewish tradition of respect for the dangers women faced in childbirth.[10]

Whatever the reasons that moved them, ministers and rabbis, along with Planned Parenthood and many courageous physicians, gradually persuaded the public that justice required that human beings have control over their own reproductive lives. This was the sacred work of that period.

Opening Skirmish between Planned Parenthood Clergy and Roman Catholic Critics

On Sunday, December 8, 1935, Cardinal Patrick J. Hayes, leader of the Diocese of New York, preached a sermon at St. Patrick's Cathedral attacking birth control. This was a most unusual action for him. He had not preached since October 1931, and he interrupted the regular schedule of preachers to make his remarks. The occasion for his upset was a proposal made at a recent birth control meeting in Carnegie Hall. Sponsored by the American Birth Control League, the gathering had heard from speakers who proposed that the government should provide birth control information for people on relief. The cardinal's tone was apocalyptic: "As Cardinal Archbishop of New York I rise to voice measured, deliberate and emphatic condemnation at the effrontery of those who . . . advocated birth control for families on relief. As shepherd of my flock . . . I feel it my duty to cry out in warning against those who would fly in the face of God and bring ruin and disaster in the land and to the civilization that some among us at least still cherish."[11]

The cardinal denounced "society women" who seemed to have little respect for his opinions on this issue: "One of these women had the audacity to say to me personally that she practiced contraception, and moreover that she had advised her domestics to practice it. That is going pretty far. Who are these people to do that?"[12]

Then he went on to the core of his remarks, which gave a comprehensive account of the teachings of the church and the Roman Catholic rejection of so-called artificial birth control. Reviewing the major papal statements condemning the practice, the cardinal made it clear that this was a matter on which there could be no compromise. Natural law ordained that the primary purpose of intercourse was procreation. Anything that frustrated that end was severely condemned. Catholics were, however, allowed to regulate family size through either the use of the rhythm method (selective intercourse which avoided periods when the woman was fertile) or through abstinence. Concerning the latter, he cited the contemporary pope's optimistic estimate of the possibilities of celibacy within marriage: "There is no possible circumstance in which husband and wife cannot, strengthened by the grace of God, faithfully fulfill their duties and preserve in wedlock their chastity unspotted."[13]

The text of his remarks was printed in its entirety in the *New York Times* the next day. Reading it through, one has the sense that the cardinal felt that he was denouncing the morality of some out-of-the-mainstream birth control advocates and that this would be the end of it. But the response to his sermon came right from the center of the mainstream.

Eight days later, on December 17, a group of thirteen New York City clergy took the cardinal to task on the front page of the *Times*. These were the leading clergy of the city. Most well known was the Reverend Harry Emerson Fosdick, the leading light of American Protestantism and pastor of the citadel of American Protestantism, the Riverside Church in Manhattan. His congregation held many influential members of the city establishment, including John D. Rockefeller, Jr. Other clergy signers of the reply to the cardinal included the Reverend John Haynes Holmes, Dr. John Howard Melish of Holy Trinity Protestant Episcopal Church in Brooklyn, and Rabbi Milton Steinberg, chair of the Committee on Social Justice of the Rabbinical Assembly of America.

This august group disagreed with many of the cardinal's arguments, including the claims that birth control is race suicide and that it leads to social decadence. But the main thrust of their argument was directed against the cardinal's theological claim—that contraception is contrary to the commandment of God. In their reply, they made it clear that they had a different theology. Using language that reflected their belief that God is disclosed in the current lives and experiences of human beings, they said: "If the Cardinal chooses to accept the literal interpretation of Old Testament statements as infallible doctrine, we register no complaint; nor should he complain if we choose instead to base our faith upon the evidence, the knowledge, and the experience available in our own time."[14]

They closed their letter with two points, that the Catholic Church should not try to impose its views on those of other religions who did not agree with it, and that the church should drop its opposition to publicly financed birth control clinics. It would be over three decades before that would happen in most places, but this was the opening salvo from the Protestant and Jewish world. Based on moral and theological convictions, it was the kind of statement, with rare exceptions, that only clergy can make.

Organizing a National Clergy Network

For the first few years after this 1935 skirmish, clergy support for Planned Parenthood grew slowly and mostly out of sight of the media. As with any movement, it took a while to grow. It took time for clergy to share their experience with each other, to learn new information, and to become familiar with the detailed particulars of contraception. But one shocking 1940 incident accelerated clergy organizing in defense of Planned Parenthood.

By 1940 the birth control movement had won some victories. The cause had also benefited from Sanger's continued work for reproductive rights. Her travels around the world made her a well-known figure. More and more birth control clinics were opening in America, some with government funding. The movement was teetering on the edge of respectability. Then came Holyoke, Massachusetts.

In October 1940, Margaret Sanger was giving a series of talks in western Massachusetts. All went well until she reached Holyoke. She was to speak at a Congregational church there, but just prior to her coming, the local Roman Catholic priest issued a letter to be read at all the masses. In it he said that those who were sponsoring the lecture were a "disgrace to the Christian community."[15] Then he called a local banker who was on the board of the Congregational church. Shortly thereafter the church withdrew its invitation and announced that "the problem of economic damage to Congregationalist members as a result of their allowing the speech to be made had to be taken into account."[16] Margaret Sanger was livid and insisted that she would speak in Holyoke. It proved impossible to rent a hall, and things looked hopeless until a female organizer for the Textile Workers' Union invited her to speak in the two rooms of their office. Some seventy-five people crowded into the space to hear her lecture. She went on to speak at eleven other cities with no further problems.

The incident was a profound embarrassment to Protestant churches and clergy. It also continued to rankle Margaret Sanger. How was it possible that one religion could control who could speak in the sanctuary of another religion? How was it possible that freedom of speech meant so little? As long as birth control could be portrayed as a disreputable subject, it would never enter the mainstream of American life, subject always to ambushes such as the Holyoke incident.

Characteristically, Margaret Sanger decided that she would fight this. She had long enjoyed the support of a number of individual clergy, and many of them had spoken out in support of her work. Yet Sanger felt that something more publicly visible was needed. So she invited seven leading clergy and five members of the Birth Control Federation of America to a luncheon at the Hotel Weylin in New York City on March 5, 1941, to talk about forming a committee that could counter these religious attacks. They all met, and the group was in something of a fighting mood. As stated in the report on their meeting, "It was the emphatic opinion of all present . . . that the time had ceased to supplicate and beg the Catholic Church to be tolerant; that from now on the Federation and church groups should adopt an active aggressive policy of demanding such tolerance, not alone on the issue of birth control but on the issues of free speech and religious assembly as well as religious tolerance."[17] Sanger had a nonreligious name in mind for the proposed group, a "National Council of Ethical Values," but what finally emerged was something different, a National Clergymen's Advisory Council, the first of three waves of clergy support for Planned Parenthood. This was to be the biggest and most influential wave of the three.

At first the coming of World War II delayed the clergy in organizing, and in November 1942, there was a second shock. A referendum in Massachusetts that would have repealed the Comstock law that made any use of birth control a crime was widely expected to pass easily. Yet a determined and well-financed campaign by the Roman Catholic Church in the last few weeks before the election defeated the referendum decisively. With this added spur, the Federation's National Clergymen's Advisory Council met on February 17, 1943, at the Town Hall Club in New York City to develop a strategy. At that meeting Kenneth Rose, who was chief executive of Planned Parenthood from 1939 to 1948, raised the question of what to do about Roman Catholic opposition to birth control. He asked the clergy for their thoughts.

Though willing to help, the clergy were getting mixed signals. Those closest to Margaret Sanger were ready to go on the offensive. Typical of this camp were the Reverend Guy Shipler, editor of *The Churchman*, the magazine of the Episcopal Church, and Bishop G. Bromley Oxnam of the Methodist Church. Oxnam was one of the boldest and most controversial Protestant leaders of the post–World War II period who, when he was not being called before the House Un-American Activities Committee, was advocating for Planned Parenthood. At that February meeting, the clergy present were willing to go beyond the defensive. Dr. Sidney Goldstein, chairman of the Jewish Institute on Marriage and the Family, said that it was the duty of clergy to take a public stand, to characterize any state or city health department that blocked contraceptive services as "undemocratic" and to expose Roman Catholic opposition as a "denial of the people's civil liberties." Furthermore they should "smoke the opposition out and expose it for what it is."[18]

But Kenneth Rose was the soul of caution and conservatism, and he did not sympathize with this clergy mood. Only two months later the Executive Committee of the Planned Parenthood Board adopted a statement, "Suggested Policy on the Catholic Church," which went in the opposite direction. Far from going on the offensive, this statement said that it would be the policy of Planned Parenthood: "To avoid religious controversy and emphasize the health and social values of Planned Parenthood. . . . The Federation realizes that it is not possible to reply directly through the medium of the Roman Catholic press to articles printed therein attacking Planned Parenthood, and believes that such attacks are best ignored. Generally speaking, a local incident should not be magnified into a national issue."[19]

On every one of these points Margaret Sanger would have disagreed; she didn't avoid religious controversy, didn't ignore attacks, and usually won the battle whenever a local incident was magnified into a national issue. The end result was a National Clergymen's Advisory Council that was somewhere in the middle between feistiness and docility. Their charge read: "The National Clergymen's Advisory Council is asked to be the spokesman for the Federation on the moral and religious values of planned parenthood."[20] In general, they followed Rose's recommendation to stress health issues and to focus on how birth control could help the institution of the family. But at times they spoke out sharply. And they did find ways to put religious opponents on the defensive.

One of their earliest efforts was a 1943 proclamation to coincide with the annual celebration of National Family Week, a program sponsored by the

International Council of Religious Education in Chicago. The clergy proclamation was entitled "Statement by Religious Leaders on the Responsibilities of Parenthood." In it they made this appeal: "As families look to their
physicians for health guidance, they look to their religious counselors for
moral guidance . . . believing that in these times it is of particular importance that the moral issues be further clarified, we join in urging. . . . [t]hat
religious groups lend continued support to the principles of responsible
parenthood and family planning as essential to the building of a strong and
vital post-war generation."[21]

They were able to secure 480 clergy signatories from forty-three states.
Signers included 17 bishops, deans, seminary presidents, and most of the
leading names in both the American Protestant and the Jewish worlds. By
1944 the number of interested clergy was so large that Planned Parenthood
decided to hold national mail balloting of affiliated clergy to elect the
twenty-five members of the national board of the Clergymen's Advisory
Council. Elected that year were figures such as the Reverend Adam Clayton
Powell, Jr., of the Abyssinian Baptist Church in Harlem, later to become a
major figure in Congress, Dr. Sidney Goldstein, and the famous Unitarian
leader the Reverend A. Powell Davies.

Once the war ended the tide of clergy coming to support Planned Parenthood became a flood. By September of 1945 New Jersey had signed up
400 clergy, Maryland 300, and Illinois an impressive 1,000. Clergy began to
assume other leadership roles within Planned Parenthood. In 1945 the Reverend Cornelius Trowbridge, the chair of the National Clergymen's Advisory Council, was elected to chair the Planned Parenthood National Board.

The next time (1946) the Clergymen's Advisory Council issued a national
proclamation, it had no less than 3,200 clergy signatures. And this time
there were hints of the combative in their identification of who was holding up public access to contraception. This petition denounced the religious
opponents, "whereas minority religious opposition to the planning of parenthood, through the use of medically approved methods of birth control,
frequently prevents boards of hospitals, nursing and welfare agencies from
recognizing this essential service."[22] They also suggested that clergy should
fight to get this service into those agencies.[23] A sense of the opposition still
to be faced can be gathered from a letter sent in response to the proclamation, "Dear Sir: Congratulations to the 3,200 Protestants and Jews who
desire to pervert nature and plan themselves right out of existence. Go right
ahead. America and the world will be well rid of you." Signed, "A Catholic
Parent of 12."[24]

Part of what made the time right for the rapid rise of clergy support was a confluence of certain trends in clergy life. First there was the obvious fact that clergy performed a large percentage of the weddings in America and along with weddings went marriage counseling. Clergy could not help but notice that many young couples were ignorant about contraception. What should be said to them? Those ministers and rabbis who weren't in denial knew that couples could suffer a great deal of emotional distress and pain from unplanned pregnancies because of this ignorance. The feeling grew that to be responsible the clergyperson should—at a minimum—be able to give them some information on how to prevent, or space, their children. If he—and clergy were almost all men in this era—didn't feel knowledgeable or was too embarrassed, he could at least refer them to Planned Parenthood. Second, involvement in marriage counseling indirectly forced even the most politically indifferent clergyperson to become aware of the religious and political opposition to the availability of birth control in the public sector. He might find himself recommending means of contraception that were banned under national or state-based Comstock statutes.

Also driving this surge was the phenomenal postwar growth of mainline American Protestantism and Judaism. During the thirties and forties religion was somewhat out of fashion. Writers such as H. L. Mencken and Sinclair Lewis had fostered the image of religious institutions as backward, superstitious holdovers from the past. But after the end of World War II and the dawn of the atomic age, people turned back to religion. Now it was fashionable to be in attendance at religious services.[25] Suburbs were on the rise everywhere and suddenly they all seemed to need churches, lots of churches. The baby boom was beginning and that fed the startling increase in church attendance. Churches whose growth had been stagnant for years suddenly were burgeoning. One minister who oversaw the rapid development of a new suburban church turned away his colleagues' praise with the wry comment, "If I had stood in the doorway and barred their way with a broom, I couldn't have kept them out." The media of the time wrote endlessly about this return to religion.[26] Every denomination, evangelical as well as mainline, experienced phenomenal growth. During the immediate postwar period, a typical mainline denomination might see its membership increase by as much as 50 percent.[27] For mainline Protestantism especially, this was its heyday.

But it was not just a matter of increased numbers. Certain Protestant leaders led a renaissance of public interest in theology and religious ethics. It was a time when theological and ethical schools received more attention than usual in the popular media. And the clergy who were at the forefront

PLANNED PARENTHOOD NEWS

501 MADISON AVENUE · NEW YORK 22, N. Y.

PUBLISHED
BY THE PLANNED
PARENTHOOD
FEDERATION OF
AMERICA, INC.

No. 17 — WINTER, 1957

United Lutheran Church Endorses Planned Parenthood

A comprehensive statement on marriage and family life, deploring "irresponsible conception" and urging couples to "plan their parenthood," has been officially adopted by the United Lutheran Church in America, largest body of Lutherans in the country.

Approved at the church's 20th biennial convention in Harrisburg in October, the new statement declared:

"Husbands and wives are called to exercise the power of procreation responsibly before God. This implies planning their parenthood in accordance with their ability to provide for their children and carefully nurture them in fullness of Christian faith and life.

"The health and welfare of the mother-wife should be a major concern in such decisions. Irresponsible conception of children up to the limit of biological capacity and selfish limitation of the number of children are equally detrimental. Choice as to means of conception control should be made upon professional medical advice."

The new code also calls upon the church's 4,400 pastors to institute regular counseling periods with engaged couples, and urges congregations to extend programs of marriage counseling. Churches are encouraged to offer marriage education training to pastors and lay leaders through special courses in seminaries, colleges and institutes.

The Church has more than 2,250,000 members.

A Moment of Discovery

Mr. and Mrs. Thomas Donald Scott
(with Zachary and Donald, Jr.):

"We thought birth control would cost too much and nobody told us about the clinic before. Shirley and I love both our boys, but we don't think it's fair to have more now—children just can't grow up right when there are too many."

The Scotts have just talked
with Mrs. Ophelia Egypt, a Planned
Parenthood community worker. For
the story of her challenging job, see

MISSION IN WASHINGTON

Pages 4-5

United Lutheran Church, the largest Lutheran church in America, endorses the principle of planned parenthood, October 1956. (Reproduced with permission from Planned Parenthood Federation of America, Inc.© 1957 PPFA. All rights reserved.)

of that movement were the very clergy who were most publicly in support of Planned Parenthood.

The most notable was Reinhold Niebuhr, professor of Christian ethics at Union Theological Seminary in New York. Niebuhr was as famous in the secular, political, and foreign policy worlds as he was in the world of religion. He led a movement known as Christian Realism, a sophisticated look at the ethical complexities of modern society. Ever since his seminal book *Moral Man and Immoral Society* had come out in 1934, he had dominated discussions of religious morality in the United States. He challenged John Dewey for being too optimistic about human nature, and he challenged the pacifists who were in ascendancy in American churches in the thirties. He warned of the need to resist the Nazis, and events appeared to prove him right.

Niebuhr's ethics were based on the idea that the central biblical imperatives were love and justice. But achieving justice in social situations was incredibly complex and required prudent calculations of a utilitarian nature. For example, Christians were to love their neighbor, but in a world of multiple relationships, which neighbor was to be loved, and what statutes or government programs would best achieve the most justice for that neighbor? Furthermore Niebuhr took human selfishness seriously and argued that people usually operated on the basis of self-interest, however much they tried to disguise it from others and themselves.

But individuals were not the only ones with self-interest. Groups, businesses, unions, and other organized bodies were moved primarily by self-interest as well. This meant that sometimes compromise, coercion, police power, and even military force were necessary to resolve the clashes of self-interest and bring about at least some degree of justice. Those following a Niebuhrian analysis looked for ways to balance conflicting power in such a way that a greater measure of justice could come about. In practice Niebuhrians often sympathized with unions and understood the need for strikes. Following the war, the Niebuhrian school of thought dominated the thinking of several generations of seminary students, and Protestant clergy became much more sophisticated about political realities.

Clergy followers of Niebuhr would likely be sympathetic to the Planned Parenthood movement, because it dealt with the realities of the sexual needs of human beings and because they recognized that denying family planning to women and families who wanted and needed it was unjust. As for Niebuhr himself, he chaired the Federal Council of Churches committee report that first endorsed birth control in 1930, as we have seen. And through the forties and fifties he remained a strong supporter of the Federation.

Planned Parenthood was so heartened by its clergy supporters that when it was time in 1946 to celebrate the twenty-fifth anniversary of the organization, it was the clergy who sponsored the dinner at the Waldorf-Astoria Hotel in New York on January 23. Two clergy—Bishop G. Bromley Oxnam of the Methodist Church and Dr. James Robinson, pastor of the Church of the Master in Harlem—were the principal speakers on that occasion. In their remarks that night, Dr. Robinson was good cop to Oxnam's bad cop. Robinson said, "No one would oppose the application of scientific skill to save the life of a mother in childbirth, nor would they deny a childless couple who desire the blessings and happiness of children the right to scientific assistance. Isn't it therefore just as right and logical to apply scientific help toward planning the conservation of the family?"[28] But Bishop Oxnam went on the attack: "When rituals declare that a child is conceived in sin and born in iniquity I say such declarations are themselves sinful and iniquitous. The love of a husband and wife is sacred. Those who insist there shall be no expression of that love except for purposes of procreation are not defenders of the family. They bring to the most sacred of human relationships a blight of an asceticism that is blasphemous."[29]

His remarks were greeted with much applause. Nobody in attendance had any doubt about whose rituals were being discussed. That applause was a mark of the hostility that Protestants and Catholics felt toward each other in the increasingly public argument over birth control. It was also an indication that Planned Parenthood clergy were becoming much more willing to take a strong public stand against the religious opposition.

The next effort of the Planned Parenthood's Clergymen's Advisory Council was to develop systematic clergy organizing. The plan was to form clergy councils in every affiliate in the country. On October 14, 1947, the executive committee of the national council approved "Cooperation with Religious Leaders," a detailed directive for building a clergy–Planned Parenthood partnership. It began, "It is imperative that every Planned Parenthood unit . . . have an active clergymen's advisory council to whom it can go for guidance, constructive criticism and support." And here—in a nonpublic forum—the executive committee was much more blunt about the resistance that would be encountered:

The only organized opposition to planned parenthood stems from the Roman Catholic Church, whose attacks on the movement have frequently abridged civil liberties and contravened the American political principles of separation of church and state. In this opposition Catholic attacks have taken the form of attempting to stifle free speech, to prevent the use of radio and press by exponents of the movement, and to bar the inclusion of planned parenthood educational and service programs by national, state, and local organizations.[30]

Realizing the critical need to dispel the ocean of ignorance and misinformation, the council urged local clergy to do all they could to further the acceptance of birth control and sex education in the public schools. It detailed plans to persuade libraries to purchase books on birth control and seminaries to include courses on marriage and family life, courses that would include specific information about contraception.

As a model of the latter, the Reverend Roy Burkhart, M.A., Ph.D., a prominent midwestern minister of the First Community Church (Congregational) in Columbus, Ohio, developed a course on "Ministerial Counseling and Planned Parenthood." But his most comprehensive work for the National Clergymen's Advisory Council was on a major course titled "Planned Parenthood through the Church." He was impressed with the quiet marriage counseling being done in many Planned Parenthood affiliates. He believed that the church could add a spiritual dimension to that counseling and be a helpful support to young couples entering marriage and to older couples experiencing problems. In his view, the pairing of the practical knowledge of Planned Parenthood and the compassionate support offered by church and synagogue was a natural combination.

He wrote curricula for seminary courses, summer conferences, and special programs. Though dated in many respects and paternalistic in tone, the materials nevertheless were willing to look at all of the real problems of sexuality, infertility, impotence, and infidelity. His was one of sharpest visions of the clear harmony of the sacred work of the church and the sacred work of Planned Parenthood. Furthermore, Burkhart was not from New York City, but right out of the American heartland.

An astonishing amount of work was done by the National Clergymen's Advisory Council in this immediate postwar period. By 1947 Planned Parenthood's clergy supporters were organized enough to speak publicly for, and act on behalf of, the right of doctors to support Planned Parenthood without losing their livelihoods. In a matter of months they would have to make that fight.

DEFENDING DOCTORS: THE POUGHKEEPSIE SEVEN

Far more dramatic than public letters and clergy petitions was the third tactic of the Planned Parenthood clergy of that period—publicly defending doctors who had been discharged from Catholic hospitals because they believed in contraception.

Health care was a major priority for the Roman Catholic Church. The church operated an extensive system of hospitals and nursing homes across the country. These facilities served not only Catholics but people of all religious backgrounds. In the postwar period the Catholic religious health care system had to come to terms with the increasing public interest in, and acceptance of, birth control. Most critical was the question of how far the church would go in opposing this reality. Obviously the Roman Catholic Church would not allow contraceptive devices to be given out within its hospitals. The church would also instruct Roman Catholic physicians and nurses on their obligation to refuse to participate in contraceptive services while serving in non-Catholic hospitals.

But how much further would they go with this? For example, what about non-Catholic doctors who had privileges at Roman Catholic hospitals? Would the church try to control the behavior of such doctors in the parts of their medical practice that had nothing to do with their work in the Catholic hospital? In this interregnum period of the forties and fifties, the answer appeared to be yes.

An early incident occurred in 1947 in Waterbury, Connecticut, where six Protestant doctors had joined the Committee of 100, a group of physicians who were lobbying the Connecticut General Assembly to pass a bill that would permit doctors to prescribe birth control to patients where pregnancy would pose a clear threat to their health. On April 7 these six physicians released a statement announcing that they had been dismissed from the staffs of three Roman Catholic hospitals in Waterbury, Stamford, and Bridgeport, because they refused to withdraw from the Committee of 100. One of the physicians discharged was Dr. Oliver L. Springfield, assistant professor of clinical pediatrics at Columbia Hospital. He was also serving on the executive board of the American Academy of Pediatrics.

The Fairfield County Medical Association issued a statement opposing the dismissals, as did the Stamford Medical Society. But the loudest protests came from the religious community. The Greater Hartford Ministers' Fellowship issued a statement insisting that no hospital who dismissed a physician for his employment of free speech on a medical issue should receive public funds. In other towns such as Litchfield, Plainville, and Milford, Councils of Churches and ministerial associations also said that state money should be withdrawn and that such institutions should not receive money from "general public subscription."[31] This battle might have gone somewhere had Dr. Springfield decided to sue. Support from the American Civil Liberties Union was offered, but in the end he decided against it, and for the most part the national press did not pick up on the issue.

Then in June 1947 four doctors were discharged from the staff of Mercy Hospital in Springfield, Massachusetts, because they were accused of providing birth control information and advice. Two hundred members of the Planned Parenthood League of Western Massachusetts met to protest the actions of the hospitals. While these dismissals caused great concern and turmoil in these small cities, and though the anger level of Protestant and Jewish clergy was rising, the issue did not reach national attention until a few years later, in a notorious case in Poughkeepsie, New York.

On the morning of Friday, February 1, 1952, the front page of the *New York Times* carried this headline: "Catholic Hospital Tells Doctors to Quit Staff of Birth Control Unit." Six days earlier, on January 26, St. Francis Hospital, a two-hundred-bed Roman Catholic health facility in Poughkeepsie, New York, had given an ultimatum to seven doctors on its medical staff— either break all connections with the Dutchess County League for Planned Parenthood, or resign from the hospital's staff. The doctors had been given oral notice by a physician on staff, Dr. Victor Brasile, who said he was acting at the behest of the superintendent of the hospital, Sister M. Anne Roberta. They were given nothing in writing, and were told they had only 72 hours to decide.

None of the doctors were Catholic. Four were Protestants, three were Jewish. Most of the doctors had been with the hospital for years. Their work with Planned Parenthood was no secret. In fact one of the physicians, Dr. Florence Gottdiener, was the assistant medical director of the local Planned Parenthood clinic. Why this sudden action? Why only three days to decide? At first no explanation was forthcoming from the administration of St. Francis Hospital. And efforts to reach the Catholic Archdiocese of New York, which had jurisdiction over the hospital, were unsuccessful. A local priest, Monsignor Michael P. O'Shea, dean of the Catholic clergy in Dutchess and Putnam counties, was in New York City and unavailable for comment.

One of the physicians, Dr. John F. Rogers, an obstetrician, stated that he would resign from the Planned Parenthood League, because he still had patients waiting to deliver at St. Francis. But he was publicly critical of the hospital: "I don't believe the St. Francis hospital policy is justified, I realize the program of the Planned Parenthood League is a controversial one, but I don't believe a hospital should bar me from its staff if I belong to the league. I don't think my interest in preventative medicine should be construed as having any bearing on the practice of my profession at St. Francis hospital."[32]

On that same Wednesday, as banner headlines in the local paper proclaimed, "St. Frances Hospital Warns Staff Against Planned Parenthood Affiliate," the local Planned Parenthood League formed a special steering committee to deal with the crisis.[33] It was made up of officers of the league and five of the doctors affected, and was chaired by two members of the league's ministerial committee. Clergy were involved from the outset and their actions would be critical in the resolution of the crisis.

Citing economic reasons, two physicians bowed to the hospital's directive and resigned from Planned Parenthood. But four others were refusing to resign. They were Dr. Albert A. Rosenberg, chair of the league's medical advisory board, Dr. Florence Gottdiener, assistant medical director of the league, Dr. William Bennett, and Dr. E. Gordon MacKenzie. Dr. Rogers, the obstetrician, made it clear that as soon as his scheduled patients had their babies at St. Francis, he would resign from the staff of St. Francis and rejoin Planned Parenthood.

On January 30, the ministerial committee of Planned Parenthood—nine ministers and one rabbi, all from Poughkeepsie—issued a strong statement condemning the hospital's action and supporting Planned Parenthood.

> The attempt to police the thoughts and personal actions of individuals in our American democracy is un-American and contrary to our cherished principles. . . . We deplore the fact that the Roman Catholic church has injected this divisive controversy at a time of crisis.
>
> We affirm and support the high ethical principles of planned parenthood. The planned family is necessary for the well being of this and every other community throughout the world.[34]

In response, Monsignor O'Shea, who had just returned from New York, put forth a strong defense of the hospital's action. Claiming that the hospital had been "lenient" toward these seven physicians, he said that "logically and in justice they should be called upon to resign from the hospital staff."[35] He was immediately rebutted by Dr. Rogers, who said that in twenty-two years of practice in Poughkeepsie he had never heard a word about a hospital policy concerning connections with Planned Parenthood.[36]

In the face of this criticism, responses coming from the Roman Catholic community were tinged with denial. Sister M. Ann Roberta, hospital administrator, claimed that there was actually "nothing new" with regard to the hospital's attitude toward Planned Parenthood. She was quoted as saying, "The hospital's policy has been in existence since St. Francis' hospital opened its doors in 1914. There is nothing new and there is no controversy between St. Francis' hospital and any other group."[37] For his part, Monsignor O'Shea seemed unable to accept the statement of the Planned Parenthood clergy. He didn't rebut their arguments or even engage them in any way. Their position appeared to be something that he could not take in. Although it was obviously untrue, he persisted in saying that all religions agreed that the Bible opposed birth control. When it was clear that there was no such agreement, he said he was scandalized that a committee of clergy would support Planned Parenthood.[38]

But the clergy were only beginning to express their opposition. On the following Sunday, February 3, the leading ministers of Poughkeepsie all preached on the ouster of the doctors and the local press gave extensive coverage to their sermons. Typical of the ministers' approach were the remarks of Dr. Philip Allen Swartz, minister of the First Congregational Church and a former secretary of the Federal Council of Churches in America. In a radio address sponsored by the Council of Churches, he outlined the problem for the community. Noting that all members of the community contribute to the hospital—and expressing his gratitude for the hospital's service to the city—he nevertheless criticized the actions of the administration: "The hospital's methods savor of medieval absolutisms rather than of an enlightened scientific and democratic society. . . . We should honor these seven men irrespective of their decisions."[39]

Press coverage also continued to increase. The *New York World Telegram and Sun* came to town and asked Sister M. Ann Roberta if she had received a specific complaint against these physicians. She refused to answer.[40] She was also asked if the hospital would extend the birth control order to cover patients. She replied that the hospital did not ask patients about their personal beliefs.[41]

Soon there were more charges leveled at St. Francis Hospital. Dr. William Meyer, medical director for the local Planned Parenthood League, noted that the hospital had not insisted that these doctors cease using contraception in their private practices, only in their work with Planned Parenthood. He questioned why there was no objection to doctors issuing contraception to private patients, but only when they issued them to poorer women at Planned Parenthood.[42]

There was also an issue of selective enforcement. Dr. Florence Gottdiener noted that nine other doctors were on the staff of St. Francis and also on the staff at Planned Parenthood. But nothing had been done to them.

As the controversy expanded, other problems emerged for St. Francis. In New York City, Dr. William Kennedy, chair of the Medical Committee of the national Planned Parenthood Federation, claimed that on August 21, 1950, Sister Ann Roberta had sent a letter to staff physicians asking them to keep patients in the hospital "for a longer stay period, when possible." The letter explained that this would help the hospital meet its requirements for internships and would also help the hospital with Blue Cross patients.[43] Dr. Kennedy gave out a copy of the letter and called on Blue Cross to investigate the hospital's practices in this regard. On February 8, Dr. William Vogt, national director of the Planned Parenthood Federation, wrote to Edward Edwards, chair of the State Commission against Discrimination, asking the state to investigate the possibility that the hospital's ultimatum had violated New York's non-discrimination laws. By February 11, even *Time* magazine was covering the story and noting that the hospital was still not forthcoming with answers to the question everyone asked—why had things gone on for so long without action?

But the bigger question was who gave the order to initiate this action. One local newspaper, *The Compass*, said that two of the people involved believed the order came from "someone higher up."[44] This could only mean the Archdiocese of New York, known to be one of the most conservative dioceses in the country. Although no hard evidence exists to prove this allegation, it seems plausible. It is highly unlikely that the decision came from St. Francis. I could find no sign that the trustees of the hospital had ever heard of the decision until it was announced. Nor is it likely that Sister Ann Roberta would decide such a matter on her own. Whether the archdiocese believed that the change of policy would simply be accepted by the community, or whether it was angry about some other policy of Planned Parenthood and didn't care about the consequences, we cannot know. All attempts to reach Cardinal Francis Spellman were turned away and the archdiocese maintained its silence throughout.

For the duration of the crisis, the defense was left to the good offices of Sister Ann Roberta and Monsignor O'Shea. But that proved to be a considerable burden. In the absence of a positive statement by the archdiocese, public opinion grew increasingly unfavorable. While the public, including the supporters of Planned Parenthood, respected the right of the church to its moral objections to contraception, they could not remain so respectful when the church moved from theological condemnation to taking specific acts against the physicians of Planned Parenthood. Here the church's moral calculus got terribly muddy. When Roman Catholic hospitals actually discharged physicians who disagreed with them about this issue, it seemed more an abuse of power rather than an exercise of moral leadership. To threaten to take away the livelihood of doctors, to force them to resign from private organizations they had freely chosen to join, was a hopeless strategy. If the doctors resisted, they looked like martyrs. If they capitulated to the ultimatum, it looked not only unfair but also a bit ominous.

This action by St. Francis Hospital did one other thing: it awakened the fears of many non-Catholics that the Catholic Church might ride roughshod over them whenever it was in a position to do so. The Poughkeepsie situation demonstrated this perfectly. Poughkeepsie was a small city. In such a place, though there will always be controversies, people in general want to get along. People become especially anxious when theological opinions seem to be affecting their health care systems. Many non-Catholics used St. Francis Hospital. They probably had few worries about it before, but now they were facing a situation where their doctor might no longer be able to treat them in that hospital. And that would not be because of the doctor's skills, but because he or she belonged to Planned Parenthood.

Given all these factors, it was not surprising that the controversy ended the way it did. As the year went on, four of the physicians, led by Dr. Albert A. Rosenberg, who continued to serve as chair of Planned Parenthood's medical committee, steadfastly refused to resign either from the staff of St. Francis or from Planned Parenthood. Nothing was done to them. The hospital took no action.

And then, quite anticlimatically, one year later the crisis was over. In January 1953 St. Francis renewed the contracts of all of the doctors. Dr. Rogers, one of the three who temporarily left Planned Parenthood, indicated that the local community of physicians was contemplating withdrawing their affiliations if the hospital did not renew privileges for all the doctors involved.[45]

The Planned Parenthood Federation issued a gracious statement praising the hospital:

> It is indeed a happy conclusion to an unfortunate situation. It also is a conclusion that reflects the reasonable attitude of the management at St. Francis hospital, giving freedom of action for the highest standards of medical practice.
>
> Our federation offers its congratulations to the seven physicians and its

gratitude to them for their consistent stand while honoring St. Francis' hospital for its part in closing the books on the Poughkeepsie incident.[46]

Consistently, the hospital had no comment. Sister Ann Roberta would not confirm that the reappointments had been made. She said only that there would be no statement from the hospital. What began with an ultimatum ended with silence.

Conclusion: The Sanction of the Sacred

In its own way, the Poughkeepsie hospital controversy epitomizes the forces that were at play all during the interregnum period. On one side was the support for birth control largely embodied in the Planned Parenthood organization and its clinics. This cause kept strengthening, because more and more people were using contraception now that it was readily available. They came to the clinics for it and were grateful to get it. Adding immensely to its growing respectability was the support of synagogues and churches. In some cities the contraceptives were being distributed at Planned Parenthood clinics located in churches. Most people responded to birth control as a liberating movement, which gave them more control and freedom over their lives. From that standpoint it was a cause that could hardly lose.

Central to the victory were the clergy. Although it is undeniable that there are many clergy who have no interest in social and political issues, a significant number of ministers and rabbis are unalterably committed to the cause of social justice, even when it is controversial. Most Christian and Jewish seminaries convey to their students the importance of the witness of the prophets, the willingness of the latter to speak against those who use their power to control others, and on behalf of those who have no voice or control over their lives. In that era, there was no constitutional right to birth control. In addition, in actual practice there were many pressures, social and emotional, which severely limited a woman's ability to control her own reproductive life. Because of this prophetic tradition, it is profoundly meaningful for clergy to feel that they are involved in something that makes life better for those who are hard-pressed. For this reason in Poughkeepsie—as well as in most other places—Planned Parenthood had the solid support of virtually all of mainline clergy.

Though clergy, especially those working with Planned Parenthood, cared about a married woman's right to have birth control, it was not the main issue in the Poughkeepsie controversy. Two other concerns, freedom of religion and freedom of speech, far outweighed it. Concerning the first, when a minister like the Reverend Philip Allen Swartz used the term "medieval absolutism," he was summoning up an image of a non-American, nonpluralistic society where one religion had its way. When St. Francis Hospital issued its fiat with no consultation, no discussion, and seemingly no interest in the opinions of the community, it seemed to have overtones of an unpleasant past. In Poughkeepsie physicians were being punished by loss of hospital privileges and the resultant income because medical advice offered in other locations was condemned by church teaching. But that medical advice might be in accordance with those physicians' own religious beliefs. To the Poughkeepsie clergy that seemed to be an indirect, but real, attack on the Protestant, Jewish, and even nonreligious views of the doctors. More was at stake than Planned Parenthood. Although the separation of church and state was not overtly involved here, this community controversy foreshadowed the New York City Hospital crisis of 1958 (see chapter 4), where separation was very much the issue.

The other driving concern of the clergy was freedom of speech. Were doctors, nurses, and educators, at Planned Parenthood or anywhere, free to talk about a subject like birth control? Comstock had tried to suppress all such speech with his laws. That had led to something most of the founding fathers never contemplated, the censorship of the mails. In 1953 the country was still living with the Comstock heritage. But that heritage was weakening, and the courts had carved out some areas of freedom. An appeals court decision of 1936 had accorded doctors the right to order contraceptives for their patients.[47] Presumably that meant they could talk to them about the subject. But in Poughkeepsie it appeared that the Catholic Church was trying, indirectly, to silence doctors in their work outside of Roman Catholic hospitals. So it was perhaps not surprising that Jewish and Protestant clergy on the Planned Parenthood ministerial committee would decry an "attempt to police the thoughts" of the physicians.

This issue remains as alive today as it was in 1952–53. The controversies that currently embroil Planned Parenthood and the women's movement involve government attempts to impose "gag rules" both internationally and domestically. These rules state that no government funding can go to clinics that inform a pregnant woman that abortion is one of her choices. That is forbidden speech. Those clergy who oppose gag rules invoke the right of freedom of speech.

But in Poughkeepsie in that era the Roman Catholic Church saw it quite differently. To the church it seemed an issue that had just as much importance as free speech; it was a matter of conscience. How could a Roman Catholic hospital support, even indirectly, a physician who worked at a clinic where women, almost certainly including Catholic women, were being taught to violate the teachings of the church? Surely the church had a right to try to stop such things.

In modern times the same dynamic is being played out in every community where a Roman Catholic hospital merges with a secular hospital. Under the terms of these mergers, the latter is required to operate under a code known as the bishop's directives. These directives come from the American Conference of Catholic Bishops and are designed to see that hospital practice does not violate church teachings. Thus a formerly secular hospital that enters such a merger is required to stop sterilizations, abortions, and issuing contraceptives.[48] In communities where such battles are occurring— and there are many—opponents of the merger, including Protestant and Jewish clergy, see it as a matter of free speech. The Roman Catholic Church sees it as a matter of conscience.

There was a certain poignancy in the Poughkeepsie controversy. Monsignor O'Shea could not understand why a moral issue so clear to him was seen so differently by other people of the cloth. To his mind, Planned Parenthood was so clearly wrong that it should be stopped or at least limited as much as possible. Opposing clergy probably wondered why the monsignor could not see what they saw, a violation of the free speech of the physician and an attempt by one religion to impose its views on those who did not subscribe to them.

In any case, the Roman Catholic Church fought a losing battle throughout this era. Conservative Protestant denominations in general were not supporters of birth control and certainly not of Planned Parenthood, but they did not join the struggle to keep contraception out of public health services.[49] This was largely because while evangelicals and fundamentalists had their differences with mainline Protestants, in this era between the Scopes trial of 1925 and the rise of the Moral Majority in the mid-1970s, the more conservative groups tended to view politics as too worldly. In addition, these denominations viewed subjects that involved sexuality with distaste. For a range of reasons, those denominations stayed on the sidelines in the 1950s and 1960s. That would change.

While there were also secular groups and individuals in America who had objections to contraception, it was the Roman Catholic Church alone that took up the cudgels to try to stop it. In the Margaret Sanger era, the church was focused on its opposition to her personally and to the fledgling groups she led. When the church made a public proclamation that birth control was "immoral," it expected that society would recognize the church's moral claims as superior to those of a secular group such as Planned Parenthood. But in the 1930s things had changed. Even in that era, such expectations proved to be groundless.

Now the church's claims were challenged by Protestant and Jewish clergy who stepped up to defend Planned Parenthood with a moral authority that was equal to that of the Roman Catholic Church. One solemn religious claim to authority has a certain force, but when it is answered in kind, that force is largely neutralized. All the petitions and public statements created a "sanction of the sacred" for the work of Planned Parenthood. In the face of conflicting religious and moral claims, the public—especially an American public—will decide for themselves and probably choose the course that seems to make the most sense. Over the course of these decades, the cause of Planned Parenthood, defended and promoted by clergy, proved to be most persuasive. Although there were still battles to be fought, by the beginning of the sixties birth control was an accepted part of American life.

CHAPTER 4

The 1958 Battle over the
New York City Hospitals

And if anyone still held the stereotype of religious leaders as men who live and work only in the realm of the spirit, he was probably [the] most amazed of all at the skill and vigor with which Protestant and Jewish churchmen dealt with a temporal conflict.

—"The Anatomy of a Victory," Planned Parenthood Federation of America, 1959

ON A PLEASANT EVENING in early December 1953, two organizations that cared about women—the Brooklyn Section of the National Council of Jewish Women and Planned Parenthood—joined together to hear an address by Dr. Louis Hellman, executive officer of the Department of Obstetrics and Gynecology at New York State University's College of Medicine. As part of his remarks, Dr. Hellman noted that of the 1,200 women who came to Kings County Hospital each year following miscarriage, nearly half were there because of complications from an illegal abortion.

Had he made these observations in the thirties or the early forties, probably nothing would have happened. But this was the fifties, and American society was no longer ignoring the widespread reality of illegal abortion as it had in the past. So it was perhaps not too surprising when Brooklyn district attorney Miles F. McDonald immediately empaneled a grand jury to investigate Kings County Hospital. The problem was that the New York City Sanitary Code required hospitals to notify the Department of Health whenever a illegal abortion was discovered or even suspected. The hospital had reported only 30 cases to the Health Department, not 600.

The district attorney's action was typical of the post–World War II period in America. During the thirties and the war years, women's reproductive behavior was relatively unscrutinized. Depression and war meant that society had bigger fish to fry. In that climate of societal indifference, contraception was slowly becoming available. Some southern states were even distributing birth control devices in public clinics. Illegal abortion was practiced openly by some physicians in large cities, and therapeutic abortions were not uncommon in hospitals, at least for middle-class and wealthy women.

But in the postwar years all that changed. In part because of anxiety about the prospects for 12,000,000 returning veterans (almost all men) and in part as a reaction to the freedom of women (financial and otherwise) working in war plants and serving in the military, society began to push women back into traditional roles. Suddenly all the sources of authority—doctors, clergy, even government officials—began to hit the same note: a woman's place was in the home; a woman's destiny was motherhood. This powerful pull toward social and sexual conservatism meant that women's ability to prevent unwanted births now came under harsh scrutiny.[1]

Dr. Hellman appeared before the grand jury several times. Although no indictments were handed down, a warning had been issued to the New York City medical community. The latter understood that they were under official scrutiny. Things soon turned grim for women. And yet before the decade was out an alliance between clergy, Planned Parenthood, and physicians would tear down one of the major barriers to women's reproductive freedom—the refusal of New York City hospitals to provide birth control for women who desperately needed it.

DESPERATE PLIGHT

In the early fifties there were only three ways a woman might limit her fertility—contraception, sterilization, or, as a backup, abortion. To consider the last first, abortion was sporadically available in two forms, therapeutic or illegal. Therapeutic abortions were done when there was a danger to the life of the woman. The New York State abortion law allowed that exemption when two physicians certified that it was necessary. Doctors sometimes interpreted the law broadly to allow nonfatal threats to the woman's health. In practice, wealthy women often had no difficulty obtaining the procedure. Illegal abortions were just that, abortions performed, by doctors or nonphysicians, that were in violation of the law.

For a long time, family doctors had been doing therapeutic abortions in their offices. Some were more liberal than others in this respect, but in any case it was a private cooperation between doctor and patient. But as medical procedures were increasingly done in hospitals, the doctor's decision was no longer his or her own. With prosecutors such as Attorney General McDonald scrutinizing them, hospitals of the fifties created a new institution, the therapeutic abortion committee. These committees now sought to limit the number of therapeutic procedures done in their hospital. Each was afraid of doing more procedures than rival hospitals lest they run the risk of becoming known as an "abortion mill." The result was that the number of therapeutic abortions declined sharply. Furthermore, the process became increasingly demeaning to women. In some cases these committees required women to undergo physical examinations and verbal inquiries from several doctors, after which they still might be turned down. The process deliberately and consciously discouraged women. At Sloane Hospital in New York City, the creation of a review committee in 1955 meant that fewer than half as many therapeutic abortions were performed over the next five years. Many hospitals followed suit.[2] The door was almost closed on this option.

At the same time, there was an unusual surge of prosecutions of illegal abortionists. Doctors and skilled nonphysicians who had practiced more or less openly for decades in cities like Portland, Baltimore, Detroit, and New York were now arrested, prosecuted, and sent to jail. In desperation, women turned to more risky alternatives, or even attempted to induce the abortion themselves. The result was that the very hospitals that were refusing to do therapeutic abortions had full abortion wards where they treated the women who came in with complications from illegal or self-induced abortions.

In theory, women could also turn to sterilization to prevent pregnancies. But in practice, this option also required them to go before committees similar to the abortion committees. Here too they were blocked by political, not medical, considerations. To begin with, a woman needed her husband's consent. Then such committees often applied something like the "rule of 120" (unless the number of living children she had—multiplied by her age—equaled 120, the sterilization was denied). Or there was the "rule of 30." A woman had to have "six kids living by the time you were thirty, five by age thirty-five, four by age forty, or have had three c-sections, and you had to have the permission of your husband, or if you were separated, he had to have been gone seven years."[3] Women had no agency in the process, but were subject to a male social and political agenda, an agenda with racist consequences.[4]

Complicating the functioning of such committees at times was a clear hostility to women and a startling lack of compassion. At one hospital a committee member—opposing a woman's petition for an abortion—remarked, "Now that she has had her fun, she wants us to launder her dirty underwear. From my standpoint she can sweat this one out."[5] It seems strange to view the birth of a child as a proper punishment for perceived misbehavior, but it was not an uncommon attitude at that time. The point seemed to be that these women should be punished and that a hospital board had the right to withhold an abortion as a punishment.

Finally, given their vanishing access to abortion and sterilization, women were left with only one way to prevent unwanted pregnancies—contraception. With good birth control, most sterilizations and abortions could be avoided. As we saw in the previous chapter, Planned Parenthood had worked hard to make contraception available, but throughout the fifties it had still not succeeded in getting birth control services into public agencies such as hospitals and welfare offices.

For millions of women in New York City, the very public hospitals that could provide them the means of contraception had an unofficial policy that forbade any physician from prescribing them. It was this policy that would be challenged by Planned Parenthood and the city's Protestant and Jewish clergy.

GENTLEMEN'S AGREEMENT

In 1958 the New York City municipal hospital system had 20,959 beds and a budget of $135,000,000.[6] In that year 210,000 people were admitted as in-patients. The system's outpatient clinics had 2,614,000 clinic visits.[7] But through an almost secret policy, birth control was kept out of the hands of all of these patients. City officials were acutely conscious of Roman Catholic objections to birth control. In deference to those feelings, they refused to provide such services. As a result, in 1958, if a woman asked for contraception, her request was denied.

When Dr. Alan Guttmacher moved to New York from Baltimore in 1953 he found it hard to believe what he heard: "I was told by chiefs of service that the nurses weren't allowed to mention contraception. One chief told me that when he had put leaflets referring patients to Planned Parenthood in the waiting room of his clinic, these leaflets were torn to shreds before his eyes."[8] Even more astonishing, he found that even private hospitals like Mount Sinai, where he had come to be head of the Department of Obstetrics and Gynecology, were intimidated. When he was interviewed by the board of that institution about his plans, he said that he wanted to start a contraceptive clinic. "One board member, a layman, said, 'Dr. Guttmacher, I don't think you should do that—you have no idea of the amount of

Catholic financial support this institution has.' I replied that I thought it would be ridiculous for us to give in to this, instead of doing what was normally considered good medicine."[9]

When Joe Kahn, a reporter for the *New York Post*, began a series on the subject of birth control in the spring of 1957, he discovered that he was up against a wall of silence. While interviewing the director of a settlement house, he was shocked at what he heard:

> I asked whether the [settlement house] was under any restrictions due to the fact that the City gave them free rent. The settlement house director whispered to me, and stressed that he didn't want to be quoted, that Planned Parenthood was not allowed to have any meetings in their center. I was shocked to learn this, because if any group of people needs this kind of help, it is the low-income families who live in public housing projects. . . . I started investigating the situation in other City departments and learned that a ban existed—an unwritten one—in every department. So here was a health measure of importance being denied thousands of people who needed it more than any segment of the population.[10]

As Kahn queried the major officials of the city's health system, each evaded the topic by either pleading lack of expertise or just pleading not to be put on the spot. The highest official, Mayor Robert Wagner, flatly denied any "gentlemen's agreement": "There is no ban on birth control information in city departments. I have never issued such an order and to my knowledge, there is no city law against it. Department heads may do whatever they believe is right to further the health and general welfare of the people."[11] But the mayor's subordinates were not going to accept his invitation. They knew that birth control was a taboo subject in New York City. The reason was obvious. The Roman Catholic Church was unalterably opposed to birth control, and 46 percent of the voters in the city were Roman Catholic. In addition, the city had witnessed a demonstration of the power of Catholic social agencies as recently as 1953. In that year, the city Welfare and Health Council, an assemblage of hundreds of social agencies, finally admitted Planned Parenthood to its membership. In protest, fifty-four Catholic agencies resigned, withdrawing their financial support. After two and a half years, the Welfare and Health Council admitted defeat and reorganized in such a way as to bar Planned Parenthood from policymaking and take away its vote. Planned Parenthood had lost.

For their part, the Roman Catholic leaders of the city denied that it had forced the city to agree to any policy. The Reverend Timothy J. Flynn, information director for Cardinal Spellman, said, "The Archdiocese of New York has no agreement with the city administration, and we are not aware of any ban on birth control information in city agencies. If such clinics were established by the city or state, naturally we would be displeased."[12] There is no reason to doubt this statement, though it is a bit disingenuous. The fact is they didn't need an agreement. A few years earlier the archdiocese had endorsed this statement by a theologian from Catholic University of America: "Prohibition to practice contraception is not regarded by the Catholic Church as one of its laws binding only Catholics. The Church proclaims this prohibition as a law of God, which binds all human beings, whether they be members of the Catholic Church or not."[13] City politicians didn't need a road map to figure out what to do.

This "gentlemen's agreement" to ban contraception seemed to need little enforcement. People were intimidated and afraid to challenge it. Joe Kahn noted this when he said, "I was inspired in a bitter sort of way, by many people who took me aside and said they were for me, but not publicly. Some of these, at first, and rather incredibly, were people in Planned Parenthood."[14] So on the eve of the battle, the city hospital policy against birth control was firmly established and, apparently, unchangeable.

CALCULATED AMBIGUITY

As 1958 began, there was some confusion about exactly what was the hospital policy on contraception. In November 1957 Dr. Louis Hellman, chief of obstetrics at Kings County Hospital, the largest hospital in the city system, had charged that departmental policy on birth control prevented patients from getting modern medical care. Dr. Morris Jacobs, commissioner of hospitals, responded, "I do not consider it the function or the responsibility of the municipal hospitals of this city to disseminate birth-control information."[15]

Then on January 7, 1958, the executive secretary of the New York Academy of Medicine, Dr. H. D. Kruse, began a correspondence with Dr. Jacobs. Specifically, Dr. Kruse asked the Board of Hospitals to make room on its agenda for a consideration of the subject of contraceptive counseling in municipal hospitals. The board did take up the subject in its meeting on April 11 and adopted a statement that said, "There shall be no interference in proper and accepted therapeutic practices nor intervention in ethical relationships between patient and physician."[16] Furthermore, despite the contradiction between this statement and Dr. Jacobs's November comments, he insisted that the hospital policy was the same as it had always been. This began a period in which Dr. Jacobs seemed to practice a kind of calculated ambiguity.

Dissatisfied with this perpetual uncertainty, some physicians in the city hospital system occasionally referred patients to private birth control clinics. They took this action when an additional pregnancy might create a medical emergency. Other physicians in the system were also dissatisfied with the situation. They believed that there had long existed an unofficial ban on contraception, and before going ahead with prescriptions they wanted a clearer authorization. They knew that the issue would come to a head if the hospital purchased contraceptive supplies with city funds. One physician actually ordered a contraceptive device for a non-Catholic patient. The order was sent by the pharmacy to the hospital director, who "referred it downtown" (meaning to Dr. Jacobs's office). When reporters asked Commissioner Jacobs if contraceptive counseling and prescription were included in the "proper and accepted therapeutic practices" or "ethical relationships" between patient and physician in which "there shall be no interference," he refused to say. He was also silent about whether he would approve any contraceptive prescription that was "referred downtown." He declined all further comment and said only that he had nothing to add to what he had said in his letter to the academy.[17]

Not surprisingly, later in the spring, the Catholic Church weighed in. Monsignor Timothy J. Flynn told the *New York Times* that "any unnatural or artificial method of birth prevention is an immoral practice." To make sure the intentions of the diocese were clear, he added that it would consider it immoral if the city began a birth control program.[18]

Now, like the opening moves in a chess game, a number of groups publicly staked out a position. Dr. William Vogt, national director of the Planned Parenthood Federation, spoke out on May 22, praising the "courageous city hospital physicians" for trying to obtain birth control services for their patients. But he pointed out that no contraceptive services would be realistic unless contraceptive materials and supplies were kept in stock.[19] He also noted that birth control had been approved by many Protestant and Jewish denominations and that they would regard spending tax money on it as quite moral. A few days later a statement came from the Protestant Council of the City of New York, an agency that would play a major role in the controversy. The Reverend Dan Potter was the executive director of the council. Speaking at a communion breakfast, he advocated access to birth control at the city hospitals and insisted that the requisite medicine and supplies should be provided as they were for any medical condition.[20] Aligning himself with the general mission of Planned Parenthood, he noted that Protestants usually accepted new methods whenever science came up with developments that improved human life.

DENIAL OF SERVICES: THE CRISIS BEGINS

Things remained quiet for several months, but on July 16, Dr. Hellman sought to fit a contraceptive device for a Protestant woman who was in the hospital with a severe case of diabetes. Claiming that another pregnancy would endanger her life, he was prepared to proceed with the fitting, using devices supplied by a pharmaceutical house, not by the city. On July 1, the Kings County Hospital Medical Board had given him authority to proceed in such circumstances. At 9:30 on the morning of July 16, Dr. Hellman told Dr. Harvey Gollance, supervisor of Kings County Hospital, of his intentions. Dr. Gollance said that Dr. Jacobs had issued orders that Dr. Hellman was not to proceed. Dr. Hellman asked that the order be given to him in writing. Dr. Gollance said that he would contact Dr. Jacobs.

Later that morning, when Dr. Hellman was back in his own office, he received a call from Dr. Gollance, who again ordered him not to proceed. But he would not put the order in writing. Dr. Hellman said,

> I was shocked. Such an action would be highly improper on the part of the hospital director. One just doesn't do this sort of thing to a responsible physician. This was about an hour before the patient was due. I immediately went to see the director and told him that any administrative interference was improper and unjustified. He said, "For goodness sake, Lou, I'm caught in the middle. Don't blame me." So I asked him for a written directive which we did not get, but we did get a call from Dr. Jacobs indicating that this was an order and I'd better obey it.[21]

At that point Dr. Hellman said that the order from Commissioner Jacobs had tied his hands and he would not resist it. But he pointed out that the order contradicted the letter Commissioner Jacobs had written to the Academy of Medicine.[22]

Appearing as it did on the front page of the city section of the July 17 issue of the *New York Times*, the story caused a mini-firestorm. A Protestant woman, being taken care of by a Jewish physician, had been refused a critically important medical service at a public hospital, and she had been refused because a city hospital was deferring to Roman Catholic opinion on the issue of reproductive control.

There was outrage for a number of reasons. First, her physician stated that without contraception, the woman might now have to be sterilized in order to safeguard her health. Second, the incident had made it clear that the calculated ambiguity of Commissioner Jacobs simply masked a hard—and secretive—policy. But people were also up in arms at the clear evidence of one religion's being favored over another in the public square. Dr. Guttmacher, who in addition to being head of obstetrics and gynecology at Mount Sinai Hospital was chair of the medical committee of Planned Parenthood Federation of America, said that he was "shocked and disgusted." Furthermore he emphasized that the incident made it clear that Dr. Jacobs's statement that there was no interference by his office with medical treatment was "not only double talk, but a total fabrication."[23]

Mayor Wagner was being dragged into the controversy. He danced carefully around the issue, saying that he would inquire about the facts of the. case from Dr. Jacobs. Meanwhile Dr. Jacobs continued to stonewall the press. At this point the New York Board of Rabbis, a collection of six hundred Reform, Conservative, and Orthodox rabbis of Greater New York, issued a strong statement against the hospital policy:

> We deplore the notion that patients in tax-supported hospitals who do not wish to adhere to the views of religious groups to whom the Dept. of Hospitals seems to be deferring, should be compelled to do so even if their very lives may be endangered. . . . Under our Constitutional principles of religious liberty government agencies may not directly or indirectly impose upon others the religious beliefs or practices of any one faith, nor as in this case may they influence the policies of tax-supported hospitals as if they were sectarian institutions.[24]

Press reaction was immediate and highly critical of the hospital's policy. Noting that the issue could have desperate urgency for the poor, the *New York Post* argued that for some people it could be a matter of life and death.[25] For the *New York World Telegram*, legality was the issue; since contraception was lawful in the rest of New York State, it must also be lawful in the city hospitals.[26] Editorially, the *New York Times* said that it would be wrong to mix up religious views and medical practice, especially for those who didn't agree with those religious views.[27]

The Protestant Council took a number of actions. First, it asked the 162 chaplains serving in city hospitals to "examine the situation" and report to the council. In particular the chaplains were asked if they knew of any direct or indirect interference with physicians. Then the council appointed a committee of five Protestant clergy and a layman and demanded an immediate meeting with Dr. Jacobs. The layperson was an attorney, Arthur Apha, chair of the council's Social Relations Department. Clergy on the committee were the Reverend Dr. Gardiner C. Taylor, president of the council; the Reverend Herbert Waldo Manley of St. Mary's Protestant Episcopal Church in Brooklyn; the Reverend Robert J. Stone of the Adams-Parkhurst Memorial Presbyterian Church; the Reverend Dan Potter; and the Reverend Paul W. Rishell, executive secretary of the Social Relations Department. But Dr. Jacobs said that he was preparing a report on the subject and declined to meet with the committee.[28]

Now counterpressures began to come from the Roman Catholic community. The Pasteur Guild, an organization of Roman Catholic employees in the Department of Hospitals, wrote to Dr. Jacobs describing birth control as "morally objectionable, subversive of nature, and as insidious as the 'snake of Eden.'" Roman Catholic nurses pointed out that they might be forced to assist in fitting birth control devices, something they believed that they, in good conscience, could not do. The National Council of Catholic Women and the National Council of Catholic Men sent congratulatory telegrams to Dr. Jacobs. The Catholic Physicians Guild expressed its opposition to a program they considered immoral. But the main statement came from the diocese itself, which cited the pronouncement of Pope Pius XI: "No indication or need can change an action that is intrinsically immoral into an action that is moral and lawful."[29]

In response, more and more Protestant denominational groups and individual clergy declared their opposition to the hospital policy. The New York Conference of the Augustana Lutheran Church;[30] the Reverend Dr. Hampton Adams, pastor of the Park Avenue Christian Church; the Reverend Dr. Carson Wasson, pastor of the huge Rye Presbyterian Church and board president of the Port Chester Planned Parenthood Center;[31] the United Lutheran Church in America; the New York Association of the Congregational Church; the group ministry of the East Harlem Protestant Parish; and the Orthodox Rabbinical Alliance of America all issued statements in opposition to the policy of the hospitals. A typical statement was that of the Baptist Ministers' Conference, which said that its members would "actively oppose any city official who flagrantly disregards the principle [of separation of church and state]."[32] But the most prophetic of all was the Presbytery of New York, which—reflecting a high degree of political sophistication—sent a letter to Dr. Jacobs stating that his support for one minority view and his "contemptuous treatment" of the views of others would not long "be tolerated by a wise city administration or by an informed electorate."[33]

This drumbeat of charge and countercharge went on for the rest of the summer. While the mayor and Dr. Jacobs might have hoped that the affair would blow over, they began to realize that these political efforts reflected powerful feelings in both the Protestant and the Jewish communities. Dr. Jacobs finally agreed to meet with the representatives of the Protestant Council on Friday, August 8. They requested that he present their case for birth control services to the Board of Hospitals at its September meeting, and he agreed. He also met with the Interdenominational Ministers' Alliance in Brooklyn on August 19. That group represented churches in Brooklyn with a combined membership of 175,000. For his part, Mayor Wagner (who could have given lessons in neutrality to the Swiss) said that on the one hand, he as a Roman Catholic was opposed to the prescribing of contraceptives in city hospitals, but that on the other hand, he would leave the decision to Dr. Jacobs and the members of the Board of Hospitals. Reporters tried to draw him out by asking if he would endorse a move by the Board of Hospitals to approve birth control therapy for city hospital patients, but he said that it was a medical matter and he would not interfere with the decision of the board.

By late August the ice was cracking a bit. Dr. Jacobs tried to propose a compromise whereby non-Catholic city hospital patients could be referred to private agencies such as Planned Parenthood. But the members of the Interdenominational Ministers' Alliance to whom he made the proposal, rejected it. Speaking the mind of the group, the Reverend Joseph May, a Protestant chaplain at Kings County Hospital, said that sending women needing birth control to private agencies made no sense. If a procedure was "improper and unacceptable" in the city hospitals, how could it be acceptable in private facilities?[34]

Interestingly enough, as the fateful September 17 hospital board meeting neared, an influential national Catholic journal broke ranks and raised questions about the policy of the New York and Brooklyn dioceses. In the September 12 edition of Commonweal, one of the editors, James Finn, noted that there had once been widespread religious opposition to birth control, but that clearly times had changed. He therefore questioned the wisdom of Roman Catholic insistence on legal directives that did not have the sympathy of most Americans. He saw a danger in a strategy that relied too much on legal coercion. It seemed to him that it produced a distorted view of the Church. Moral persuasion would seem to be a wiser course.[35] Nor was *Commonweal* alone in its estimate of the situation. Writing in the *Catholic Messenger*, Monsignor J. D. Conway also pointed out the futility of the hospital policy. Monsignor Conway felt that the church had already lost the struggle. To continue to pursue it was counterproductive.[36]

On September 12, Planned Parenthood and the clergy each made their final effort. The Medical Advisory Committee of Planned Parenthood reminded the public of an ethical injunction of the American Medical Association which warned that medical care must never be based on "exclusive dogma or a sectarian system." At the same time the Protestant Council made a formal request that the policy be changed. And it did so in the strongest moral terms:

> Failure to recognize the need of sex relations in married life, separate from the intention for pregnancy, is a serious misunderstanding of the nature of man created by God to be bound together, wife and husband, in the spiritual union that God has made possible. . . . The responsible use of contraceptive devices is, therefore, approved by most Christian leaders. . . . According to the Protestant view, the use of contraceptives practiced in Christian conscience in planning parenthood fulfills rather than violates the will of God.[37]

Now it would be up to the Board of Hospitals. This was a group of five physicians and five laypeople, plus Dr. Jacobs. There were two Roman Catholic members, John J. Lynch and Dr. Charles A. Gordon. But one member, Mary Lasker, was vice-president of the Planned Parenthood Federation. Other lay members were Judge Lewis Goldstein; David M.Heyman, financier; and Anna Rosenberg, former assistant secretary of defense. Other physician members were Dr. Willard C. Rappeleye, Dr. Howard A. Rusk, Dr. Peter Marshall Murray, and Dr. George Baehr.

VICTORY: THE POLICY CHANGES

Although there had been some signs of change, it nonetheless came as something of a surprise when the board on September 17 changed its policy by an 8 to 2 vote. In just two paragraphs, the board set out a completely new policy:

> When there are clearly defined medical decisions in which the life or health of a woman may be jeopardized by pregnancy, it is generally recognized

by the medical profession that contraceptive measures are proper medical procedure.

Municipal hospitals should provide such medical advice, preventive measures, and devices for female patients under their care whose life and health in the opinion of the medical staff may be jeopardized by pregnancy and who wish to avail themselves of such health measures.[38]

Consistently—and astonishingly—Dr. Jacobs continued to insist that this statement did not constitute a change of policy. Proclaiming that it was merely a "clarification and elaboration" of his original letter to the Academy of Medicine, he said, with admirable understatement, that there had been "considerable airing of the subject" and that had led to this recommendation.[39] Mayor Wagner made no public comment.

The Protestant Council of course was pleased with the new policy. Its members welcomed what they saw as an end to discrimination against women who had been denied medical services to which they had no moral objection. The American Jewish Congress also welcomed the board's action, seeing it as a commitment that the city hospitals would operate on medical principles and let each person affected make her choices—with or without the involvement of religion. Planned Parenthood was also pleased and saw the decision as a victory for the people of New York, one that would have significance for the rest of the country.[40]

But it was the joint statement of the Archdiocese of New York and the Diocese of Brooklyn that offered the most insight into what this victory meant. At first glance their response seemed to be no different from the traditional Roman Catholic opposition to contraception. In its condemnation of the new hospital policy, it stressed the old natural law argument which stated that the primary purpose of sexual intercourse was procreation. Presumably, any device which frustrated that purpose was wrong. It also attacked the morality of the clergy who had opposed it, accusing them of "basing morality on individual decision."[41] The statement continued: "Catholics are rightly distressed at this [removal of the ban on birth control which] introduces an immoral practice in our hospitals that perverts the nature and dignity of man. It uses public funds for corrupt purposes, contrary to the manifest will of a large number of taxpayers. . . . All Catholic personnel of our hospital are reminded of their grave obligation in conscience to, in no way, cooperate with such procedure."[42]

But there was another dimension of the letter that had considerable historical interest. The church took pains to explain that it was not unmindful of the problems of marriage, of the need for the expression of love between husband and wife, of the dangers that childbirth could pose to the mother. Here the tone was defensive, indicating that at some level the church realized that it had lost the battle for public opinion. Criticism like that from the *Commonweal* article had made it clear that even the American Catholic world was no longer that supportive of coercive anticontraceptive public policies. After all, this was 1958. A new reform pope, Pope John XXIII, was in office. A Vatican Council was coming, as was a completely new form of birth control—the pill. And the scientist most associated with its development, Dr. John Rock, was a Catholic. The times were changing.

Ironically the most striking portion of the statement was the assurance that abstinence was not the only acceptable practice when a couple wished to avoid children. Couples could also practice the rhythm method that allowed intercourse during "periods of natural sterility." That the church felt compelled to offer its own method of contraception was the clearest evidence that the birth control movement had changed even it. Margaret Sanger had recognized the profound human need for birth control, and in the end, despite years of bitter opposition, the Catholic Church had had to follow her lead and find a method of birth control it could sanction.

CONCLUSION

Four factors led to this victory. First, public acceptance of contraception had steadily grown since the 1930s, when Protestant and Jewish denominations first defended it. It was moving out from private clinics into public hospitals. Not only Planned Parenthood affiliates but also private hospitals and gynecologists now prescribed birth control to their middle-class patients. Given that reality, it was hard to argue that distributing it to poor people in public hospitals was somehow immoral.

Second, courageous physicians had forced the issue before the public. Doctors like Dr. Louis Hellman were unwilling to accept the old policy. They played a part that brought about a public confrontation that placed the old policy in a horrendous light.

Third, Planned Parenthood had wisely pursued a coalition strategy. It did not want this to be the usual battle between birth control advocates and their religious opponents. So it formed a partnership with the clergy, who, in this case, were highly motivated. Then the Federation stayed in the background, furnishing information to other professional groups fighting the hospital policy. This strategy was a long time coming. In the thirties the groups that Planned Parenthood sought alliances with, like the Eugenics Society, had held them at arm's length. They had had better success in building alliances with physicians. Then there was the period of the forties and fifties when the Federation developed a clergy network, but did not learn how to use it effectively in a controversy. In the Poughkeepsie struggle (chapter 3) there was no effort on the part of the national office to have its clergy network make a statement of support of the doctors whose hospital privileges were threatened. But in 1958 Planned Parenthood saw how clergy could be effective in transforming public policy. As the controversy began, Planned Parenthood gave support to both the Protestant Council and the New York Board of Rabbis as they challenged the hospital's policy of denying family planning. When these respectable religious bodies publicly supported the family planning work that was epitomized by Planned Parenthood, they conferred a kind of blessing on the organization. The coalition strategy implied that Planned Parenthood was no longer a strange radical group but rather part of mainstream society and acceptable to many religious groups and individuals.

But the fourth factor, and the most critical element, was the political effectiveness of the clergy. At a panel discussion on November 18, 1958, the national director of Planned Parenthood, William Vogt, acknowledged this: "No organization was more important than that of the religious groups which protested domination by one sect."[43] For decades city hospitals had refused to change, primarily because of their awareness of the strong feelings of the Roman Catholic Church. By default the church held a monopoly of the sacred on this issue. And Americans are sensitive to religious considerations. But in this 1958 controversy, the church lost its monopoly. Two other religious traditions presented a different religious morality. In the Protestant and Jewish traditions, contraception was highly moral, even God-ordained. With the entry of these faiths into the field, the morality issue was neutralized.

This religious presence gave political cover to bureaucrats like Dr. Jacobs and politicians like Mayor Wagner. They could risk offending the Catholic Church because the conflicting moral claims of other religious bodies had entered the public debate in a strong and assertive way. In a situation of such conflict, politicians could now do what politicians are meant to do, forge a compromise that would satisfy public opinion while giving something to each of the conflicting parties. The Catholic Church was reassured that its doctors and nurses would not be forced to do anything against their conscience. And the hospitals were told they could bring the contraceptive services into the hospitals.

Ultimately the victory came because the issue of justice was so clear. When Dr. Jacobs ordered Dr. Hellman not to give medical services to a diabetic woman who needed them desperately, the injustice was unmistakable. Dr. Jacobs was operating within a religious, not a medical context. What was religion doing in a public hospital determining the fate of a Protestant woman who had no religious objections to birth control? In the end there was no moral defense of such an action.

The New York City hospital controversy of 1958 differs strikingly in one respect from modern reproductive struggles. In 1958 the voices of women were silent. There was no National Organization of Women or National Abortion Rights Action League to issue public statements and arrange demonstrations. In the absence of a strong feminist voice, the debate was carried on instead in terms of the separation of church and state or the favoritism of one religion over another. And yet despite this difference in argumentation, the issue was really justice for women.

It was the case of that one diabetic Protestant woman that galvanized both Planned Parenthood and the clergy. Planned Parenthood had been helping such women for thirty years. Protestant and Jewish clergy had always worked with women like her in their pastoral counseling. Both the clergy and Planned Parenthood were committed to the sacred work of justice. Planned Parenthood had the experience and the clergy had the theology to defend the organization's work. As in the earlier alliances of the thirties and forties, these two groups found themselves working together. It would not be the last time.

CHAPTER 5

Sacred Work in Baltimore, 1961–1965

Concern with planned parenthood therefore is not an option in the Christian way of life. It is a moral and religious obligation for the sake of healthy mothers and wanted children, for the sake of spiritual growth through the expression of love in the relation between husband and wife . . .

> —From a sermon, "Planned Parenthood: A Christian Responsibility," preached by the Reverend Alfred B. Starratt at Emmanuel Church in Baltimore on the Sunday before Lent, February 8, 1959

FOLLOWING THE SUCCESS OF THE New York City hospital fight, a surge of clergy enthusiasm led to a reborn national clergy committee with a new name, the Clergymen's National Advisory Council. Chairing the committee this time was one of the brightest and most colorful American members of the clergy of the 1950s and 1960s, Bishop James Pike, the bishop of the Episcopal Diocese of California. Beginning his life as a lawyer, Pike found himself bored with the law and fascinated by the mysterious power of religion which, despite all its flaws, seemed to him to have the capacity to make human lives richer and more just. In 1952 he was appointed to the position of dean of the Cathedral of St. John the Divine in New York City. Though less well known than St. Patrick's Cathedral, St. John's is far larger. The position of dean offers a pulpit, literally and figuratively, from which the occupant can enter the political and social dialogues of the time. From the time he became dean, Bishop Pike had a knack for capturing the public imagination.

He had spoken out on behalf of Planned Parenthood in 1953 when the New York City affiliate of Planned Parenthood was being forced out of the city's Welfare and Health Council. By 1960, when he assumed the chair of the new Clergymen's National Advisory Council, he had become the Episcopal bishop of California. This council retained some members from the original group, including Dr. John Bennett, the Reverend Harry Emerson Fosdick, and Bishop Oxnam. Now they were joined by Rabbi Edward E. Klein of the Stephen Wise Free Synagogue in New York City, Rabbi Maurice Eisendrath of the Union of American Hebrew Congregations, the Reverend Donald Harrington of the Community Church in New York City, and the famous popular writer Dr. Norman Vincent Peale, pastor of the Marble Collegiate Church in New York City and author of *The Power of Positive Thinking*. Under Pike's leadership, in April 1960 the council published "The Ethics of Family Planning," in which members presented anew the Protestant and Jewish justifications for contraception: "The ethical conviction of Protestants and Jews that family planning fulfills the will of God is rooted in the religious conviction that there are two primary functions of sexual intercourse in marriage, the unitive and the procreative. . . . The first may be rightly sought apart from the second. The sexual act sacramentally expresses and nourishes the love and commitment that partners in marriage give to one another."[1] An affiliate clergy committee in Baltimore was about to use those words and many others like them to end a long social injustice.

MARYLAND 1961: TOLERANCE AND INTOLERANCE

In 1649 the Maryland Colonial Assembly passed an Act of Toleration whose second part proclaimed that no one who followed Jesus Christ "shall from henceforth be in any ways troubled, molested or discountenanced, for or in respect to his or her religion, nor in the free exercise thereof, . . . nor in any way compelled to the belief or exercise of any other religion against his or her consent."[2] It was no empty statute. In Maryland not only Catholics but also other outcast Christian groups such as Quakers were welcomed. Both Protestants and Catholics served as governors, and the colony had the reputation of having a strong climate of religious tolerance. Nevertheless, this brief strand of Maryland history—however positive—can be misleading. This gesture toward religious freedom simultaneously held serious consequences for non-Christians. For even this unique Act of Toleration granting freedom of worship to all Christians had a section that said that those who were not Christians could be imprisoned or executed. But despite this irony so apparent to us today, the act still had a spirit of tolerance that was advanced for its time.

A similar irony was abundantly present in Maryland in 1961 when it came to the practice of family planning. Because of powerful religious opposition from the Roman Catholic hierarchy, public apathy, and little or no interest in the subject by other religious groups, the Maryland State Department of Welfare was forbidden to offer family planning services to any welfare clients in the entire state of Maryland—even if they asked for them. Since many—probably most—clients were not Catholics and were not bound to follow any Roman Catholic doctrine or social ethics, this amounted to a clear violation, if not of the letter, certainly of the spirit of the Act of Toleration.

The organization that would challenge this state of affairs was Planned Parenthood of Maryland. In 1925 a distinguished psychiatrist from the faculty of the Johns Hopkins University School of Hygiene and Public Health, Dr. Adolph Meyer, joined Margaret Sanger's national board. That same year people from Maryland invited Sanger to speak in Hagerstown on the topic "'Rational Motherhood' or 'Birth Control.'" It was her first speech in the state and drew a crowd of over a thousand people. The interest generated led to the formation of a planning group for a "Clinic on Contraceptive Advice" in 1926. On November 2, 1927, the Baltimore Birth Control Clinic was opened. It was the first such clinic in the state of Maryland.[3]

Shaping the form and operation of the clinic was a strong personality of those times, Dr. Bessie Moses. She came from a rigid aristocratic family whose members were social leaders of the influential Baltimore Jewish community. Her parents opposed her going to medical school, but supported her financially nonetheless. Influenced by friends, she finally broke away from them enough to take on this work. Ironically, in reality she was as rigid as her parents, but in this situation that quality served a purpose: her intimidating demeanor probably helped to keep the law at bay.

She had gone to New York in 1926 to meet Margaret Sanger, and Sanger came to Baltimore several times in subsequent years. Something clicked between these two women and a close bond was formed. Dr. Moses said that she drew strength from those visits. When the clinic opened in 1927, the first patient was an African-American woman. In the custom of the times in Maryland, the clinic was segregated. African-American women came on Thursdays. White women came two other days a week. While Dr. Moses honored the custom, she was not in agreement with it.[4] She provided training for an African-American gynecologist, Dr. N. Louise Young, and later helped her start her own clinic. However Dr. Moses was quite strict about providing services only to married women.

Diaphragms and other contraceptives came in only by truck or rail, despite the fact that the Comstock laws prohibited shipment by mail. No public appeals for funds were made. Individuals donated, and Bessie Moses raised money from her friends. The women who came to the clinic paid what they could—often nothing—for the materials. Essentially, Dr. Moses gave up obstetrics to devote her life to this clinic. She directed the Baltimore affiliate for almost thirty years until her retirement in 1956 and became so much of a presence in the city that a jingle grew up about her, "When your man proposes, go see Bessie Moses."[5]

From this modest beginning, Baltimore's Planned Parenthood grew until it had a number of satellite clinics, a large central clinic, and a network of relationships with the medical community. By 1961 the Baltimore affiliate was seeing thousands of women per year. Yet that reality was almost unknown, because it was struggling with a certain kind of invisibility.

THE INVISIBILITY OF PLANNED PARENTHOOD

In the mid-nineteenth century Queen Victoria demonstrated the power of invisibility when an unruly mob of Bolivians burst into the British embassy and forced the ambassador to ride on a mule. The indifferent response of the Bolivian government did not please her majesty. So she decided that Bolivia simply didn't exist. From that point on, whenever Bolivian citizens presented their passports at a point of entry into England or a British possession, it would be handed back to them with the words, "There is no such country." When Bolivian currency or bank drafts reached a British bank, they would be refused with the same sentiment. It was not long before the Bolivians had to sue for peace. If the goal is to suppress something, few strategies are more effective than virtual invisibility.

In Maryland in 1961, Planned Parenthood was like Bolivia—it was invisible. The State Department of Welfare and the city hospitals had unwritten policies against referral to Planned Parenthood. The major Baltimore newspapers, *The Sun* and *The Evening Sun*, would not carry the announcements of the organization. The Health and Welfare Council and the Union of Voluntary Agencies in Baltimore continued to reject Planned Parenthood's application for membership. Among the political leadership of the city, the attitude toward Planned Parenthood seemed to be one of genial dismissal. The mayor's Coordinating Council for Health Services made a statement that became famous among the staff of Planned Parenthood clinics of that era. The council said that Planned Parenthood was not really a health agency at all, or if it was, it was "just about like the Boy Scouts, who have a first aid course that they teach the Cubs."[6]

For things to change, Planned Parenthood would have to confront the

power of the Roman Catholic Diocese of Baltimore. The instrument would
be the Clergymen's Advisory Board. These two protagonists—the Diocese
of Baltimore and the Clergymen's Advisory Board—would bring two widely
differing religious perspectives to the subsequent debate.

ROMAN CATHOLICISM IN MARYLAND

Roman Catholicism in Maryland had a different history than in the other col-
onies. In the latter, the Protestants were well ensconced as the land-owning
establishment when the majority of Catholics arrived as poor immigrants.
But in Maryland the Catholics were the aristocrats from the very beginning.
Unlike other early American cities, Baltimore was a city founded by Catholics. In the 1960s many of the leading families of Baltimore were Catholics
with long and proud lineages in the state. This small state had well-respected
Catholic colleges such as Loyola College in Maryland, Mount St. Mary's
College, and the College of Notre Dame of Maryland This was a heritage of
which the Catholic citizens of Maryland could be justifiably proud.

When it came to contraception, the Diocese of Baltimore had, like all
Catholic dioceses, opposed Margaret Sanger and Planned Parenthood for
decades. When Dr. Alan Guttmacher opened an infertility clinic in Baltimore
in 1946, rumors went around that the clinic was a Planned Parenthood
"trap." The Catholic Church called a mass meeting at the Grand Ballroom
of the Knights of Columbus building for the night of March 27, 1947. Lenore
Guttmacher, Dr. Guttmacher's wife, went to the meeting with a friend, who
took shorthand notes. Before a huge crowd in a packed hall, the chairman
of the meeting warned that while Christian civilization has been threatened
many times, "one of the most insidious dangers facing us today is the
Planned Parenthood movement."[7] While the language was extreme, the fear
and hostility were real. It was a hostility not easily overcome.

Despite this history, the early sixties were to be years of fateful change
for Roman Catholics everywhere. The Vatican Council called by Pope John
XXIII would convene in a matter of months. This was to be a monumental
attempt to move the church into the modern world. It would change relationships between Catholics and non-Catholics, between priests and the laity,
and greatly revise church rituals and liturgy. Change was in the air. Dr. John
Rock, a Roman Catholic physician, had been principally responsible for the
development of the birth control pill. Though there had been wide internal
discussion of oral contraception, the Vatican had not definitively ruled on
it yet.[8] Some respected Catholic scholars and many laypeople thought that

the church might actually change or modify its position on the issue. In addition there were signs that the church was losing its stomach for the birth control fight. While in the forties figures like Cardinal Richard Cushing of Boston defended legal prohibitions of contraception with statements such as "We owe it to God and to the general community to keep up our fight for the retention of sane fundamental legislation," by the sixties, he had changed his position.[9] When the Supreme Court's *Griswold* decision (affirming a constitutional right to birth control for married people) came down in 1965, he said, "I have no right to impose my thinking, which is rooted in religious thought, on those who do not think as I do."[10]

Yet in 1962, on the eve of the debate before the Maryland State Board of Welfare, these changing tides of Catholic opinion did not moderate the opposition of the Baltimore diocese to family planning in general and Planned Parenthood in particular. That opposition was still both powerful and focused.

PLANNED PARENTHOOD'S CLERGYMEN'S ADVISORY BOARD

On the other side of the issue stood Baltimore Planned Parenthood's Clergymen's Advisory Board. Unlike the Diocese of Baltimore, it had no two-hundred-year history. It had begun in the immediate post–World War II period (1945–1953) by the executive director of Planned Parenthood of Maryland, Virginia Kirchoff.[11] She began with her own Methodist minister, and he led her to others. In the sixties two longtime members, Rabbi Abraham Shaw and Rabbi Samuel Glasner, were joined by an Episcopal priest, the Reverend Al Starratt, who would become one of the leading Planned Parenthood of Maryland supporters in subsequent years. Starratt and many of the clergy gave lectures on family planning to private secondary schools. Nor did they hesitate to preach on family planning to their congregations.[12] Starratt and Shaw were remarkable clergy and served as outstanding and imaginative leaders. By 1965 the board had sixty-five clergy members.

These were the years when Baltimore clergy asked Planned Parenthood to open clinics in their churches, a fact, which had it been widely known, might have positively affected public opinion. This process began in 1958 when the Reverend Edgar Ward of the Cherry Hill Community Presbyterian Church of Baltimore offered the church facilities to begin a satellite clinic. Soon other clinics were opened in other Baltimore churches, such as the Graceland Methodist Church in 1959, the Metropolitan Methodist Church in 1959, and the Douglas Community Memorial Church in 1962. And the influential downtown Brown Memorial Presbyterian Church carried out an extensive survey to see how it might help Planned Parenthood provide family planning services to its neighborhood.

It was not only individual churches but also the Baltimore Council of Churches that took an active interest in contraception. In 1960 the council, at the urging of Planned Parenthood's Clergymen's Advisory Board, sponsored a series of seminars for clergy on family planning. This long history of active participation by the Clergymen's Advisory Board had generated in its members a passion and concern for the issue that would serve them in good stead in the coming struggle with the Roman Catholic Diocese of Maryland.

CLERGY ADVOCACY FOR CHANGE
BEFORE THE STATE BOARD OF WELFARE

At the beginning of 1961 the Planned Parenthood board was anxious to change the Maryland Board of Welfare policy that prohibited the referral of welfare clients for family planning services, even when they requested it. But the affiliate wanted to find out what lay behind the prohibition before proceeding, and asked the Clergymen's Advisory Board to hold three strategic meetings: one with representatives of the Roman Catholic Church, one with the heads of the two publicly supported hospitals, City Hospital and the University of Maryland Hospital, and one with the directors of the city and state Departments of Welfare. The clergy arranged the meetings quietly.

The first Clergymen's Advisory Board meeting was with representatives of the Roman Catholic diocese to hear them explain their position. They told the visitors that they wanted frank discussion. They certainly got it. The two priests stated that they believed the Roman Catholic Church had the right "not only to block this information from being given to their own parishioners, but to use any means, fair or foul, to keep any word of birth control from reaching anyone in the city."[13] The sheer chutzpah of the statement was startling, but the sentiment was not totally unexpected. Although the Catholic Church was on the verge of great change, the church temperament in Baltimore was still defensive and the priests who came to the meeting seemed to have little interest in ecumenical discussions on a subject such as this. It was still a time when Protestants were referred to as "non-Catholics." Vatican II would make them into "separated brethren."

No spirit of rapprochement had yet been awakened. Consequently, it is understandable that these representatives would be both defensive and defiant. They had a situation in which the policies favored by their church were being challenged. Seeing no injustice in these policies, they didn't want them changed.

Then came what turned out to be the most critical meeting, the meeting with the welfare officials. The latter said yes, there was pressure to keep the policy against birth control, and yes, they admitted, they bowed to that pressure. When asked why, the answer was clear. "We are public servants," they told the clergy, who had to go to Annapolis every year and fight for the funds needed to provide services. They did not want to risk those funds without good reason. Then the clergy were given a lesson in political effectiveness. The welfare officials said,

> Why is it that all pressure comes from the Catholics? Why is it that the majority is unable to assert its position as skillfully? Why is it that Monsignor Dorsch of Catholic Charities is the one who always argues for welfare budgets, who is a mainstay and support to the Department of Welfare in all of their activities, and therefore has the potential for pressure? Where are the Protestant and Jewish clergymen when the budget is up for a hearing?[14]

Clergy took the lesson to heart and vowed to take a greater interest in the department's welfare.

Planned Parenthood then began a months-long concerted effort to raise public consciousness of the issue. A series of educational teas with Planned Parenthood speakers was carried out. A newsletter was begun, to be sent to all financial contributors, volunteers, and leaders of social agencies. Personal contacts were made with people from the Domestic Relations Court, Urban Renewal, and many other civic groups. In this intensive campaign, the affiliate sought to build support from community leaders across the board.

In this sixteen-month period from February 1961 to June 1962 there was also a series of serendipitous supportive developments. First, the Baltimore grand jury specifically recommended that welfare clients be referred to Planned Parenthood of Maryland. This came about because the grand jury was moved by the many serious social problems that were present in the lives of the people they were seeing. Members of the grand jury had inquired about Planned Parenthood services and were impressed by what they heard. Many letters to the newspapers endorsed that recommendation. In addition, the Governor's Commission on Illegitimacy had recently (1961) recommended birth control as a means to reduce out-of-wedlock births. Planned Parenthood's views could now no longer be characterized as either marginal or eccentric.

In late spring of 1962, the CEO and medical director of Planned Parenthood met with the director of the Department of Welfare. The latter suggested that the affiliate could ask for a hearing before the State Board of Welfare to request that the policy of silence be changed. Planned Parenthood expected that such a meeting would be in the fall, but it was scheduled for July 20. That gave the affiliate only three weeks to prepare. With everyone working flat out, they were able to meet the deadline.

In its presentation on July 20, Planned Parenthood explained its work and the available services. A significant number of favorable letters from community leaders were produced, from agencies such as the Department of Health, the Johns Hopkins School of Hygiene, the Council of Churches, and the local public school system. Planned Parenthood also stressed that many people wanted to write letters but were afraid to speak out because of their positions. The final section of the presentation was on the religious support for the affiliate. Here a member of the Clergymen's Advisory Board spoke at the meeting and made it abundantly clear that not only did other religious groups not share the Roman Catholic position, but many denominations felt that it was far more than just permissible, it was actually a religious obligation for families to practice birth control in their family life. For the State Board of Welfare to ignore that reality was, in effect, a form of religious discrimination.

The presentation impressed the board and on September 28, 1962, it abolished the old policy of silence. The cautious resolution the board issued said that "under circumstances where child-spacing becomes desirable, the worker shall make referral to the Planned Parenthood clinic or to the family physician for child-spacing information, as a normal resource made available to the community to married parents."[15] The victory was sweeping. The decision by the board not only benefited welfare clients but also meant that the Health Department and the public hospitals would also follow suit and refer people for contraceptive services.

The next day Dr. John Whitridge, chief, State Department of Preventive Medicine, sent a letter to county health officers across the state telling them of the new policy and asking them to ready their clinics for referrals. Planned Parenthood helped several of the counties develop the services and even, in some cases, supplied the physicians to render them.[16]

Catholic reaction was swift and angry. Monsignor Dorsch reiterated his opposition to the Department of Welfare's dispersal of birth control information to any client. He sought to re-open the issue, but this time he could not persuade the board to rescind its decision. The new policy stayed firm.

Reversing the Moral Argument

Many factors contributed to this major policy change. A critical element was the strong support for Planned Parenthood by one member of the State Board of Welfare. Howard Murphy, editor of *The African American*, a Baltimore newspaper, had long been a gadfly to the Department of Welfare board on the subject of birth control. Several years earlier, as a member of the Governor's Commission on Juvenile Delinquency, he had wanted the commission to recommend birth control as a way of combating the problem. As a leader in the African-American community, he had been outspoken in defending Planned Parenthood against charges that birth control was a form of genocide. Having advocated for Planned Parenthood on the State Board of Welfare for years, he was finally able to bring the majority with him.

Success before the State Board of Welfare was also the result of a broad-based and sophisticated approach. Careful preparation and the support of key members of the board itself were factors that helped to end the policy of silence. But perhaps the key to the change was the religious and moral voice of Jews and Protestants.

Any religious institution, synagogue, temple, church, or mosque has a certain moral presence in a community. People wanting to begin any kind of humanitarian work in a town almost always contact the religious institutions, because they assume they will be sympathetic. It is also presumed that religious institutions care about the welfare of children, of the helpless, of the poor, and so on. Immoral behavior by clergy is automatically news, because it is presumed they will behave morally. Given this background, when the Catholic Church said that its morality was offended by all forms of contraception (except natural family planning), public officials took note. The size, the tradition, the historical involvement of the church in welfare policies and the sheer political strength of the church meant that politicians had to pay attention. For decades the anti-contraception policy had enjoyed a moral monopoly because no one challenged it on those grounds.

But a large, organized, and articulate group of Jewish rabbis and Protestant ministers was now doing just that. In effect, they reversed the moral argument. Their positions were as clear as the Catholic position, albeit

diametrically opposed. On their side they pointed out that the World Council of Churches, Jewish leaders, and Protestant denominations had all said
that family planning was a necessary requirement. Birth control was not just
a moral issue; it was a moral imperative. The differences had been outlined
in the 1946 Planned Parenthood Clergy Advisory Council resolution (see
chapter 2), signed by 3,200 clergy nationwide. After pointing out that religious opposition to family planning had been successful in the past in preventing hospitals and social service agencies from providing this essential
service, the statement went on to say: "Be it therefore resolved that Protestant and Jewish clergymen . . . seek the inclusion of planned parenthood
services in hospitals and other agencies . . . and . . . that favorable policies
be sought to permit professional staff members in other health and welfare
agencies to make maximum use of these services."[17] Thirty-four Baltimore
clergy signed that resolution in 1946. Sixteen years later, others were following through on it.

The social context of contraception had already been changed by the
simple reality that the pill was widely available to those who could afford
it. Now the concept of family planning as a religious obligation, an obligation being denied by the State Welfare Board, was a new and startling point
of view in which denial of services could be construed as immoral. What
do public officials do when religious groups with different moral views
press their opposing arguments on them? Generally they try to accommo-
date both groups. In this case they made an accommodation by expanding
their services in a way that acknowledged the moral position of Jews and
Protestants. The presence of the clergy gave them political cover. The moral
presence of the Catholic Church was balanced by the moral presence of
the Protestant and Jewish denominations. Change became possible and the
clergy were the key to that change.

Round Two: Help for the Unmarried

In 1962 the new policy of the State Board of Welfare was a victory, but only
partially so. It allowed family planning information to be given solely to
married people. This reflected the conflicting attitudes of society as it slowly
accepted family planning. From the nineteenth century on the great danger
put forward by contraception's opponents was that it would lead to promiscuity. Presumably, sexual intercourse freed from the likelihood of pregnancy
would lead men and women—married or unmarried—to frequent and
casual sex with numerous partners. Many opponents reasoned that if you

couldn't block birth control entirely, the first line of defense was to limit its use to the married.

Buried within such policies was the primal conviction that the fear of pregnancy worked to keep people from having sex, or alternatively, that if a woman became pregnant from out-of-wedlock contacts, then the pregnancy was a proper punishment. Also embedded in such attitudes for some was a deep sexism which believed that the fear of unwanted pregnancy was a powerful force to constrain the sexual behavior of women.

From today's vantage point it seems a strange philosophy. If people are so irresponsible about bringing unwanted children into the world, would it not be in society's self-interest to furnish them the means to prevent giving birth to children they do not want and that society will have to support? Why withhold those means?

Nevertheless, many people in Baltimore in the early sixties did not want the means and materials of contraception given to unmarried women. Indeed even one of the churches that housed a Planned Parenthood clinic objected to any service to unwed mothers. In March 1961, the minister of the Cherry Hill Community Church (United Presbyterian) wrote to Anne Huppman, the director of Planned Parenthood, to express his concern

> that there are unwed mothers who are being allowed the services of Planned Parenthood without our knowledge. This is immoral, in opposition to the principles of the Christian Church and should not be continued.
>
> Throughout the country, Planned Parenthood is in a struggle to become accepted as a creditable part of modern civilization; let us not defeat the gains we have made by attempting an easy solution to sexual immorality.[18]

On the surface, the Planned Parenthood affiliates of the time formally limited their contraception services to married women. Undoubtedly, many people in the movement felt that this was a good policy. The feminists of the late sixties strongly criticized it.[19] Yet as the minister's letter indicates, at least some unmarried women were in fact getting birth control from Planned Parenthood despite its formal policy and despite the Board of Welfare's policy forbidding it. In practice how did Planned Parenthoods enforce such a protocol? Did they insist on seeing a marriage license? Did the woman have to be accompanied by her husband? Clearly some affiliates did enforce it. But in fact did other affiliates and the women seeking their services dodge the policy? Were there many affiliates that just accepted an unmarried woman's word when she said she was married? Almost certainly some affiliates had sympathetic staff who didn't ask too many questions about a client's marital status. In a long ministry I have heard many anecdotes to that effect. Planned Parenthood is a woman's organization, and in more than a few affiliates there was compassion for the predicament of many unmarried women.

But affiliates who might have wanted to publicly change their policy on this issue still had to move carefully. It was dangerous to get too far ahead of public sensibilities. In that era, even health services at leading women's colleges were unwilling to provide contraceptives for their students lest they be considered to be sanctioning premarital intercourse. Ultimately this was also a moral question. And in Baltimore here too it was the Clergymen's Advisory Board that was able and willing to reexamine the issue and raise questions about this long-settled policy of denial of services to the unwed.

Members began by looking carefully at all aspects of the lives of unwed mothers. On January 10, 1963, the clergy committee convened and noted a report by Dr. Robert Farber, the commissioner of health, which stated that "illegitimacy is one of the biggest public health problems of the city." The clergy next looked one by one at how the agencies of the city dealt with unwed mothers. First they discovered that the schools took a punitive attitude toward a pregnant girl. When a girl was pregnant she had to leave school. After the baby was born it was up to the individual principal to decide whether the girl could return to her school. If she married she had to withdraw and enter the evening program. The Department of Welfare had a caseworker for unwed mothers who was oriented toward helping the mother place the child for adoption. Once the baby was adopted, the mother was dropped from services.

As they learned about the situation and began their discussions, the clergy were by no means in agreement. One minister wanted the Welfare Department to mandate that an unwed mother on welfare be required to accept counseling with a "minister of her choice." He believed that she must be brought back "into the church and into moral roads."[20] He even argued that if she became pregnant again, she should be sterilized. Another opposed such sterilization, but believed it was immoral to give contraceptive information to young girls.

But attitudes began to change as the clergy looked at the specific facts of the lives of unwed mothers. It was not unusual in Baltimore for pregnant girls to drop out of school at age twelve.[21] An examination of the "Family Life Education" curriculum in schools revealed that it contained little or no realistic sex education. In time it became easier for board members to ask what kind of morality it was that denied poor young women the knowledge to protect themselves from pregnancy and sexual disease, and kicked them out of school when they became pregnant. These specifics moved them away from abstractions such as "promiscuity" and "sexual immorality."

Above all, they struggled with the question of prevention. How could these young women be helped? Throughout 1963 the clergy board arranged meetings with leading educators and public health officials. They asked themselves, what agency could provide the services that could prevent unwanted pregnancies? They decided that however they might want to, the churches and synagogues could not do it, because studies indicated that most unwed mothers were unchurched. Realistically they felt that most parents, even if available and concerned, could not provide what was needed. Only public agencies had the sources to provide both counseling and the needed referrals.

From 1963 to 1965 they debated the issue, winning over reluctant clergy until they had created a consensus for change. Part of the process was discovering that the Baltimore grand jury was moving in the same direction. On December 4, 1964, the jury reported that

> We are impressed by ambivalent attitudes and procedures of our society which, on the one hand, condemns the parents of out-of-wedlock children, and yet appears to offer little, if anything, as a preventive or positive program. It has been proven that where there has been counseling help for the unwed mother, the likelihood of her repeating the pattern has decreased. Of the 6,730 illegitimate births in Maryland in 1963 less than 400 received counseling, all of this from private agencies.[22]

Was a grand jury to show more compassion than churches? The clergy had the same concerns as that jury. It was obvious that most of these births were unwanted. What was the morality of compulsory pregnancy? When people believed they could not care properly for additional children, was it moral to withhold the means of contraception from them? Middle-class people, people not on welfare, had access to those means through private physicians. The morality of the whole situation was certainly open to question. Rabbi Abraham Shaw captured the tragedy of the situation when he called the unmarried mother the "forgotten soul."[23]

By 1965 the Clergymen's Advisory Board had reached a consensus. It was voiced publicly by Rabbi Shaw. He said that the board had gone through "considerable soul-searching, particularly in view of the challenge made in some quarters that planned parenthood encourages promiscuity. After much discussion and even debate we have come to the conclusion that the problems of the unwanted child far overshadow the possible extension of the problems of promiscuity."[24] They concluded then that whenever unmarried women were referred by responsible agencies or clergy, Planned Parenthood should provide them with contraceptive services.[25] The State Welfare Board accepted this recommendation and started referring unmarried people to Planned Parenthood, which then provided the services.

The swiftness of the turnaround seemed to indicate that society had been moving in the direction of allowing contraceptive services to unmarried women, but it's reasonable to argue that, in that time and place, the clergy were the ones who could make it happen. (The Supreme Court did not establish the right of single women to contraception until 1972.) When Rabbi Shaw and the other clergy spoke of a poor, unmarried woman as a "forgotten soul," they were making apparent the humanity of these women, a humanity that was obscured by all the remainders of Victorian morality that lingered even in the America of the early sixties. The board members lifted up the sadness and loneliness of those women and made society pay attention to them. The strength of these clergy came from their willingness to look closely at and to feel the suffering of the outcast person. It moved them from indifference and judgment to compassion. In turn they were able to help the society move more in that direction. These clergy saw that unmarried women are no less deserving of access to reproductive services than married people, and this vision helped to diminish the stigma of deeming a woman to be acting improperly and immorally if she chose to be sexually active before marriage.

THE BALTIMORE EXPERIENCE

The Planned Parenthood successes in Baltimore occurred for three core reasons. First, that affiliate, like the New York affiliate before it, learned that much can be accomplished when there is a close partnership between an affiliate and the clergy. In 1977, following many more battles, Planned Parenthood of Maryland acknowledged the critical importance of clergy support.

> In each of these major breakthroughs we used the good services and advice of our active Clergymen's Advisory Board which we cultivated and nurtured

to include representatives from each of the Protestant and Jewish denominations. This respected group held workshops and discussion sessions to inform
the community about our program and actually spearheaded the drive for the
[Department of Public Welfare] change in policy, the inclusion of sexuality
education in the schools, and—most important—the setting up of the Pregnancy Testing and Counseling Center which was established adjacent to a
church in downtown Baltimore.[26]

The second reason for the success of the Planned Parenthood alliance was
that both clergy and the affiliate leaders learned how important it was to
organize. In the 1958 hospital fight in New York City, organization was not
as essential, because the issue was so immediate and media-driven that
people came together without having to be recruited. But usually no serious political effect can be expected unless an effective and cohesive group
has been organized. The Clergymen's Advisory Board in Baltimore was that
kind of effective organization. People who confront a difficult and controversial issue over a long period of time either fall apart or bond together
into a unit where there is a serious measure of respect for one another.
The minutes of the meetings and the public statements make it clear that
the Clergymen's Advisory Board had such a bond.

The third lesson was the same one learned in New York—that the defense
of Planned Parenthood and the women it serves should be made on the
basis of justice. Too often that defense has been almost entirely confined to
the issue of rights. The language of rights is certainly valid, but when it is
asserted, opponents invariably cite other and opposing rights. At that point
the debate can become muddy. But justice is a biblical term and religious
people understand it. The Baltimore clergy could sense that it was unjust
on its face for social institutions dominated by men (and composed almost
entirely of men) to make legal, moral, and religious decisions defining the
lives of women.

No era is more excoriated in current political debate than the sixties, but
the Clergy Advisory Board of the Baltimore affiliate is the clearest refutation of that notion. Here was a group of clergy who emerged from the usual
somnolence of the churches in regard to controversial social issues. In this
remarkable partnership with Planned Parenthood, they took the time and
expended the energy necessary to turn themselves into not only an effective
political body but also a thoughtful agent of social change.

CHAPTER 6

Victories in the Sixties

We believe that husband and wife act responsibly when they decide, within the providence of God, that there are compelling reasons against child-bearing: specifically when the birth of a child would likely injure or destroy
• the health of the mother
• the economic, emotional, or spiritual well-being of the household, and especially of other children
• the family's ability to lift its life above the level of chance, accident, or grim necessity, into the realm of freedom and personal decision before God.

—Statement of the Metropolitan Church Federation of St. Louis, February 26, 1960

THE SECOND WAVE OF CLERGY organizing touched many more places than Baltimore. In many cities, affiliates used their clergy connections to good effect. But clergy cannot take too much credit. It was the sixties, after all, and social change was in the air. The Montgomery bus boycott and the lunch counter sit-ins in North Carolina had launched the civil rights movement, and it was accelerating. Progress was being made, though it was by no means automatic. Nevertheless in every section of America, Planned Parenthood found that a determined effort—often led by clergy—would bring birth control services into hospitals and welfare offices where people could be helped. The struggles in St. Louis, Denver, and San Francisco were typical of what happened in affiliates across the country. Richmond, Cleveland, Tucson, or many smaller towns could just as easily have been selected.[1] Finally, the stigma of being a "cursed" organization seemed to be fading away.

DENVER: THE "BIG PUSH"

When Margaret Sanger crossed the country speaking in 1916, she was most impressed with the spirit and confidence of the women of Denver. Those women had had the vote for some years and had used it wisely. Male politicians in Denver had learned to pay attention to their concerns. Sanger came back again in 1923 and 1930, speaking to civic groups and professionals. She loved the Denver audiences. The first clinic dispensing birth control services and information in Denver was opened in 1926. It was located in the First Reformed Church. A clinic historian described the conditions it faced:

> The majority of the women served had twelve children or more. Volunteers took mothers back and forth to the clinic, while other volunteers attended to the children at home. The clinic opened at 8 A.M. . . . . The courageous women who helped start the clinic were Mrs. T. C. Cunningham, Mrs. Imogene Daly Genter, Mrs. Montgomery Dorsey, Mrs. Charles Kassler, Mrs. Verner Reed, Mrs. James Rae Arneill and Mrs. V. L. Board. Only loyalty, courage and imagination kept the idea and work afloat because these women encountered continual opposition and ridicule.[2]

But the church supported them. Two additional clinics opened in Denver. Others were begun in Greeley, Colorado Springs, and Pueblo by 1935, and in 1951 Planned Parenthood opened a large new clinic in Grace Community Church in Denver.

In March 1961 Planned Parenthood of Denver, inspired by the 1958 victory in the New York City hospital system, renewed its determination to get birth control services into Denver General Hospital. They called it the "Big Push." Their proposal read in part:

> The Denver Chapter of Planned Parenthood, Inc., a charitable corporation duly organized and existing by virtue of the laws of the State of Colorado, through its Board of Directors hereby respectfully requests the Board of Health and Hospitals of the City and County of Denver to authorize the inclusions of family planning services as part of the maternal care program presently established and operating in Denver General Hospital, Denver, Colorado, and to include the same in other public health facilities under the jurisdiction of said Board of Health and Hospitals.[3]

They wanted to put a nurse with Planned Parenthood training into the obstetrical clinics of the hospital. Planned Parenthood would pay for the service; it would cost the taxpayers nothing. An earlier effort in November 1957 had been blocked when Dr. Francis Candling, a veterinarian, and the sole Roman Catholic member of the hospital board, threatened that he would sue the Board of Health, resign from the board, and remove all Roman Catholic physicians from the hospital. Apparently the threat was

effective, because nothing happened until March 1959, when Planned Parenthood was finally allowed to have a nurse in the hospital prenatal clinic two
mornings a week. This was something, but far short of the real help that
many patients needed.

So a second effort was mounted and here, as in New York, clergy were to
be the spear point to change the policy. Esther Shoemaker, the executive
director of the Denver chapter of Planned Parenthood put it this way:

> This preliminary skirmish led us to believe that if an actual clinic was ever to
> be allowed in the Hospital we must have strong and united Protestant and
> Jewish support, as well as medical support, in order to provide the necessary
> "backbone" for our city fathers and administrators. In other words, in this
> matter (as well as in many others) they allow themselves to be governed to
> a great extent by public opinion, and we felt the situation was not likely to
> change until the Board of Health was impressed by the strong weight of
> Protestant and Jewish religious opinion.[4]

The Denver chapter of Planned Parenthood had a dedicated Clergymen's
Committee with about thirty clergy members, Protestant and Jewish. A subcommittee of that group prepared a statement and then submitted it to the
governing boards of their respective congregations for support. Not surprisingly, the clergy framed it as a matter of justice:

> The responsible choice of parenthood is one of the important areas in which
> men and women are called upon to make conscientious decisions under
> God. As a rational being with a capacity for making such decisions, man is
> able to assess right and wrong, interpret God's will and thereby to determine
> his own actions. To forfeit this ability is to abuse one of God's most pre-
> cious gifts.
>   . . . if a couple prayerfully decides they should not have a child at a given
> time, they should be free to use the most effective and acceptable medical
> methods to prevent conception. They would be morally remiss if they did not
> exercise control of this situation.
>   These are our positive convictions. We believe that public policy which
> does not take account of these convictions does injustice to many citizens,
> probably to a majority. However, we respect the rights of those who differ, and
> we do not believe anyone should be coerced to accept our principles if they
> are contrary to his personal religious and ethical traditions.
>   Since, further, the giving of medical advice for family planning is permitted

by law, we believe it is the responsibility of public health programs and government hospitals and clinics to provide this service to those requesting it.

We, therefore, respectfully request that medically approved family planning services be allowed in public health facilities in Denver.[5]

When the statement was approved, it was given to Planned Parenthood.

But the "strong weight of Protestant and Jewish religious opinion" involved much more. The Denver Council of Churches also sent a copy of the statement to all the member churches in the area seeking their endorsement. When all the religious statements had come in, thirty-five local congregations had approved the statement. All of the religious endorsements were added to similar endorsements from the medical community, and copies were sent to each member of the Board of Health and Hospitals, one to the manager of health, one to the mayor, and—most critically—one to each of the two local newspapers. It was essentially the same strategy used in Baltimore.

In its submission statement Planned Parenthood also took up the theme of justice when it noted the inequity of the current situation: "In Denver, contraceptive care is admittedly available to those in favorable economic circumstances. However, with the exception of the Planned Parenthood Clinic and Colorado General Hospital, no birth control information or service is available to low income and medically indigent families in the City of Denver because it is not offered in the tax supported clinics and hospitals where they of necessity must receive care."[6]

The affiliate noted that contraceptive clinics had been already established in a range of states, including California, Delaware, Maryland, Michigan, Illinois, and New York. It also used religious terms to describe its conviction that "the objections of some must not be permitted to deprive others of contraceptive assistance which is scientifically authoritative, and which may be required of them when in conscience they believe birth control fulfills the will of God."[7] Planned Parenthood supported this argument.

The affiliate then contacted the manager of health and asked for a place on the agenda of the first board meeting in October. This he agreed to (the law required that he had to consider all such requests), and ten days before the meeting copies of all supporting documents were given to each board member. They needed to have the lead time because—as Esther Shoemaker, the executive director of Planned Parenthood, tartly put it, "without looking it over carefully [board members] could not be properly impressed with the breadth and force of our local backing—from religious and medical sources, and from social service agencies."[8]

Alerted by the information from the affiliate, the *Denver Post* was at the October meeting. Ironically, Dr. Candlin, who had prevented anything from happening in 1957, was now the chair of the board. True to form, that night he prevented any consideration of Planned Parenthood's request. But he overreached a bit. When, following the meeting, a reporter asked him when the issue would be given a full hearing, he said, "If I have my way, never." Clearly his response was evidence of unreasonable obstructionism, and it drew a highly critical editorial from the *Denver Post* entitled "Let Planned Parenthood Be Heard." The editorial cited Planned Parenthood's proposal as a priority and, acknowledging the political advantage of delaying the proposal until after the November elections, urged the board that for critical health reasons it was imperative that Planned Parenthood be heard.[9] With that, the battle was essentially over. Dr. Candlin appointed a subcommittee to hear the Planned Parenthood proposal. It reported favorably and at the full meeting on October 27 the board granted permission—by a vote of 4 to 2—for the clinic to be opened in the hospital. Dr. Candlin voted against the plan.

After only four months it was clear how much the service was needed and, sadly, how many women had gone without help in the years that the clinic was delayed. In that four-month period, of the 210 women offered contraceptive services in the hospital by the Planned Parenthood nurse, 200 accepted help.

As in New York, it was clear that while the services in question were medical, the obstruction was religious. Here, as there, only an opposing religious coalition could overcome the barriers.

St. Louis

In all the contentious battles to make contraception available to Americans, few places have been stonier ground than St. Louis and the state of Missouri as a whole. Decades of conflict were foreshadowed in an incident in the summer of 1916 when Margaret Sanger came to speak in St. Louis. A hall had been booked and paid for, but when she arrived the doors were locked. According to the *St. Louis Post Dispatch*, Catholic priests and laypeople had protested against her being allowed to speak. The management of the theater had caved in to their wishes. But there were 1,500 people waiting outside to hear her, and so she tried to address them from the seat of her car. An officer stopped her. The police seemed to be concerned that her speaking would anger the Catholics. She shouted to the crowd, "We're not in St. Louis, we're in Russia!" The crowd shouted back, "Go on! Go on!

The Catholics run the town."[10] But her driver was worried about a riot and drove off.

In reaction to the situation, the *St. Louis Post Dispatch* and the *St. Louis Globe Democrat* both editorialized against the boycott as a dangerous attempt to stifle free speech. The St. Louis Men's Club, which had little interest in the subject of birth control but knew a hot topic when it saw one, invited her to speak. She addressed a crowd that was larger than the one Theodore Roosevelt had drawn at the club. Forty Catholic members resigned in protest. But whether through sympathy with her cause or concern about boycotts, one hundred other men joined the club for the first time.[11]

By 1932 the state's first prototype of Planned Parenthood was formed. It was called the Maternal Health Association of Missouri. Perhaps encouraged by the fact that Protestant and Jewish denominations were beginning to issue statements in support of birth control, it was willing to face the powerful opposition of two churches, the Roman Catholic and the Lutherans. But while some Lutherans spoke against it, other Lutheran churches gave the association clinic space.

In 1945, Roman Catholics and the Missouri Synod Lutherans tried to force the Chamber of Commerce to drop Planned Parenthood of St. Louis (they had changed their name in 1942) from its list. It didn't happen, largely because of the clergy. In St. Louis, the most prestigious religious organization was the Metropolitan Church Federation, made up of the mainline Protestant denominations. It presented the chamber with a letter of support for Planned Parenthood signed by the Episcopal bishop of Missouri, the president of Eden Seminary, and prominent rabbis and ministers of the largest congregations in town. What is striking about the language is the specific identification of Planned Parenthood values with Christian and Jewish values: "The aims and the practices of the Planned Parenthood Association have been presented to the Charities Committee by a person well-qualified to speak for that organization. We stress the point that a vast number of sincere Christians and Jews are heartily in sympathy with those aims and practices. If endorsement is given to agencies sponsored by religious bodies who do not share this point of view, it must also, in fairness, be given to agencies supported by religious bodies who do share it."[12] Furthermore, the clergy made it clear that they saw the situation as a *religious* issue: "the Charities Committee is—in reality—being asked to pass judgment in a religious controversy. The charge against the Planned Parenthood Association is not that it fails to meet medical and social work standard

business practices. . . . But the charge is that the Planned Parenthood Association, in its philosophy and practice, runs counter to the religious beliefs
held by Roman Catholics and certain minor Protestant groups."[13]

On June 12, 1946, the chamber held a meeting at which the Knights of
Columbus and the Missouri Synod Lutherans would be given an opportunity to voice their objections. Planned Parenthood would have a chance to
respond. When it was over, the chamber was unimpressed with the com-
plaints. They unanimously renewed Planned Parenthood's membership.

While resistance remained strong throughout the forties and fifties, so
did clergy support. One of the best examples of such support came in
February 1949, when the Reverend James Clarke, minister of the Second
Presbyterian Church of St. Louis, prepared a radio talk that generated many
requests for copies. It was called "The Ethics of Planned Parenthood."
He linked Planned Parenthood directly to the situational ethics of Jesus:
"Planned Parenthood is a Christian idea because it is helpful to the spiritual happiness and physical well-being of both parents and children. It em-
phasizes the sacredness of personality as Jesus did. He declared that to judge
whether a thing was right or wrong its effect on human beings would reveal
its nature. If it lifted them up, it was good; if it degraded them, it was bad."[14]

He went further and expressed the famous Planned Parenthood slogan,
"Every child a wanted child," in Christian terms: "The Christian conscience
demands that children be conceived wisely, so that like the child Jesus,
they may increase in stature and wisdom and in favor with God and man.
Planned Parenthood is Christian because this is its aim and achievement."[15]
This radio talk was typical of the increasing clergy support in this era. In
1957 Eden Theological Seminary in St. Louis even invited Planned Parenthood to come on its campus and offer a series of lectures for students who
were to be married that summer.

But all these preliminary skirmishes were merely laying the groundwork
for what promised to be the biggest fight—getting contraceptive services
for the poor into public hospitals and welfare offices. This was a serious
socioeconomic issue as well as a matter of reproductive freedom. A wall of
bureaucratic inertia, hostile politicians, and enormously powerful religious
opponents made this look like a tough uphill struggle. Here, as in Denver,
Planned Parenthood made careful preparations. After preliminary meetings
in 1963, the interested citizens—a coalition of Planned Parenthood supporters and others sympathetic to the cause—formed a group called Citizens
Committee for Family Planning through Public Health Agencies. The group
was essentially Planned Parenthood in a different guise. It was chaired by

Dorothy S. Roudebush, vice-president of the St. Louis Planned Parenthood Association. As was the story with many unsung women in Planned Parenthoods across the country, her leadership on this issue was noteworthy. In the *St. Louis Globe Democrat* of February 22, 1964, she announced that the Citizens Committee for Family Planning through Public Health Agencies believed that St. Louis public health facilities provided no birth control services for poor families and that this was discriminatory.[16] The Citizens Committee went ahead and asked Governor John Dalton, Mayor Raymond R. Tucker, and St. Louis County supervisor Lawrence K. Roos to provide these services. On April 7 Supervisor Roos responded he had no intention of doing so, saying that "such a move is unpalatable" to many county residents who would be "upset" by such action on something that was so controversial.[17]

But if St. Louis and its politicians hadn't changed much, other things had, in both the secular and the religious worlds. St. Louis in 1964 was going to be different from Denver in 1961, because the War on Poverty was beginning. In 1964 President Lyndon Johnson was taking the first steps to create the Great Society, a stunningly broad effort to end poverty in America. According to the thinking of some of the planners, poverty could be reduced if the 5.2 million poor women in America could have access to family planning services. This would mean fewer children born out of wedlock to people dependent on welfare and fewer children born into poor families. The states had already begun to move in this direction. After decades in which no state outside the South would do anything in this area, in 1961, California began offering family planning services. In 1963 eleven states followed its lead, and in 1964, eleven more joined the effort.[18]

The key agency in Johnson's plans was the Office of Economic Opportunity (OEO), headed by Sargent Shriver. Shriver, a Roman Catholic, was tasked by the president with maintaining good relationships with the National Catholic Welfare Conference.[19] The president was anxious not to upset the Roman Catholic leaders, but he was hopeful that, for the sake of reducing poverty, they would not object too much to family planning. It was already clear that some cities were going to accept federal grants for family planning services. Would St. Louis?

For its part the Roman Catholic world was experiencing astonishing change. Pope John XXIII had brought in a Second Vatican Council, which was in session from 1962 to 1965. From September to December of each of those years, almost every Roman Catholic bishop in the world came to Rome to deliberate. American bishops had a chance to talk with bishops who took a much more nuanced view of difficult social issues. During the council, the church's stance toward people of other faiths was transformed. In the new Catholic world of Vatican II, outsiders were no longer lumped together as "non-Catholics"; Protestants and Jews were now termed "separated brethren." Attitudes changed as remarkably as the terms. American priests who had spurned membership in the local Council of Churches were now willing to join. Both sides began to discard traditions of disdain and suspicion. Indirectly, it made Roman Catholics much more open to a Protestant-dominated group such as Planned Parenthood. The church still rejected what it called "artificial contraception," but Planned Parenthood was no longer evil personified. They were just another manifestation of the world of "separated brethren."

Finally, there was a revolution in the technology of contraception: an oral contraceptive had been developed. Its creator was a devout Roman Catholic doctor, John Rock, who argued in his book, *The Time Has Come*, that the "pill" was not in conflict with the church's position on family planning. In one way he saw it as a device that could make the rhythm method work more successfully.[20] Because of Rock's credibility in both scientific and religious circles—and because a decision had to be made about this new method—it was not surprising that in June 1964, Pope Paul VI appointed a commission of clerical and lay Catholics to study the issue of family planning and make recommendations for change, if change was called for.

And in a final stroke of good fortune, the Roman Catholics of St. Louis were led by a remarkable spiritual pastor, Joseph Cardinal Ritter. Renowned for his courageous leadership on racial issues in a city known for its racial strife, he successfully and peacefully brought about an early integration of the city's parochial schools. In 1961, when problems became too much for the parochial system, he stopped school construction and informed the St. Louis public school authorities that in the future most of the Catholic pupils would be coming to the city schools. Then he urged Catholics to support the public schools strongly and vote for the tax hikes that would be needed to pay for the influx of Catholic students. At the Vatican Council of 1962–1965 he was the preeminent American church leader.[21] Embodying the best of the new spirit of Vatican II, he was regarded as a progressive, humane man, and he generated real affection in many circles of St. Louis society.

On September 6, 1964, Dorothy Roudebush wrote to Cardinal Ritter describing Planned Parenthood's hopes and intentions. Then she did something that was unthinkable against the background of decades of Planned Parenthood experience—she asked him for his support:

Knowing your deep concern for the welfare of the total community, We are writing to ask your guidance in a project, which we think, is of supreme importance. We believe that the planning of children is the cornerstone of responsible healthy family life. We know that those who must use public facilities for medical care are being denied access to knowledge and materials, which would enable those who so desire to plan their families according to their individual moral judgments. Because we believe that there is basic agreement between the position of the Catholic Church and our position on the need for family planning, we are eager to explore the possibilities for such a public program with a member of your diocese. . . . Would you be kind enough to put us in touch with such a representative?[22]

All of these factors combined to form an "era of good feeling" in the family planning wars of St. Louis. In February 1964, Dr. Rock came to St. Louis to speak to a Planned Parenthood fund-raising dinner and said that the Catholic Church should join forces with the nation's Planned Parenthood associations. He called for the Catholic Church to give moral sanction to oral contraceptives. It was his conviction that the church would change its interpretation of natural law and accept the new technology.[23]

Meanwhile, unaware of how these trends were going to bring them success, the Planned Parenthood people were still rounding up clergy support for the effort to bring contraceptives into public health facilities. In April 1964 they asked for the backing of the St. Louis Metropolitan Church Federation. The federation gave its support in a somewhat less than stirring statement to the mayor of St. Louis in June: "We do not advocate an indiscriminate use of contraception, but when a physician prescribes contraception for an indigent patient we ask that that prescription be filled at the City Hospital pharmacy and paid for in the same manner that other prescriptions are paid for."[24] Individual clergy from all Protestant denominations, plus many rabbis, were also registering their support. Almost every clergy letter referred to the discrimination against the indigent. As in Denver, the issue was seen as a matter of justice and a denial of needed services to the poor.

Everything changed in January 1965. At the national level at that time, the Office of Economic Opportunity was receiving funds that were to be funneled down to individual communities. In St. Louis a nonprofit agency, the Human Development Corporation, was created to receive the grants. That agency was quite supportive of Planned Parenthood and had put in for grants that would include funding for family planning. Both Planned Parenthood and the Citizens Committee for Family Planning through Public Health

Agencies were immensely heartened by these developments, but also concerned that the Diocese of St. Louis would use all its formidable political
power to make a public fight. On January 15, 1965, Dorothy Roudebush and
other Planned Parenthood representatives were suddenly summoned to the
Office of the County Supervisor. The latter had just come from a high-level
meeting at the diocesan Chancery Office. His news was stunning: the cardinal had said that he would make no objection "to the inclusion of birth control programs in the Human Development Corporation request for funds."[25]
The group was jubilant. In return for the cardinal's decision, Planned Parenthood agreed to let this happen without issuing any public statement of its
own. Instead the public agencies made the announcement. On July 2, 1965,
city papers carried the headline "Anti-Poverty Funds Are Approved for Birth
Control Project Here." Now poor women had access to contraceptive services.

In all likelihood the Office of Economic Opportunity and the Human
Development Corporation would have gone ahead with their plans even if
the diocese had objected. But that would have meant a painful public battle that the diocese would probably have lost. Cardinal Ritter's statesman-
ship avoided all that.[26]

Although poor women could get government-funded contraception in
city hospitals, Missouri's Welfare Department still refused to let its staff
discuss birth control. But in 1967 the state legislature was considering a
repeal of the 100-year-old law forbidding the sale of contraceptives. On an
icy night the redoubtable Dorothy Roudebush and three others flew down
to Jefferson City in a plane loaned by a Planned Parenthood supporter to
lobby for the bill. They were successful, the law was passed, and the repeal
took effect in October 1967. At that point the director of the Welfare Department—who had resisted Planned Parenthood appeals for years—now not
only instructed his workers to discuss family planning with clients, but also
paid the bills for their contraceptives.

In a matter of a few years in this era of good feeling, St. Louis had caught
up with New York City, Baltimore, and Denver. And this had been achieved
in large part through the sustained support of Protestant and Jewish clergy,
and—in this case—one very important member of the Roman Catholic
clergy.

San Francisco

As in so many other cities, birth control work in San Francisco began when
a woman, Ida Leverick, who had met Margaret Sanger in India, began a

chapter of Sanger's American Birth Control League in Alameda County (Oakland-Berkeley) in 1923. Many socially prominent people were in this chapter, including the president of Mills College, three Superior Court judges, and a young lawyer destined to be governor of California and Chief Justice of the Supreme Court, Earl Warren. Across the Bay in San Francisco, the local chapter of the American Association of University Women had been operating a "Mother's Milk Fund" to provide milk free of contamination for the poor children of the city. In 1929 this program was expanded to include birth control instruction. These two neighboring clinics—which would merge many years later—were the origin of what would become Planned Parenthood of the Golden Gate.[27]

Today this affiliate reflects a wide range of diversity and intense political commitment to defend women's rights, but in its earliest years both the strengths and the weaknesses of its founders shaped it. It reflected an irony present in the formation of Planned Parenthood in many American cities. In those first years Margaret Sanger soon realized that no money or support for birth control was going to come from state, local, or national governments. Desperate poor people who needed birth control had neither money nor social power. Here in San Francisco, as in the establishment of the American Birth Control League in New York, the only option was to turn to socially concerned wealthy people and professionals such as physicians. These were the people who had the means and skill to open a real clinic. Like Dr. Bessie Moses in Baltimore, they would use their own money or raise it from people of means. The strengths and commitment these people brought to this work cannot be overstated.

But the downside was a "lady bountiful" approach to the work. In the San Francisco affiliate during the early years, the gap between the world of its board and the life of the patients was as wide as San Francisco Bay. While board members met in a private residence and dined elegantly, the actual clinic (which most board members had never seen) was in a less desirable part of the city.

An additional characteristic of such support proved to be a serious limitation. Often these wealthy backers had little taste for public controversy and conflict. Socially conservative by temperament, it is not surprising that they were unprepared to deal with a public crisis when it came.

In 1937 officials for the Golden Gate Fair suddenly asked the American Birth Control League of San Francisco to withdraw its exhibit. The Roman Catholic archbishop who was to bless the buildings housing Catholic exhibits said he would not do so if groups advocating contraception were included in the fair. Seemingly in a state of shock, the affiliate offered no resistance. Margaret Sanger urged it to take the matter to the courts, but it chose not to. Ironically, as affiliate historian Tom Saunders points out, the directors of the fair were sympathetic and expected the affiliate to fight.[28] Had it done so, the directors would have supported them against the archbishop.

It was a classic example of differing strategies. The Sanger policy of fighting for one's rights would have used the exclusion to provoke a public controversy and put the archbishop on the defensive. The clinics could have protested that one religious point of view was being allowed to determine what people of other faiths—or no faith—could see. And precisely on this issue alone, they could have found many clergy supporters. Out of that flap might have come much publicity for the cause and the discovery of many additional adherents. By not resisting their expulsion, the opportunity was lost. Twenty years later they did fight, and this time the clergy supported them strongly.

By the early 1960s Planned Parenthood of San Francisco had a Clergy-men's Advisory Council of about thirty members. Reflecting the influential Asian populations of the city, the council included Japanese and Chinese churches as well as a representative from the city Council of Churches. In 1964, that Clergy Advisory Council was prepared when a great public birth control battle erupted on the front pages of the San Francisco papers. Dr. Elgin Orcutt , the newly appointed chief of obstetrics at San Francisco General Hospital (and a member of the San Francisco Planned Parent-hood Medical Advisory Board) was given a little "guidance" by the hospi-tal superintendent. In a comment typical of the climate of that time, the superintendent told Dr. Orcutt that he didn't want "any funny stuff in the operating room. I know that some of you gynecologists have been getting away with doing sterilizations. I've got my nurses in the operating room watching for that."[29]

Dr. Orcutt wanted to begin a birth control program in the outpatient clinic. But the hospital superintendent also told him that he wasn't very "hot" for birth control. When the doctor requested a budget line item of $10,840 (a number that would become famous because of this controversy) to initiate the contraceptive services, the hospital's chief administrator cut the item out. Planned Parenthood, however, organized public support, and the administrator put the item back in the budget. But when the budget went to Mayor John F. Shelley, he took it out again. Then the fight became public, with banner headlines on the front page of both the *San Francisco Examiner* and the *San Francisco News Call Bulletin.*

Twenty-four Methodist ministers weighed in with a statement that proclaimed, "It is our firm conviction that such a policy [publicly provided
birth control] is consistent with human welfare."[30] Leading the clergy voices
was none other than the Reverend James Pike, Episcopal bishop of San
Francisco and the chair of the Planned Parenthood Clergymen's National
Advisory Council. He had left the Cathedral of St. John the Divine in New
York City to become bishop of California. As he had used the St. John's
pulpit to address some of the most contentious issues of the decade in New
York, he was now ready to make the same kind of witness in San Francisco.

From the time he was in New York and continuing on into his ministry
as bishop of San Francisco, Pike devoted enormous amounts of energy to
Planned Parenthood. A person always restlessly searching for humane theology, it bothered him greatly that there was so much religious opposition
to the simple public provision of birth control. However he was heartened
by what he believed would be a shift in Roman Catholic attitudes. With so
much of his heart invested it was inevitable that he would take a leadership
role in persuading the mayor to change his mind about $10,840.

The controversy rolled on. When the president of the County Medical
Society accused the mayor of blocking decent medical care for the poor
people of the city, the mayor argued that he had cut the funds because it
wasn't clear how the money was to be allotted and managed. But the attorney for Planned Parenthood said it was "hard to believe this deletion was
done on any ground other than religion—the other excuses are so miser-
ably weak."[31] As if to confirm the truth of that, Catholic doctors, laypeople,
and the archbishop registered strong opposition to a public birth control
program.

Controversy was renewed with another front-page headline in late April
1964, when a San Francisco woman offered the Board of Supervisors of the
city of San Francisco a certified check for $10,840 to fund the program. Once
again, Planned Parenthood organized public pressure to ensure that the
Board of Supervisors would accept the money. Although two Catholic members of a subcommittee of the board voted (2 to 1) to reject the gift, the full
board did accept the money, and with that "*l'affaire* $10,840" was over. In San
Francisco, it was Planned Parenthood that finally—after the usual tortured
struggle—brought birth control into the public hospitals of San Francisco.

Here, in this public debate as in Denver and St. Louis, the clergy functioned as a religious and moral force, which took away whatever lingering
"scandal" still clung to the issue of contraception. If clergy were not scandalized, if, in fact, clergy reframed the issue as a denial of justice to poor

women and families, political leaders were enabled to let change happen. In effect, the Planned Parenthood clergy were saying, it is time for society to grow up, to recognize the real needs of real people. In political terms it was a winning strategy. In religious terms it was an embodiment of the prophetic word, "Let justice roll down like waters" (Amos 5:24).

THE ERA OF GOOD FEELING

In Denver, St. Louis, San Francisco, and in many other cities and towns around the nation, the sixties were to be a period of immense change for the movement begun over fifty years earlier by Margaret Sanger. Planned Parenthood clinics emerged as the most knowledgeable contraceptive services in the country recognized as public agencies. Though still controversial, they had achieved a certain respectability, and even their religious opponents were reevaluating their own positions.

The changes in Roman Catholicism in the 1960s could legitimately be called astounding. Following the death of Pius XII in 1958, the College of Cardinals, the body charged with selection of a pope, was deadlocked between several strong candidates. As was their historical pattern in such cases, they decided to select an elderly candidate to (in a famous Italian phrase) "keep the seat warm" for a few years until time would resolve the deadlock. The person they selected, Angelo Roncalli, Pope John XXIII, stunned the world by transforming the church. In a famous gesture reported around the world, he threw open a Vatican window and said that it was time to let in some fresh air.

With this kind of pope things began to change even before the Vatican II Council convened. By 1960 American Catholic intellectual leaders such as John Courtney Murray, the leading American theologian of the fifties and sixties, were beginning to say that it was no longer wise to defend anti–birth control statutes like the Connecticut law.[32] Roman Catholics began to discuss the population issue, and when Bishop Pike suggested that the National Institutes of Health begin intensive research to improve all contraceptive methods, including the rhythm method, Father John A. O'Brien of Notre Dame said, "I commend highly the friendly and constructive spirit in which Bishop Pike made his timely proposal."[33] He went on to say that he hoped the results of such a study would end the controversy over birth control and bring to an end the hostilities of the past.

This new spirit led to invitations by each side to speak at the meetings of the other. In the spring of 1964 a Roman Catholic priest, Father John L.

Thomas, S.J., of St. Louis University, addressed a national Planned Parenthood meeting. It was the first time a priest had spoken at such a gathering. In 1963 Planned Parenthood representatives and Roman Catholic leaders met at the University of Notre Dame to discuss population issues.[34] The climate was improving so fast that in 1966 Dr. John T. Noonan, Jr., director of Notre Dame's Natural Law Forum and one of the world's leading Catholic scholars on contraception, said that the conflict of the past would yield to a recognition by Planned Parenthood of the Church's concern for "life, dignity, and love" and a reciprocal recognition by the church of Planned Parenthood's "moral concerns."[35] Old Planned Parenthood hands must have thought they were seeing a vision.

But the window of peaceful coexistence between two periods of intractable struggle passed too swiftly. Two developments brought it to an abrupt close, the 1968 papal encyclical *Humanae Vitae* and the emergence of the abortion issue.[36]

Throughout the sixties, as the papal commission studied whether to recommend approval for the oral contraceptive, the situation in the Catholic Church remained fluid. Many believed the Church would change its long-standing opposition to contraception. Vatican Council II had changed so many things that it was not unreasonable to think that more change was coming, particularly in an area where there was such a gulf between the laity and the hierarchy. That belief had made it far easier to get birth control into the hospitals and welfare departments of St. Louis and elsewhere.

But on July 25, 1968, Pope Paul VI surprised the world by rejecting his commission's recommendation that he accept the oral contraceptive. Instead he reaffirmed the old condemnation and applied it to Dr. Rock's pill as well. Women—and men—in many Catholic churches in America walked out as the decree was read. The disappointment among Catholic women was palpable. In the years since the encyclical was issued, the response of American Catholic women has been to ignore it and use contraception to the same extent as non-Catholic women. As one Catholic woman put it, "Before *Humanae Vitae*, I used birth control and felt guilty. After *Humanae Vitae*, I used it and no longer felt guilty."[37] So in St. Louis, Denver, and all American cities, the rapprochement was ended. Catholic priests found that they were still expected to condemn Planned Parenthood.

But even if the pope had not issued the encyclical, the days of cooperation would almost certainly have ended because of the emergence of the abortion issue. In the late sixties feminism was burgeoning and women were demanding reform of the nineteenth-century laws that made abortion a crime. States like Colorado and California were reforming their abortion laws. Alarmed, the Catholic Church began to oppose them politically. When, in 1969, the Planned Parenthood Federation of America supported repeal of existing abortion laws, the split between the two camps returned, and it was to be deep and prolonged. The era of good feeling was over.

CHAPTER 7

Planned Parenthood and the Clergy Consultation Service on Abortion, 1967–1973

Therefore believing as clergymen that there are higher laws and moral obligations transcending legal codes, we believe that it is our pastoral responsibility and religious duty to give aid and assistance to all women with problem pregnancies. To that end we are establishing a Clergymen's Consultation Service on Abortion which will include referral to the best available medical advice and aid to women in need.

—Statement of Principles, Clergy Consultation Service on Abortion, May 22, 1967

IT IS A GROSS MISPERCEPTION that all American religious denominations are hostile to a woman's right to choose to have an abortion. In the late 1960s nearly two thousand American clergy formed a network to assist women to find safe, if not legal, abortions. From 1967 to 1973 they helped over a hundred thousand women find doctors who would help them, and when New York State legalized abortion in 1970, clergy arranged the opening of the first legal abortion clinic in America.

THE ABORTION ISSUE BURSTS UPON THE NATIONAL SCENE

In that ephemeral era of good feeling in the mid- to late sixties when Planned Parenthood was solidifying its new gains toward public acceptance, women began to engineer a monumental societal change that would make the Federation controversial once more. Since entering the postwar era women had been trapped by a societal portrayal that insisted that they were not capable of determining their own lives. Regarded as being in need of constant enlightenment by religious traditions, moral arbiters, physicians, psychologists, even magazine editors, women were told that biology was destiny; that they were to be wives and mothers. The only professions they were encouraged to join were teaching and nursing. And those were only things to do until the children arrived. Over and over from every quarter, women were told that the home was their appointed sphere.

Much of what trapped them in this position was their inability to control their reproductive life. Dr. Jane Hodgson, a Minnesota physician who was arrested in 1970 for performing a therapeutic abortion on a woman exposed to rubella, described a woman's predicament this way,

> Before 1960, when they didn't have anything but a lousy diaphragm, women were helpless creatures. They were just victims of circumstances, so many of them. They'd come in; I'd have to wipe off the tears. And then, when they began to get [better contraception] you could just see them getting into jobs, planning their lives, and I think that, plus the legalization of abortion, when contraceptives failed, has been the biggest factor in the feminist movement. . . . I think it [reproductive freedom] will be considered one of the biggest issues, the most important movement of this century.[1]

Abortion in the fifties was invisible, unspeakable, yet ubiquitous. For society to reach the point that Dr. Hodgson refers to—the legalization of abortion—a long legacy of social attitudes had to be radically altered. Although abortion had been widely practiced and basically accepted or ignored during the first two-thirds of the nineteenth century in America, that situation changed in the1870s when a phalanx of physicians persuaded legislatures to criminalize the practice. And though societal attitudes took decades to shift in favor of that criminalization, shift they did.

But the situation was complex. While abortion was out of sight and unremarked, it had some popular support, but by the middle of the twentieth century polite society considered abortion to be an atrocious crime. Virtually no one wrote about it. In Hollywood, the Motion Picture Production Code, which set the standards for the censorship of films, discouraged any mention of it and, if it was referred to even indirectly, required that it be condemned.[2] Abortion was not to be discussed in social gatherings. It was literally an unspeakable matter.

In the 1950s, as physicians who had provided abortions for years with no opposition were being raided by the authorities, things became much worse for those women and families wishing to end an unwanted pregnancy. As discussed in chapter 4, hospitals that had performed a number of therapeutic abortions every year now created committees to screen applicants for the procedure. Under these committees, the number of abortions became less than a third of what had been sanctioned in previous years. Doctors felt the authorities looking over their shoulder and protected themselves accordingly.

With both illegal and legal practitioners dwindling, the consequences were tragic. Typical was Cook County Hospital in Chicago. In 1939 about one thousand women were treated for complications from illegal abortions. By 1959 that number had increased to three thousand. Only three years later, in 1962, they served five thousand women in those circumstances.[3] And the death rate from illegal abortions, which had been declining for years, started to rise. New York City statistics reveal that twenty-seven women died from complications each year in the early fifties, but by the early sixties the death toll had reached fifty-one per year.[4]

Serious people in the law profession wrote things that are stunning in their attitudes toward women's lives. In 1962, when the American Law Institute first began to float some modest abortion reform measures (these were known as the ALI proposals, and generally allowed abortion in cases of rape, incest, and for the health of the woman), the *Georgetown Law Review* published an article by Eugene Quay opposing such proposals. Quay was critical of any woman who would have an abortion to save her health. He said, "It would be in the interests of society to sacrifice such a mother rather than the child who might otherwise prove to be normal and decent and an asset."[5]

Religious opposition to any relaxation of the abortion statutes was no less intense. In an incident that seemed to anticipate the later Protestant-Catholic split over abortion, the 1961 New Hampshire legislature attempted to make what seemed to be a small change in its state law. Every state had criminal laws concerning abortion, but each made at least one exception: the procedure would be allowed in those cases where it was necessary to save the life of the mother. Every state, that is, except New Hampshire, where even that type of abortion was a crime. The New Hampshire Medical Society proposed an amendment that would allow an abortion at up to twenty weeks to save the mother's life. In one of the first signs of pro-choice Protestant interest in the issue, the New Hampshire Council of Churches and the Manchester Ministerial Association joined the doctors in support of the bill. It passed the state senate 15 to 8, and the house of representatives 259 to 156. But the Roman Catholic bishop of Manchester opposed the bill, and the Republican governor vetoed it. Because the legislators were unable to pass the amendment over the veto, the bishop's view prevailed and the law remained as it was.[6]

Despite these rather heartless attitudes, women who sought abortion were undeterred. In 1953 the researcher Alfred Kinsey noted in his famous study *Sexual Behavior of the Human Female* that 22 percent of all married women who reached the age of forty-five testified that they had had at least one abortion. He also cited the fact that over the course of the reproductive life of this cohort of women, the average number of abortions was not one, but two. American women were not behaving as helpless victims. They rejected the abortion laws and went out on their own seeking an abortion.

Against this background of hostility, it is doubly amazing how quickly American public attitudes toward abortion changed in the sixties. A startling event and a startling new organization were responsible for much of the change. The event in question occurred in the summer of 1962 and involved Sherri Finkbine, a young mother of four who had been taking some headache tablets that her husband had brought back from a trip to England. She discovered that the pills contained thalidomide, a drug banned in America and which had been responsible for some hideous birth defects in Europe. Some women in Europe who had taken the drug gave birth to babies with tiny flippers instead of arms, or with faces that were paralyzed or with no ears.[7] Horrified, Finkbine contacted her doctor who recommended a therapeutic abortion and quietly made arrangements at a local hospital. That might have been the end of the issue except for the fact that she thought she should contact a media person in order to warn any other women who might have inadvertently taken the drug.

The story led to a media furor. Local authorities were successful in preventing the hospital from proceeding with the abortion, and the Finkbines flew to Los Angeles to see if they could obtain an abortion in Japan, where early abortions were legal. When that was delayed they abruptly flew to Stockholm to petition for help. They landed in Sweden on August 7, but had to wait ten days for the Royal Medical Board to meet and authorize the operation. The board gave consent and the abortion was done. The doctors confirmed that the fetus had indeed been grossly deformed.[8] For its time, it was the perfect media story. Photographers and reporters followed the Finkbines every step of the way, and the public stayed riveted to each new development. Vatican Radio denounced the Finkbines, everyone had an opinion, and they received threats against their young children who had to receive police protection as they went to school each day.

Whether the account of Sherri Finkbine's experience changed public opinion or simply brought forth support for abortion that had been dormant is not clear, but this story changed forever the way the American public thought about abortion. Until this saga, the media represented a woman seeking an abortion as furtive, unmarried, possibly a prostitute, or of otherwise dubious character. But Sherri Finkbine was the perfect suburban mother with four small children. She even worked on television as the teacher on "Romper Room," a highly popular children's program of that era. Although she was fired from her job on "Romper Room," after the abortion episode, a poll indicated that 52 percent of the public thought she did the right thing.[9] The laws that forced the Finkbines to go through this ordeal now looked more than outdated, they looked cruel. Many Americans either began to think differently about abortion or began to voice openly opinions they had previously held quietly.

But an even more major change agent on the issue of abortion appeared in California in the fall of 1961, when a woman named Patricia Maginnis started an organization called the Society for Humane Abortion. With two other colleagues, Lana Phelan and Rowena Gurner, Maginnis proposed radical change. As noted, the American Law Institute had proposed reform of the existing laws. But the women of the society pointed out that reform of the abortion laws would not touch the real problem. The proposed reforms would merely broaden the grounds on which physicians and moralists might grant or reject a woman's petition for an abortion. The woman would still have no say in the matter. Instead the Society for Humane Abortion proposed a flat repeal of the laws. They argued that abortion was a woman's right. Although it wasn't the first time the claim had ever been made, this time it was going to become a popular grassroots movement, a movement that would totally transform the place of abortion in American society. These three women began to do exactly what Margaret Sanger had done some forty-eight years earlier, they began to speak about the unspeakable. First, they spoke openly about their own abortions in great detail. Maginnis had had one abortion and then induced two others. Lana Phelan had barely survived her abortion.[10] It was a harrowing account. It was not just that they spoke, but the blunt language they used that really transformed the social climate. Just as Sanger's speech about birth control opened the door for other women to speak, their narratives evoked similar stories from women who had vowed never to speak of their abortions. Everywhere the leaders of the society went they brought literature the likes of which had never been seen before. Included were precise instructions on how to talk to abortionists and to make sure they washed their hands in sterilizing soap, instructions on how to talk to the police, how to negotiate with cab drivers who worked with abortionists and who might try to cheat the women, and instructions on all methods of abortion then in common use, including—under certain medically circumscribed limits—self-induced abortions.[11] They made the cause even more publicly provocative when they stood on street corners passing out pamphlets with the names and addresses of Mexican abortionists.

These three women and the movement they began were one of the major reasons women in America began to talk with each other about abortion. After they talked to each other they began to speak out publicly. Women no longer waited to see what male-dominated professions might or might not grant them. Instead they broadcast their own experiences with illegal abortions. And they spoke with authority. They, not the doctors or the legislators, had suffered the anxieties, the fears, the anger, the pain, and the police harassment. When doctors would not help them, and when legislators labeled them criminals, they had been left alone with the full responsibility. Maginnis and the Society for Humane Abortion had shown women how to transform that abandonment into authority. And that authority was moral in tone. Women invaded legislative hearings on the subject of abortion where only men were scheduled to speak and demanded to be heard. Stunned legislators sat helplessly as women stated their views.[12] In many settings around the country women said it was not right that they be denied a voice in what was to happen with their bodies. It was immoral for society to prosecute anyone who would help them. It was unjust for male legislators and church leaders—who could never experience what women faced in pregnancy—to pass cruel and restrictive laws. Women who could easily be saved by a competent abortion in any local hospital were dying and that was evil.

Their experience trumped the abstract arguments of the moralists. They spelled out the specific details of what they had been through, and they did it in the public arenas of legislative hearings, television news, and rallies. The silence was over. Judges, legislators, and the public began to listen. Simply by virtue of the fact that these women had found their voice, they transformed the political environment. Throughout this sea change in American attitudes, the women found an unexpected but strong and faithful ally—Protestant and Jewish clergy.

THE CLERGY CONSULTATION SERVICE ON ABORTION

For years in Connecticut, where it was a crime for anyone even to possess contraceptive devices, Protestant ministers had helped women evade the law by driving them across state lines to Planned Parenthoods in New York

State, where it was legal to prescribe a diaphragm for a married woman. And all across the country, many clergy had counseled parishioners who had had experiences with illegal abortions. In the past those women and their families had told ministers what it was like to go before hospital committees to beg for permission to have a therapeutic abortion, or to go across the border to a place like Tijuana where a doctor might or might not be a doctor, might or might not know what he was doing.

Clergy also were well aware of something else that all thoughtful Americans noticed in that era, that the country did not much care about enforcing the laws against criminal abortions. Yes, there had been enough sporadic crackdowns on abortion doctors in the forties and fifties to create a chilling climate and frighten doctors into drastically reducing the numbers of therapeutic procedures they performed, but illegal abortions were still plentiful, still underground, and seldom prosecuted. In some of America's largest cities there were physicians who performed them more or less openly. Everyone in the city knew about them. There was no antiabortion movement, though the doctors doing the procedures would have been defenseless against one. Consciously or subconsciously, many clergy absorbed the feeling that the laws making abortion illegal were a hangover from the past. And there was one more critical factor. No one knows how many clergy had already had the direct experience of finding abortions for their wives and daughters. If we apply Kinsey's figure that 22 percent of American wives in this era had abortions, then that probably means that roughly 22 percent of clergy families had already sought and found abortions. They had the experience to understand what women and their families faced. All of these realities plus decades of support for Planned Parenthood had laid a certain groundwork for the Clergy Consultation Service on Abortion, the first organized clergy group that would help women find safe, if not legal, abortions.

It began this way. In New York City the Reverend Howard Moody had come to town from Texas to become pastor of Judson Church on Washington Square. The church had a long tradition of social activism, and Moody kicked it up a notch. Early in his ministry there a woman came from out of town and asked him for help in locating an abortionist. He tried to do what he could, but when they went to the probable location, the door was slammed in their face because they didn't know the code words to say. Chastened by the experience, Howard Moody brought together many of the leading city clergy to listen to a few women relate their experiences. Some described how they were blindfolded during their abortions, procedures usually done without any anesthesia. These ministers and rabbis—all male—

tried to imagine the desperation that would lead a person to take such a chance. The more they heard the more it seemed clear to them that the existing abortion laws existed primarily to punish women. Rejecting suggestions that they study the issue at length, they decided that they as clergy had a particular responsibility to act. Moody said:

> Those of us clergy who had gathered together at the Washington Square Methodist Church in the early spring of 1967 did so out of some strong convictions that leadership for the reform of that heartless and inequitable law should come from those of us who preached justice without demanding it and admonished mercy without giving it. It seemed to us only right that the counseling, encouragement, and assistance which women needed under this unjust law should come from that institution, the Christian Church, so responsible for the origins and perpetuation of that law.[13]

Eventually they formed a plan. They discussed the risks with a lawyer, who advised them never to imply—in statements or in writing—that what they were doing was illegal. Then they went through a meeting with a pathologist, who showed them exactly what was involved in a dilation and curettage abortion (the usual procedure at that time), the potential difficulties, and the pain. It was a sobering experience. Next they sought out-of-state physicians who would do abortions. Howard Moody's colleague Arlene Carmen volunteered to be the person who would check out such doctors. Posing as a pregnant woman, she visited them and assessed their concern for women, their skill, and their willingness to charge a reasonable fee. Without Arlene Carmen, there would have been no Clergy Consultation. Finally the clergy decided they were ready to go public with their service.

On May 22, 1967, the front page of the *New York Times* announced—in a story that included Howard Moody's picture—the initiation of the Clergy Consultation Service on Abortion. Twenty-one clergymen, nineteen Protestant ministers and two rabbis, announced that they would help women find safe, if not legal, abortions. They maintained that they were not breaking the law, but they operated cautiously. There was a phone number listed that any woman could call. Different clergy were on call every week. When the women came in to see the clergy, it would be under the rubric of the confidentiality of pastoral counseling. This was their defense should authorities go after them. They thought it highly unlikely that a prosecutor would try to break the confidentiality of a pastoral relationship. At those meetings women would be given the number of a doctor who would help them. It might be outside the country—Tijuana, Puerto Rico, Japan, or England. In order to minimize the risk of arrest, they would refer only to places outside New York State. Above all, the clergy members of the Service would take no money for their services. This also provided a measure of protection from legal challenge. No one could say that they were profiting from this work.

They also issued a statement of purpose:

Clergy Statement on Abortion Law Reform
and Consultation Service on Abortion

The present abortion laws require over a million women in the United States each year to seek illegal abortions which often cause severe mental anguish, physical suffering, and unnecessary death of women. These laws also compel the birth of unwanted, unloved and often deformed children; yet a truly human society is one in which the birth of a child is an occasion for genuine celebration, not the imposition of a penalty or punishment upon the mother. These laws brand as criminals wives and mothers who are often driven as helpless victims to desperate acts. The largest percentage of abortion deaths is found among the 35–39-year-old married women who have five or six children. The present abortion law in New York is most oppressive of the poor and minority groups. A 1965 report shows that ninety-four percent of abortion deaths in New York City occurred among Negroes and Puerto Ricans.

We are deeply distressed that recent attempts to suggest even a conservative change in the New York State abortion law, affecting only extreme cases of rape, incest, and deformity of the child, have met with such immediate and hostile reaction in some quarters, including the charge that all abortion is "murder." We affirm that there is a period during gestation when, although there may be *embryo* life in the fetus, there is no living *child* upon whom the crime of murder can be committed.

Therefore we pledge ourselves as clergymen to a continuing effort to educate and inform the public to the end that a more liberal abortion law in this state and throughout the nation be enacted.

In the meantime women are being driven alone and afraid into the underworld of criminality or the dangerous practice of self-induced abortion. Confronted with a difficult decision and the means of implementing it, women today are forced by ignorance, misinformation, and desperation into courses of action that require humane concern on the part of religious leaders. Belief in the sanctity of human life certainly demands helpfulness and sympathy to women in trouble and concern for living children many of whom today are deprived of their mothers, who die following self-induced abortions or those performed under sub-medical standards.

We are mindful that there are duly licensed and reputable physicians who in their wisdom perform therapeutic abortions which some may regard as illegal. When a doctor performs such an operation motivated by compassion and concern for the patient, and not simply for monetary gain, we do not regard him as a criminal, but as living by the highest standards of religion and of the Hippocratic oath.

Therefore believing as clergymen that there are higher laws and moral obligations transcending legal codes, we believe that it is our pastoral responsibility and religious duty to give aid and assistance to all women with problem pregnancies. To that end we are establishing a Clergymen's Consultation Service on Abortion which will include referral to the best available medical advice and aid to women in need.[14]

Even for the outspoken sixties, this was a strong statement. They pointed to the racism and classism in the way the laws played out. They did not hesitate to say that the fetus was not a living child. They gave their support to physicians who performed therapeutic abortions "which some may regard as illegal." They proclaimed that they regarded such a doctor as "living by the highest standards of religion." And they stated their intention to live by higher laws and moral obligations, which—they believed—transcended legal codes. Finally, they were going to help women find safe, reasonably priced abortions, regardless of the criminal statutes.

The clergy were on the front page because they were news. Most women who were seeking abortions felt that the last person they would take this problem to was a minister or rabbi. Women facing an unplanned pregnancy assumed that, in concert with popular opinion, the clergy would condemn them and simply try to talk them into bearing the child. But they were wrong. How did clergy get to this point? They came to—or, in more proper biblical language, were led to—this juncture because women had shared their suffering with them. And the essence of the vocation of a minister or a rabbi is the imperative to show compassion, to help the people who come in pain and fear. In 1967, unless such clergy lived in a world of denial (and many of course did), you could not be a savvy minister for long without becoming aware of the fact that any sizable city contained at least one doctor who would do abortions and that middle-class and upper-class women went to that doctor. But hearing of the actual experiences first hand changed the lives of these ministers and rabbis and built in them an ever-deepening commitment to abolish such "heartless and inequitable" laws.

Within hours of opening, the Clergy Consultation Service received twenty calls. Although there is no exact record of how many women contacted them in the first week, it was far beyond their planning. They felt overwhelmed. Women called from all over the country. It was clear that many thousands of women were seeking abortions. In those early days of the Service, clergy often worked six or seven hours a day counseling women. From May to the end of 1967, they helped eight hundred women. In 1968 the number rose to three thousand, and by 1969 it was ten thousand per year.[15] Almost all of the women who came had already decided they wanted to go ahead with an abortion, but they were frightened because they had no idea of what the procedure would be like. Here is where the clergy were able to be helpful. As Howard Moody put it, "We told them what would happen to allay some of those fears and to give them some confidence that what they were doing was not the most horrible thing in the world."[16]

In a relatively brief time, the Clergy Consultation Service became a sophisticated movement involving legal advice, medical consultations, and careful planning for a variety of contingencies. In the next few years, the Service spread across America until between 1,400 and 2,000 clergy were involved.[17] Ministers from many different denominations participated. As it grew, the Service gathered in a number of college chaplains who had been helping students find abortions for years. Among them was the Reverend J. Claude Evans, the head chaplain at Southern Methodist University, who established the Clergy Consultation in the state of Texas, and the Reverend E. Spencer Parsons of the University of Chicago, who did the same in the state of Illinois. Other recruits were clergy who had been supporting Planned Parenthood for years and who now simply added their work with the Service. Still others were ministers and rabbis who had become activists through the civil rights movement and who now fought sexism in addition to their ongoing work against racism.

As noted earlier, illegal abortions were rarely prosecuted (laws against abortion were rarely enforced), but when they were, they brought media attention and made headlines. Over the next six years there were two arrests. The first was a Presbyterian minister from Ohio, the Reverend Robert Hare. He had referred a woman for an abortion to a physician in Massachusetts. When that physician's office was raided by the authorities, the woman's name was discovered and a zealous Massachusetts prosecutor from Middlesex County went to Ohio to question her. She admitted that the Reverend

Hare had given her the doctor's name. On June 6, 1969, a grand jury issued a warrant for his arrest. The charge was aiding and abetting a criminal abortion, and following legal advice, he waived extradition and went to Massachusetts to appear.

Many religious people who supported the Clergy Consultation on Abortion were outraged, and there was a wave of religious protest against his arrest. In a development typical of the sixties, the Presbytery of Cleveland, an ordinarily staid association of Presbyterian churches composed of 50 percent clergy and 50 percent laypeople, insisted that they be arrested too. Declaring that if he was guilty individually, they were guilty corporately, they went on to point out that when the Reverend Hare referred that woman for an abortion, he "was acting on the basis of his ordination vows and the confessional position of this Church."[18] The city's leading newspaper, The *Cleveland Plain Dealer*, was also outraged and used the case to editorialize against the Ohio abortion law. On March 23, 1970, the Reverend Hare appeared in Middlesex Superior Court, where his attorney said that the Massachusetts abortion statute denied the right of women and the right to ministerial counseling. The judge dismissed all charges, but the state appealed to the Massachusetts Supreme Judicial Court. The case was pending for several years until the *Roe v. Wade* decision of January 1973 made it moot.

A second arrest, this time of a rabbi, occurred on January 6, 1970. Police used an undercover detective to pose as a woman seeking an abortion. Rabbi Max Ticktin, the Hillel director at the University of Chicago, met with her and referred her to a doctor who did abortions in Oakland, Michigan. Armed with a search warrant issued by the district court in Oakland, Chicago police entered Rabbi Ticktin's apartment and carried off some folders. Rabbi Ticktin himself was in Israel.

As with the Reverend Hare's arrest, this incident produced quite a reaction. The University of Chicago and the Chicago Board of Rabbis supported Rabbi Ticktin. In Michigan, the Reverend Robert Marshall of the Unitarian-Universalist Church in Birmingham told the prosecutor who had brought the case, "You will have to jail every rabbi in Oakland County, every Unitarian cleric, at least half of the Protestant clergy and even a few Catholic priests."[19] There were many other protests, and on January 24, 1970, the prosecutor announced that he would not seek to extradite Rabbi Ticktin to Michigan.

Also in Chicago, another minister ran into trouble. Howard Moody had persuaded the Reverend E. Spencer Parsons to become the leader of

Chicago's Clergy Consultation. The Reverend Parsons was the dean of Rocke-feller Chapel at the University of Chicago. Early in 1971, when he was speak-ing about abortion before the Illinois legislature, he said that fifty to sixty thousand illegal abortions were performed in the state of Illinois each year. Furthermore, he said that he knew thirteen doctors in the state who did abortions. Congressman Henry Hyde, then an Illinois legislator, demanded that Reverend Parsons give up the names. The dean refused on the grounds that such information was a part of his confidential pastoral ministry. Henry Hyde wanted the legislature to cite him for contempt. When that failed, the Reverend Parsons was called before two grand juries, but he was never indicted.[20]

Despite these few scares, the Clergy Consultation Service had little trou-ble. Since the pattern was to have each woman meet confidentially with a member of the clergy, where she would be given the telephone number and the name of a doctor who would perform her abortion, district attorneys were reluctant to try to force information out of such a meeting. In fact, many prosecutors as well as police had little interest in enforcing the laws. One minister in the Clergy Consultation Service in New York had a star-tling moment when he helped one couple find an abortion. The husband was most grateful and told the minister to please call upon him if he needed anything. The minister asked the man what he did. He said he was a cap-tain in the New York City Police Department.[21] Clergy learned that the wives and daughters of police and judges also wanted abortion services.

By 1969 the Clergy Consultation Service in New York City began to openly advocate for repeal of the abortion laws. They took the same posi-tion as most feminists. Early experience with reform laws such as the one passed by the California legislature and signed by Governor Ronald Reagan in 1967 revealed that such measures helped women very little. So these clergy, whose cause was now being endorsed by larger church bodies,[22] went beyond reform and aimed to abolish the laws completely. In New York State the repeal movement was backed as strongly by the State Council of Churches as it was by the newly formed National Association for the Repeal of Abortion Laws (NARAL). In April 1970 the repeal forces succeeded when the New York State legislature passed the law: abortion up to twenty-four weeks was to become legal in the state for any woman, resident or not, on July 1, 1970.

The Clergy Consultation Service was prepared. Long before legalization, members knew from their experience that there would be a tremendous demand for abortion services in the first state to legalize. They had decided that their next step was to open an abortion clinic. By December 1969 they had a plan for a "Reproduction Crisis Facility," a nonprofit clinic in which any woman could obtain an abortion under the legal grounds that two physicians had certified that she was suicidal. In New York abortion was already legal when necessary to save the woman's life. The clinic would use only psychiatrists who would certify that *every* woman seeking an illegal abortion was, in this curious sense, suicidal.

Most remarkably, this clinic was to be housed in a church. The Judson Church board met on March 24, 1970, and approved the proposal. Brave as its members were, the church did not have to go forward because it was only a matter of a few weeks before the New York State legislature repealed the abortion statutes and set July 1, 1970, as the first day that abortion up to twenty-four weeks would become legal. The clergy—no longer needing the subterfuge of the two psychiatrists—made a much more ambitious plan to open a clinic that could meet their standards of safety, courteous treatment, and a cost that even poor women could afford. Dr. Hale Harvey, a New Orleans physician who had been doing abortions for the Service for years, offered to come to New York and open such a clinic. On July 1, Dr. Harvey, with the help of Barbara Pyle, who was in the process of earning her doctorate in philosophy at New York University, opened the Center for Reproductive and Sexual Health, known locally as Women's Services, at 133 East 73rd Street. The Clergy Consultation Service did not own this clinic; Dr. Harvey owned it. But the Service dictated the policies and provided almost all of its referrals.[23] It was, in effect, the Service's clinic.

It was none too soon. Clergy knew from their three years of experience in the consultation service that New York State was about to be inundated by women coming from all over the world to obtain a legal abortion. Although the New York State Department of Health and most doctors were arguing that abortions could only be done safely in hospitals, the Clergy Consultation Service knew that this was clearly untrue. By 1970 they had referred over 100,000 women for abortions that had been performed not in hospitals but in doctor's offices, and there had not been a single fatality.[24]

Another issue was the cost. At first, hospital abortions cost $600 and up. Again the clergy knew that this figure was ridiculously high. Because the Clergy Consultation Service had a vast referral network, it had the power to reduce the price. Dr. Harvey agreed to charge only $200. Women's Services became a model that eventually brought the cost down even lower. In addition, at Women's Services, those who could not pay anything were still helped.[25]

Finally, the clergy knew that there was a spiritual aspect to abortion. Women had powerful feelings about what they were going through. They needed not only information and a quick, safe procedure, but also decent human support. In the Women's Services clinic, they received that support from women counselors, volunteers who had had an abortion themselves. It was a new type of medical facility.

And it was just in time. So many women came to New York City that there were actual lines of women on the street outside the offices of doctors who were offering abortion services. Women's Services remained open from 7 A.M. to 11 P.M., seven days a week. Usually 100 abortions were done each day.[26] In the first thirteen months of its operation, the center performed 26,000 abortions without a fatality.[27] It was the model for the many freestanding clinics that were to come after it all across the country.

But after the *Roe v. Wade* decision in January 1973, the leaders of the Clergy Consultation Service also knew that their work was essentially over. They had been a major force behind a transformation of society's view of women seeking abortions. For so long such women were seen as criminals. But clergy—after being taught by the experience of suffering—did not see them that way. They made common cause with them and now society also saw them differently.

By 1973 women no longer needed clergy help. They now had clinics and physicians who could openly offer the services they needed. Clergy turned to other issues, feeling that the problem had been resolved. They were, of course, quite wrong.

PLANNED PARENTHOOD AND THE
COMING OF LEGAL ABORTION

Where was Planned Parenthood in all these developments? The Federation had played a role in laying the groundwork for the changes that were occurring. In the baby boom era of 1955, twelve years before the Clergy Consultation, when no one ever spoke of abortion and the stigma was even more powerful, Planned Parenthood held the first public conference on the subject. Forty-three men and women, mostly physicians, met in April and June at the New York Academy of Medicine. Their final report was prepared and released by Mary Calderone, M.D., the medical director of Planned Parenthood. Among the luminaries at the conference were Alfred Kinsey, author of the twin studies of the sexuality of Americans, *The Sexual Behavior of the Human Male* (1948) and *The Sexual Behavior of the Human Female* (1953);

Dr. John Rock; and Dr. Alan Guttmacher, a physician who was to become
the president of PPFA from 1962 to 1973. But the participants also heard
from L. Cottrell Timanus, a physician who had performed thousands of
illegal abortions in his office in the Baltimore-Washington area for many
years until he was arrested and served time in jail.[28] He was a rare source
of knowledge on and experience with nonhospital abortions.

Perhaps because of the scarcity of women physicians at that time, some
of the doctors in attendance could see abortion only in the narrowest medical terms. They were as far from feminism as one could imagine. One
doctor said flatly, "A woman is a uterus surrounded by a guiding personality."[29] But others demonstrated that they—like the clergy—had learned
from their experience with women. One physician pointed out that adverse
emotional reactions to abortion were nothing compared with adverse reactions to an unwanted pregnancy and the experience of being forced into
unwanted motherhood. In regard to the latter another doctor put on the
table perhaps the most salient fact in the world of abortion: "A large part
of my practice is concerned with helping the infertile couple, and I know
the terrific frustration of a woman who wants a child and cannot have one.
It does not compare with the intensity of emotion and determination of the
woman who does not want a child, is pregnant, and *won't have it.*"[30]

By merely holding such a conference, the Planned Parenthood Federation began the process of destigmatization. Finally, serious professionals
were talking about abortion responsibly and publicly.

But things in the late sixties were moving too quickly for Planned Parenthood to adjust. Ever since Margaret Sanger's time, Planned Parenthood had
stressed that contraception was important because it could prevent abortions. That position alone made it hard to see abortion in a more sympathetic light. But even more relevant was the simple truth that the culture of
caution and conservatism developed in the forties and fifties had produced
an organizational climate that could not be easily moved to support such a
drastic and controversial change. Part of the problem was that the organization was such a diverse entity. Although some leaders at the national level
might be conversant with, and comfortable with, the new challenge of abortion services, affiliates scattered all across the country were far more conservative. In April 1964, when Alan Guttmacher was asked whether Planned
Parenthood was going to join the drive to reform the abortion laws, he said
that he was doubtful that he could persuade them to do so.[31] He was correct about their mood. The Reverend Howard Moody once noted the irony
of the fact that when the Clergy Consultation announced its existence in

May 1967 on the front page of the *New York Times*, the response of Planned Parenthood of New York City was exactly the same as that of the Roman Catholic Diocese of Manhattan—total silence.[32]

Concerned about a reputation for respectability that had taken a long time to earn, and comfortable with its new acceptance as a vehicle for government birth control services, Planned Parenthood was not prepared in the late sixties for the surge of feminism. That said, the Federation did slowly begin to come around on the issue. In addition to Dr. Guttmacher, the organization's able legal counselor, Harriet Pilpel, became increasingly interested in abortion law reform. In 1962, when the American Law Institute put forward modest proposals to reform the abortion laws by allowing exceptions for rape, incest, and the health of the woman, Planned Parenthood supported them. But as the sixties unfolded, the Federation came to a more radical view. First, it saw that the California abortion reform in 1967, which was modeled along the lines of the American Law Institute proposals, had been a failure. Very few women could qualify for an abortion under its strict terms. Second, it could not help but be affected by the fact that the Clergy Consultation referral service looked like something that they should be doing. By 1969 the Federation came out in support of repealing the abortion laws.

This complex issue brought out the diversity of the whole Planned Parenthood movement. Many of the affiliates were not in sympathy with the policies of the national office. They either did not agree that Planned Parenthoods should provide abortion services or were fearful that it was too controversial. But in 1968 the national office, looking at the road ahead, hired a woman named Francine Stein and assigned her to its Field Division to set up a Pregnancy and Counseling Referral Service. The Federation urged the affiliates at least to provide a referral for women who sought abortions. Some affiliates began to make such referrals to England or Japan, where abortion was legal for the first trimester.

In 1970 Planned Parenthood of New York City (PPNYC) realized that it might be at the center of the storm if the state abortion laws were repealed. Impressed by the work Francine Stein had done in setting up an abortion referral service for Planned Parenthood nationally, they hired her to begin work with them in February of that year. When the laws were repealed, she was ready with an extensive telephone referral service. Sixteen trunk lines operated out of PPNYC offices at 300 Park Avenue South. They were staffed by ten people, four of them nurses, who could refer women to doctors and clinics that would do the procedure. In the flood of women who came into the city in the first days of legalization, the hotline was often swamped.

On April 10, 1970, Dr. Guttmacher warned that New York City doctors and hospitals were "totally unprepared" for the number of women who would be coming to the state.[33] He proposed that freestanding clinics with ties to a nearby hospital be created to meet the need. At the same time, the American Association of Planned Parenthood Physicians released a study indicating that abortion could be done safely and with a much lower cost at such facilities.

When the law took effect on July 1 there was only one New York State affiliate (out of seventeen), Planned Parenthood of Syracuse, that began an abortion service. But after a year of planning, PPNYC opened the first Planned Parenthood abortion clinic in the city on December 15, 1971.

Following *Roe v. Wade*, a few other Planned Parenthoods also began abortion services. In 1973, affiliates in San Francisco, Aurora (Colorado), Houston, Ann Arbor, and Nashville started up. In 1974 they were joined by eight others: Cincinnati, Charlotte, Memphis, Baltimore, Pittsburgh, Kansas City, Columbia, Missouri, and Des Moines.[34] Then the pace slowed. By the end of 1979 35 Planned Parenthood affiliates were performing abortions. But 155 were not. Furthermore, among those 155 was the strong feeling that Planned Parenthood should not become known as an abortion provider. From the perspective of the Clergy Consultation Service, it often seemed that Planned Parenthood was too slow in adapting to the rapidly changing situation.

A typical situation was that of St. Louis. The Clergy Consultation there started later than many in the East. Still, it not only had referred women, but had actively found abortionists, to do the procedures. As with the Women's Services clinic in New York, the goal in St. Louis was to have a nonprofit agency that could serve poor women who could not afford the higher cost of a hospital abortion. Having done the work for a long time, the Clergy Consultation expected the *Roe* decision in 1973 to mean that Planned Parenthood would take it over. But when those running the Service called the local Planned Parenthood officials, the latter were clearly reluctant. It was obvious that Planned Parenthood was a long way from initiating anything. People who worked with the Clergy Consultation then went ahead and set up their own clinic.[35]

BRINGING IN THE CLERGY—AGAIN

But although the cultures of the Clergy Consultation and Planned Parenthood were different, and there were times when mistrust ruled, eventually their common concern for justice for women—and their common adversaries—brought them together.

As if to acknowledge the two groups' common interests, some Planned Parenthood leaders realized that their organization was failing to keep up with the fast pace of social change and turned once again to the clergy. In May of 1967, a member of the Federation's National Medical Committee sent a memo to Alan Guttmacher. The committee was struggling with the question of whether the organization should liberalize its policy of serving only married women. Some affiliates were serving unmarried women, but many others were not. The doctor raised the question of whether the Federation should adopt a policy that made birth control services available "openly and freely to all women regardless of age and marital status."[36] If the answer was going to be yes, then the author of the memo thought it was time to start another national clergymen's committee, because some affiliates had found that "a clergymen's committee aware of national problems will endorse programs that otherwise could be on 'shaky ground.'"[37] Whether the doctor was aware of what the Baltimore clergy had achieved in this area in 1965 is not clear from the memo, but he recognized that clergy had a certain power in the determination of these delicate social issues.

By July 1970—the precise time when the organization was under the most pressure to change and provide abortion services—Planned Parenthood created a committee of clergy and laypeople. Instead of being known as the "Clergymen's Advisory Council," the group's name was changed to the Religious Affairs Committee. Its main charge was to set up channels of communication with the Clergy Consultation Service. The minister who would chair the committee pointed out that Planned Parenthood was "getting a bad name" because it was doing so little about abortion services. Presumably, the committee would try to help the Federation become more open to providing abortion services. But it had a wider charge:

(a) To engage in specialized clergy activities.
(b) To promote Planned Parenthood as a social change agent.
(c) To recommend innovative actions for the Federation, rather than spend time refuting accusations against the Federation.
(d) To provide leadership for Church bodies.
(e) To help people understand the population problem.[38]

Committee membership was quite different from the PPFA clergy committees of the past. Only one-third of the members were clergy. One was a

Jesuit priest who was also serving on the national board of Planned Parenthood. The rest of the members were laypeople, some of whom worked in the national offices of major denominations. For the first time in Planned Parenthood history, a few women were included, although none of them were clergy or physicians.

The clergy who were on this committee brought a strong measure of feminism to their work while providing a religious defense of a woman's right to an abortion. In 1972 the Religious Affairs Committee published a seminal pamphlet, "Abortion, Birth Control, and the Ethics of Limiting Reproduction in the Framework of Religious Thought." In this pamphlet the clergy insisted that in some situations, "mature religious judgment may indicate the advisability of abortion."[39] Here was a defense of a woman's right to choose an abortion that came from clergy within the Planned Parenthood family. The pamphlet was sent to all affiliates and was invaluable to them in their relations with local communities. In that same document, clergy also staked out new positions for Planned Parenthood services. They argued, for example, that it was important to allow minors to be given pregnancy counseling and medical treatment for venereal disease without parental consent.

Clergy influence grew within the Federation until 1974, when, for the first time, a program on religion and family planning was presented to an annual meeting of Planned Parenthood. And yet shortly thereafter the committee ceased functioning. As quickly as the need for it seemed to arise, it was gone. It is hard to say exactly why. People in Planned Parenthood may have felt that the *Roe v. Wade* decision had resolved the issue of abortion and the debate would fade away, much as the debate about birth control seemed to fade after the Supreme Court *Griswold* decision in 1965. Absent a crisis over morality, there may have seemed to be no need for clergy. It would be almost twenty years before clergy work returned to the Federation.

But before the Religious Affairs Committee vanished from the scene, it made one final contribution to clergy–Planned Parenthood relationships. In November 1973 the committee sponsored a conference at Yale Divinity School on "Sexism, Family Planning, and Religion." The clergy and the Federation had been allies in social conflicts for decades, and the opportunity to meet in the academic setting brought a new dimension to their ongoing alliance. They were there to talk about their common foe, sexism. But it would have been unusual if they had not also spent some time talking about and thinking about the nature of their long alliance. In the closing address of the conference, the Reverend Howard Moody captured the essence of that alliance in a few trenchant comments.

He began by acknowledging that the relationship between the religious community in America and family planners had not always been untroubled; those in the church, he said, sometimes felt that Planned Parenthood might be "tampering" with people's morality. Conversely, he assumed that those in Planned Parenthood often felt that the best they could hope for from the churches was silent neutrality. But he insisted that "we are more alike than we are different." Ironically, he noted that Planned Parenthood had some of the attributes of a church, with Margaret Sanger as a patron saint, Alan Guttmacher as a patriarch, and a host of affiliates with a local autonomy "that would put the Baptists to shame."[40] But more seriously, he insisted that both groups shared common assumptions, often unspoken, about the importance of human sexuality and the right of people to be able to make their own decisions in that area. And he closed by stressing that the two groups were going to need each other in conflicts over such matters as in vitro fertilization and a host of other issues that lay in the future.

In this era of the coming of legal abortion it was the clergy who were earliest in the field and more prescient than Planned Parenthood in their understanding of the implications of "sacred work." But as the decades of the seventies and eighties unfolded, both groups would find themselves coping with challenges from those churches and individuals whose understanding of sacred work did not include a woman's right to control her own body and her own destiny.

CHAPTER 8

The Post-*Roe* Era,
1973–1992

On January 22, 1973, the day the *Roe v. Wade* decision was handed down, a young minister, the Reverend Betsy Davis, a founding member of Southern Adirondack Planned Parenthood, was driving through a bitter snowstorm on her way to Albany, New York, to lobby. She was a member of the Executive Committee of the State Council of Churches, a group which—along with NARAL—had led the fight to pass the New York State abortion law in 1970. Ever since its passage the law had been under attack from anti-abortion religious groups. And because the pro-choice folks had "gone home" as far as lobbying was concerned, the legislature had actually repealed the law in the 1971 session. However, the Republican governor, Nelson Rockefeller, had refused to sign the repeal and so the law remained in force. But the situation made it imperative for those on the State Council to continue their lobbying. Because of the foul weather she stopped on the way down to call the offices of the State Council of Churches to ask, "Are we still having the meeting?" They told her about the Supreme Court decision and said, "Yes, we are still meeting, but now it's a celebration!"[1]

The Backlash

Although *Roe v. Wade* appeared to close the door on any state attempt to recriminalize abortion, the pro-choice clergy of New York State had already learned that victory leads to apathy. On the right-to-life side the lesson had been that apathy had led to defeat, but defeat could be turned into effective opposition.[2] It was soon apparent that this historic Supreme Court decision was going to galvanize abortion opponents into creating a powerful political surge known as the right-to-life movement, better known now as the pro-life movement. It began almost immediately. On January 30, 1973, Maryland representative Lawrence J. Hogan stood up on the floor of the U.S. House and introduced a constitutional amendment to overturn the *Roe v. Wade* decision and declare that a fetus was a "person" from the moment it was conceived. The first stratagem of the movement had been launched. It had taken only eight days since the reading of the *Roe v. Wade* decision.[3]

Leading the charge was the hierarchy of the Roman Catholic Church. In the first few weeks after the decision, they called for civil disobedience against the ruling and made it clear that any Catholic having an abortion or assisting in one would be excommunicated. To demonstrate their determination—and muscle—in August 1973 the United States Catholic Conference launched a protest against any CBS affiliate showing an episode of the sitcom "Maude" in which the aging central character elects to have an abortion. The response to the protest was impressive: twenty-five CBS affiliates refused to air the episode.[4] Seven months later, in March 1974, four U.S. cardinals— Timothy Manning, John Cody, John Krol, and Humberto Medeiros—testified before a Senate subcommittee about a constitutional amendment that would ban abortion. No one in Washington could remember a time when four cardinals—or even one—had testified before Congress. The four men revealed the depth and extent of their convictions by the fact that they would not even support an antiabortion amendment proposed by Senator William Buckley of New York, because it would allow an abortion to save the mother's life. Even that time-honored exception in American law was no longer acceptable.[5]

But the most powerful action came in November 1975, when the church hierarchy announced a comprehensive plan for Catholic Church advocacy against legal abortion.[6] Every diocese and every parish would be required to have a right-to-life committee that would undertake lobbying at both the state and the federal level. Since every parish had offices, mimeographs, address lists, and workers, this amounted to the overnight creation of an extensive, well-equipped, grassroots political movement. The Roman Catholic Church had never taken such drastic action on any other public issue. This was something new in the American debate over reproductive freedom.

By the end of the seventies, Congressman Henry Hyde of Illinois had secured an amendment to the Medicaid program that blocked any federal payment for abortions for poor women unless the procedure was done to save the woman's life. Opponents of abortion could not get around *Roe v.*

Wade unless they passed a constitutional amendment, but they could stop public funding of abortion, at least on the federal level. Congress passed the Hyde Amendment and the Supreme Court upheld its constitutionality. This was a major victory for the antiabortion movement. In addition, states were passing a variety of measures—parental consent laws, mandatory counseling—to limit, restrict, and hamper the practice of legal abortion.

The changed political landscape became apparent in the first presidential election since *Roe v. Wade*. In that 1976 contest between President Gerald Ford and the Democratic challenger, Jimmy Carter, Ford said that he supported abortion only in cases of rape, incest, and the life of the woman. Furthermore, he said he would support a constitutional amendment that would override *Roe* and give the power to set abortion laws back to the states. Carter was not strongly pro-choice and was worried about offending the Catholic hierarchy. Although both candidates met with a committee of six Roman Catholic bishops, President Ford's views appeared to be closer to those of the bishops. From this point on in American presidential elections two realities became apparent: first, the antiabortion stance of the Republican Party brought it closer to views of the Roman Catholic hierarchy, and second, the church hierarchy seemed to give greater weight to candidates' views on abortion than to their views on other political issues traditionally important to Roman Catholic ethics, such as fair housing, minimum wage, labor union rights, welfare legislation, and the death penalty.

With the election of America's first antiabortion president, Ronald Reagan, in 1980, things became much worse for Planned Parenthood and the pro-choice movement. The Republican Party put an antiabortion plank into its platform. An organization known as the Moral Majority emerged around the same time, through which Protestant fundamentalist denominations like the Southern Baptists now began to organize antiabortion activities in the states where the influence of the Catholic hierarchy was weak. With the addition of the political influence of these denominations and with the Senate in Republican hands, a constitutional amendment to ban abortions nearly passed the Senate in 1982.

Pro-Choice Religious Response

In the mid-seventies almost no one had seen this wave of opposition coming. It took time for Planned Parenthood and other pro-choice organizations to develop a strategy to combat such formidable opposition. By the time they got themselves together they looked out upon a political landscape that had been transformed by right-wing religion. Those denominations that had been front and center in the battle to repeal the old abortion laws were much more aware than secular pro-choice groups that the right-to-life movement was going to put up quite a struggle. Like the canary in the coal mine, the Board for Homeland Ministries of the United Church of Christ warned as early as May 1, 1973, that "the opponents of the right to choose are way out ahead of us, waging a full-force well-calculated campaign aimed at the Congress."[7] In their letter, board members noted that congressional mail was running 500 to 1 in favor of a constitutional amendment prohibiting abortion. They reported that eight states had already petitioned Congress for such an amendment. The letter closed with a pessimism that was to be amply justified. "[We] realize and empathize with all of you who have no desire to get back into the political arena and re-open old wounds, . . . but we also have a responsibility to witness to our position even when the odds look overwhelming."[8]

By the end of 1973 most mainline Protestant and Jewish denominations had taken pro-choice stands and were on record as opposing any movement to criminalize abortion. But there were parts of these denominations that were much more committed than others on this issue. The Women's Division of the United Methodist Church, the National Council of Jewish Women, the B'nai Brith Women, and other similar women's groups in African-American churches were the driving forces in creating an effective pro-choice instrument. On December 30, 1973, sixteen Jewish and Christian religious groups formed the Religious Coalition for Abortion Rights (RCAR), a national organization that worked to defend a woman's right to choose a legal abortion.

With organized affiliates in over twenty states, RCAR (now known as the Religious Coalition for Reproductive Choice) became the most overt expression of the religious pro-choice views of the mainline Protestant and Jewish world.[9] RCAR's activities and publications reassured the public that there was strong religious support for any choice a woman might make when faced with an unplanned pregnancy.

In the years immediately following the *Roe* decision, RCAR worked with limited resources to help the pro-choice movement defend *Roe*. For example, the group provided pro-choice religious voices, such as Rabbi Balfour Brickner, to testify against an antiabortion amendment at the 1974 hearings of the Senate Subcommittee on Constitutional Amendments.[10] They also published an impressive list of biblical and theological studies on abortion to answer the religious pronouncements of the right-to-life forces.[11] Above all, RCAR made a great effort to bring together people of faith to oppose the Hyde Amendment that would deny Medicaid funds to poor women seeking abortions. But they were not able to stop the measure's passage.

African-American women from mainline denominations have been a vital part of RCAR since its inception. Through their "Women of Color Partnerships" and, since 1997, their annual National Sexuality Summit for church leaders at Howard University, they have been able to mobilize African-American Christians as a vital part of the pro-choice movement and of RCAR in particular.[12]

Another, and perhaps the most significant, early religious pro-choice response was Catholics for a Free Choice. Organized by three Catholic women, Joan Harriman, Patricia Fogarty McQuillan, and Meta Mulcahy, the group set out to correct the popular understanding that Roman Catholics were working-class people who were overwhelmingly obedient to their bishops and church directives and opposed abortion. Operating with imaginative flamboyance, the group crashed onto the public consciousness on the first-year anniversary of *Roe v. Wade* in 1974, when Patricia Fogarty McQuillan had herself crowned pope on the steps of St. Patrick's Cathedral in New York.[13]

In those early years, with limited resources and no central office, Catholics for a Free Choice groups conducted guerrilla-like actions that were quite effective. They would appear as counterdemonstrators in the midst of a right-to-life protest and steal all the publicity. Many press people were intrigued by Catholics who were pro-choice. This organization cited polls to show that they and not the bishops represented the stance of most lay Catholics.[14] In 1984 the group attracted significant attention right in the middle of a presidential campaign. The Democrats had nominated Walter Mondale for president and he had startled the country with his nomination of Geraldine Ferraro for vice president. In his words, "I sought the best man for the office and I found her." But almost immediately Cardinal John O'Connor of the New York diocese criticized Ferraro for her pro-choice views. Many Catholic women were upset because the cardinal had not been nearly as critical of prominent male Catholic politicians such as Governor Mario Cuomo and Senator Ted Kennedy. They also wanted to make it clear that the church leaders did not speak for them.

The dramatic way that Catholics for a Free Choice chose to make their views known to the public was to place an advertisement in the *New York Times* on October 7, 1984, entitled "A Catholic Statement on Abortion." The statement claimed that there was more than one Catholic position on abortion and called upon church leaders to stop punishing Catholics who did not agree with the bishops. Included among the ninety-seven signatories were twenty-four nuns, two brothers, and two priests.[15] After the election was over, a Vatican office, the Sacred Congregation for Religious and Secular Institutes, demanded that the nuns and brothers who signed the statement retract their signatures. Two Sisters of Notre Dame de Namur, Barbara Ferraro and Patricia Hussey, refused to recant and, after a protracted struggle, resigned from the order. Catholics for a Free Choice supported them in their long struggle. Since that time the organization, under the leadership of Frances Kissling, has been a key part of the pro-choice movement. Their efforts are effective in making it clear that religious differences about abortion exist not only outside antiabortion churches, but also within them.

PLANNED PARENTHOOD'S UNCERTAINTY

Where was Planned Parenthood going in this post-*Roe* period? It was certainly not as bold as the Religious Coalition or Catholics for a Free Choice in its defense of abortion rights. It is perhaps understandable that there would be some hesitation about taking such a step. Not only was the organization in most places directed by boards of conservative business and professional people, but it was also clear within a year of *Roe* that the opposition to legal abortion was going to be formidable. People were intimidated. As the organization that would actually have to provide the abortion procedures, it had to develop a certain resolve.

In the eighties the growth of Planned Parenthood abortion services slowed considerably. Between 1980 and 1986, only two or three affiliates began services each year. A significant factor was the violence against abortion clinics, which by the mid-eighties had reached a level no one had expected in 1973. It became even more daunting to initiate services.

Yet, in spite of, or even because of, the violence, a cultural sorting-out process eventually took place within many affiliates and the pace picked up. In one town or another, one city or another, a Planned Parenthood board of directors would see other abortion services drying up or being priced out of reach. They could see things getting harder for women, who had to drive farther, pay more, and wait longer to get a needed abortion. The need was becoming more urgent. When such a board finally decided that in good conscience—and in consonance with the Federation's traditional commitment to the needs of women—they would vote to begin abortion services, those who could not agree usually left the board and were replaced by people who were more supportive of the decision. Much the same process took place with the clinic staff. Over time the organization's commitment to providing safe abortions deepened and strengthened. By 2000 over half of the Planned Parenthood affiliates in America were providing abortion-related services.

THE RIGHT-TO-LIFE MOVEMENT AND VIOLENCE

Throughout the rest of the seventies the right-to-life movement increased its political activity and added sit-ins and demonstrations at Planned Parenthood and other women's clinics. Tactics became increasingly ugly. Demonstrators would check license plates of staff and patients to find out who they were and where they lived or they would rummage through clinic garbage to find any paper that might produce patient names. They would then use the information to call private homes to tell parents their daughter had had an abortion. Soon every Planned Parenthood clinic in America was forced to buy a paper shredder, an example of one of the many steps Planned Parenthood would take to protect its services and its patients. Demonstrators shouted at patients. They boomed their denunciations through bullhorns so that women inside the clinics could hear them. The public became conscious of the movement as one some of whose proponents seemed to believe that they were doing God's work and that extreme tactics were justified. This latter trait began to register strongly on the sensitivities of some pro-choice clergy.

The extent of the violence was startling. In his 1990 study on abortion, *Abortion: The Clash of Absolutes*, the jurist Lawrence Tribe noted: "There has been a remarkable, although not much-remarked upon, rise in the incidence of such antiabortion violence. Since 1977 extremists in the United States have bombed or set fire to at least 117 clinics and threatened 250 others. They have invaded 231 clinics and vandalized 224 others."[16]

One event in particular set off the loudest alarms to clergy. During the Christmas season of 1984, there were bombings of women's clinics in Pensacola, Florida. Buildings were torn to pieces. One of the women arrested called the attacks "a gift to Jesus on his birthday."[17] Finding the words so blasphemous, so naively inhuman, a number of clergy felt that a line had been crossed and signs of pro-choice clergy organizing began to appear. It retrospect it was possible to see how an abortion controversy in a small upstate New York city became part of a grassroots movement that would revive widespread clergy support for the work of Planned Parenthood.

PRO-CHOICE CLERGY BEGIN TO ORGANIZE:
"THE BATTLE OF SARATOGA"

In November 1984, Southern Adirondack Planned Parenthood, a small four-county affiliate just north of Albany, New York, was awaiting a decision by the Saratoga County Board of Supervisors, the governing body for county affairs. The decision concerned a "pass through" grant, that is, a vote to allow a grant from a state bureau to pass through county government into the hands of the designated agency or designated private group. In this case the grant was for $14,400 from the New York State Department for Youth, and it was to go to Southern Adirondack Planned Parenthood. The purpose of the grant was to continue an adolescent education program in Saratoga County that had been running since 1980. In previous years the county had passed the money through after adding a stipulation that none of the funds could be used for abortions. That had not been a problem for two reasons: first, the New York State Department for Youth audited every penny and knew that the money went only for counseling, and second, Southern Adirondack Planned Parenthood did not provide abortion services.

But that year there were stirrings of opposition. Before the Board of Supervisors met on Tuesday evening, November 20 the local paper of the city of Saratoga Springs, *The Saratogian*, wrote that opponents were making plans to come to the meeting to protest.[18] Prior to the meeting the opponents carried out a well-organized telephone campaign to persuade the supervisors to block the grant. Those calls, plus the presence of one hundred protesters, turned the November 20 meeting into a rout for Planned Parenthood. With strident antiabortion rhetoric, the protesters made the argument to the board that Planned Parenthood should never receive any public grants. In a meeting that went on for several hours, the tone of the opposition was dramatic. *The Saratogian* reported that one clergy opponent told the supervisors, "There is no way anyone can speak for all these diverse groups [who are present]. . . . But I can speak for our Lord Jesus Christ. Protect our country against the spreading disease of moral decay promoted by SAPP [Southern Adirondack Planned Parenthood] in place of chastity and fidelity. SAPP is a malignant cell in our community."[19] In opposition to the grant one supervisor took out his Bible and read from it. Other opponents, including supervisors, made the case that even though Southern Adirondack Planned Parenthood did not perform abortions, any grants given to it would free up money for abortion.

In defense of the grant, the director of Planned Parenthood pointed out that in the four years of the program, the teenage pregnancy rate in the county had dropped from 371 per year to 322. The number of teenage abortions had gone down 10 percent and live births to teens by 12 percent. A sympathetic supervisor, a former president of the school board in his district, said, "it seems somewhat incredible to me that they've gone to 28 schools, 12 parent groups, 31 PTAs and six church groups and I've never heard any one of these people come back to us to say they are doing anything wrong. I think this thing has gotten out of hand."[20] It was a valiant attempt to urge reflection, but it had no chance. When the vote came, only six supervisors supported Southern Adirondack Planned Parenthood and seventeen opposed. The grant was rejected.

On November 23 the editorial writer of *The Saratogian* took a stand: "Shame on the Saratoga County supervisors who voted this week to put the Southern Adirondack Planned Parenthood out of business by refusing to let it use available state money. And shame on those who played on parents' fears and the horror of abortion to twist the issue."[21] But nothing was going to change the supervisors at that time.

Mulling over their defeat, the supporters of Southern Adirondack Planned Parenthood tried to prepare a strategy for requesting funds from the board in the next year. The question at hand was whether such opposition was a one-time phenomenon or whether the climate had changed for the indefinite future. When budget time rolled around in early November 1985, the affiliate urged friends and supporters to make calls to their respective supervisors. This time the request was for $8,000 to help pay for medical exams, cancer tests, and family-planning services to low-income residents. Barbara Thomas, the director of Southern Adirondack Planned Parenthood, explained that because of the previous year's cut, the agency had had to raise fees for such cancer tests for low-income residents from $13 to $19.[22]

At first things looked promising. On November 15, 1985, the law and finance subcommittee added the $8,000 to the 1986 budget by a vote of 6 to 1. Two of the positive votes had been negative votes the previous November. But at the full board meeting eight days later opponents greatly outnumbered supporters and the board again rejected the funds. The board chairperson, Almeda Dake, spoke in support and pointed out that Planned Parenthood offered these medical tests at a very low cost. Chairman William Sewell of the public health committee said that because of overhead costs no hospital could offer the tests as cheaply as Southern Adirondack Planned Parenthood.[23]

But none of that appeared to matter. This small affiliate was attacked as a promoter of masturbation, a cause of young people taking drugs, and— over and over again—a purveyor of abortion.[24] A number of supervisors insisted that any money given to the agency by the county would only free up funds for abortion. It made no sense. Why would Southern Adirondack Planned Parenthood take its money and send it to some affiliate who did do abortions? Affiliates didn't send money around that way. But it was clear that no factual information was going to change any minds. Despite the likelihood that no county agency would replace Planned Parenthood in offering these medical tests, the grant was once again voted down, 16 to 4. Supervisor David Meager captured the meaning of the meeting in one sentence: "We've lost a very good program simply because it was offered by Planned Parenthood."[25]

THE ADIRONDACK RELIGIOUS COALITION FOR CHOICE

For local clergy watching this rematch, Meager's words summarized it all. In effect, Planned Parenthood was now seen as an outcast organization. People working there, many of them members of local congregations, knew that while Planned Parenthood was as much a part of the community as the Red Cross, the Kiwanis, or the Salvation Army, those groups were not under attack. Ministers, rabbis, or congregations could endorse those organizations without a problem, but if they supported Planned Parenthood, there would be criticism, both from outside and from within the community of faith. One minister watching the process joked sadly that "if Southern Adirondack Planned Parenthood was the only agency in the county willing to plow snow off the highways, the highways would go unplowed!" The clergy who had been at the Board of Supervisors meetings realized that they were seeing something new, a powerful new right-to-life grassroots surge. It was highly effective, and most strikingly, religious passions were the fuel of the movement.

Persuaded that such demonization of a woman's agency was poison to politics, whether local or national, these local pro-choice clergy decided that they would organize to counter such a movement. They began by concentrating on pro-choice clergy in a five-county area, Saratoga, Warren, Washington, Fulton, and Montgomery. All of these counties were located to the north and west of Albany. Four of them were essentially rural. Except for Saratoga County, each one had fewer than 50,000 people. The original organizers were the Reverend Betsy Davis (United Church of Christ), the

Reverend Jane Borden (United Methodist), the Reverend Joyce DeVelder (Reformed), Rabbi Linda Motzkin (Union of Reformed Congregations), the Reverend Bill Pattison (United Methodist), and myself (United Church of Christ). During the spring and summer of 1986, each of us worked our denominational contacts, seeking to find out where our colleagues stood on this contentious issue.

After we gathered the names of those who might be sympathetic, we started visiting them. It was an intriguing and, at times, a moving learning experience. Each visit involved a one-on-one talk with a minister or rabbi in the area. Three realities were apparent from the start. First, the vast majority of mainline ministers and rabbis were supportive of a woman's right to choose an abortion, Conservative and Reform rabbis almost unanimously so.

Second, clergy seemed to sense that this issue was different from almost all other social justice issues that commanded their attention. There was the obvious realization that an issue like abortion can be enormously divisive in a congregation, but it was more than that. It was their awareness of the sometimes-unreasoning anger and hatred, so apparent on the national scene, that the issue seemed to churn up. For those of us clergy who had been active in the South in the sixties it was reminiscent of the anger of the segregationists. One striking similarity was an intemperate and unrestrained reaction to a major Supreme Court ruling. In that earlier era the segregationists had put up billboards saying "Impeach Earl Warren." Now at least one right-to-life clergyperson was praying for the death of Supreme Court Justice William Brennan.[26]

It was all a form of cursing. The segregationists had cursed the NAACP and Martin Luther King: right-to-lifers were cursing Planned Parenthood. In the biblical sense, to curse is to call down the wrath of God upon a person or a group, to petition the deity to make terrible things happen to those who are seen to be evildoers. In secular terms, to curse an organization is to denounce it as intrinsically evil and to place it outside the bounds of cultural acceptability. It is to make it a group to be shunned by all good people. Tragically, in practical terms the effect of cursing is to turn the outcast group over to violence at the hands of people who cannot control the fears that have been awakened. Cursing is a depressingly familiar historical strategy that has been used against many other justice movements. The sixty-year history of Planned Parenthood in America can be seen in biblical terms as an organization's enduring response to "cursing." Despite these concerns, most mainline clergy were still willing to join a pro-choice clergy group.

A third factor in recruiting clergy to join the pro-choice movement was the particular life experience of each clergyperson. Some had unique issues that held them back. A few had been unable to have children and had adopted. They were convinced that had abortion been legal at the time they adopted their children those children might never have been born. One minister said that his head was with us, but his heart couldn't get there because of his adopted children. Those were feelings that had to be respected. All kinds of other feelings and experiences emerged. Some couples had had abortions while in seminary so that they could finish their education. They had no regrets and worked solidly with us. Some women clergy had had abortions while in seminary and had never talked to anyone about it. But in this situation they felt compelled to share their experience in the light of right-to-life opposition. Most clergy didn't welcome controversy, but their seminary training and their constant contact with scripture made them aware that occasionally they might have to speak a word that their congregation and the public might not want to hear.

Finally, while those of us doing the interviews didn't usually seek out clergy who were openly opposed to choice, we wanted to listen to a number of them to make sure we understood their strong feelings on the issue. We had interviews with a few who were excellent ministers, known for their compassion toward their congregation. Although we didn't agree with their antiabortion views, we could respect their right to see the issue differently. These right-to-life clergy lacked neither eloquence nor passion in giving both biblical and theological grounds for their views. But a certain practical dimension of the issue was missing. They had never thought about what it would mean for them as ministers if their views became law, that is, if abortion were once again a criminal act in America. Because a few of us had lived in that situation, we pushed them on it.

In one case, I posed a hypothetical case to a staunch clergy opponent of choice. Imagine we are in a future era when abortion has once again been made a criminal act. Suppose a working-class family from your church, without too many resources, were to come to you and say that their sixteen-year-old daughter is pregnant and, while they don't approve of abortion, they feel deeply that she is too young to have a baby. They have reluctantly decided to obtain an abortion for her. Since they don't know where to turn, where to find a doctor, they ask you for help. What would you do? The minister to whom I posed this case said that of course he would try to change their mind. I said that I was sure he would, but I pushed again and asked him to assume he couldn't dissuade them. With sadness they tell you they are going ahead. They ask you to help them. I told him, "I know you. You are one of the best pastors in this area. Are you just going to say nothing?" He thought for a while and said, "I might send them to you." There was the irony; he wanted a law that he would break, if forced to. When he saw that a family he cared about could be at risk of potentially great harm, his compassion was stronger than his theology. Instinctively he started doing what clergy in the old Clergy Consultation Service had done; he tried to find a way to help them. He thought he was adamantly against abortion, but he just hadn't thought it through. And he wasn't the only one. We learned that underneath many professed antiabortion convictions, more than a few such clergy had not thought about the effect of such laws on individual lives.

Armed with these experiences, the organizers called their first five-county meeting in September 1986, in the New England Presbyterian Congregational Church in Saratoga Springs. Both the church and its pastor, the Reverend Jay Ekman, had long been committed to social justice issues. Twenty-five clergy from the five counties attended. First we acknowledged that the work of the Clergy Consultation on Abortion had long passed out of the public memory. Religious antiabortion forces had created a false public perception that all religions were opposed to a woman's right to choose. We were determined to change that perception.

The determination to go ahead was strong, so the clergy leaders of the denominational groups (known as judicatories) were invited by the Saratoga pro-choice clergy to a meeting in Saratoga in November 1986. At that meeting we would formally organize. At that meeting were the Reverend Jim Miller, executive presbyter of the Albany Presbytery (a grouping of all the Presbyterian churches in a geographic region); the Reverend Bill Lasher, who occupied a similar position in the Troy Conference of the Methodist Church; and the Reverend Ron Kurtz, head of the Hudson Mohawk Association of United Church of Christ local churches. The New York State Religious Coalition for Abortion Rights sent two representatives from their Syracuse chapter. After some discussion the group took the name the Adirondack Religious Coalition for Choice. Technically it was a subgroup (called an "area group") of the New York State RCAR group based in Syracuse. But unlike most RCAR groups, which were composed primarily of laypeople, we would focus on the particular role of clergy in this justice movement.[27]

There was a bit of irony here. Since neither Protestants nor Jews stress the differences between laypeople and clergy, they do not generally make a big deal over clergy; it seemed strange to be emphasizing our clerical role. But there was no denying the reality that in the American public mind, for a number of reasons, clergy are seen as figures of some authority. That meant that the opposition to choice of so many high-ranking Roman Catholic clergy and Protestant fundamentalist clergy had to be balanced by clergy speaking for choice. This group wanted to create a structure that would be clergy centered. It would welcome lay members into its ranks, but the Adirondack Religious Coalition was going to focus resolutely on clergy organizing, clergy theological study, and in time, clergy speaking out. The goal was to create a public presence to make it clear that the opposition to a woman's right to choose had no monopoly on the sacred. To realize that goal, the organization would do two things simultaneously: theological study and public advocacy.

A clear opportunity for letting the public know of our existence arose. The city's only hospital, Saratoga Hospital, was being picketed because it provided limited abortion services. A letter of support was drafted and circulated to our new local clergy members. To our delight fifteen signed on. The letter of support went to each member of the hospital board and the local press. On July 23, 1987, it was the lead story on the front page of *The Saratogian* under the banner headline "Area Clergy Back Abortion Policy at Saratoga Hospital."[28] It drew a spate of letters that questioned the validity of our ministries.

Within a year the membership grew to fifty-four clergy. It included rabbis, ministers of the Presbyterian, Methodist, Baptist, Reformed, Lutheran, Episcopal, and Unitarian churches, and the United Church of Christ. In the years that followed, the executive committee of the coalition brought pro-choice clergy, other religious people, and Planned Parenthood staffers together each autumn for theological study. The format was a one-day colloquium at the Surrey Inn on the campus of Skidmore College in Saratoga Springs, New York. The focus was always on the religious roots of choice. From 1987 to 2000, speakers included theologians or religious activists such as Dr. Beverly Harrison of Union Theological Seminary; Frances Kissling of Catholics for a Free Choice; the Reverend Howard Moody of the Clergy Consultation on Abortion; Virginia Ramey Mollenkott, author of *Human Responsibility and the Bible*, and *Godding*; the Reverend Ignatio Castuera, author of *Dreams on Fire, Embers of Hope*; and the Reverend Paul Simmons of the Southern Baptist Louisville Seminary. Each presentation was videotaped by the Reverend Bill Pattison so that clergy living in the rural counties of upstate New York could also have the opportunity to be a part of colloquium.

Next the coalition began to publish a quarterly newsletter, *Conscience*, which printed many articles critiquing the antiabortion interpretation of the

the Saratogian

A Gannett Newspaper Serving Saratoga, Warren and Washington Counties

Thursday, July 23, 1987

25 Cents

A.M. update

Debt limit legislation languishes in Senate

WASHINGTON (AP) — An urgently needed increase in the national debt ceiling languished Wednesday in the Senate as talks broke down over a proposed bipartisan amendment to revive the Gramm-Rudman budget-balancing law.

The Treasury, because of Congress' inaction, has been without authority to borrow money since last

Area clergy back abortion policy at Saratoga Hospital

By MARY CAROLINE POWERS
Senior Writer

A group of clergy, including 15 ministers and rabbis who serve Saratoga Springs congregations, want Saratoga Hospital to continue providing abortions to women.

In a letter to administrators, the hospital's Board of Managers and its foundation Board of Trustees, members of the Adirondack Religious Coalition for Choice stated, "We are willing to speak out on your behalf and to organize public support for Saratoga Hospital."

"Some of our members are strongly against abortion but believe choice should be preserved," said Rabbi Linda Motzkin of Temple Sinai in Saratoga

Springs. "We are not saying that abortion is an answer for everyone, but it must be kept a legal option."

A religiously based group opposed to abortion formed in Saratoga County in January. Among their activities, members of the United Churches for Life picket Saratoga Hospital each month to protest its abortion policy.

Please see ABORTION, page 8A

Adirondack Religious Coalition for Choice clergy defend Saratoga Hospital abortion services, July 23, 1987. (Reprinted with permission of *The Saratogian*.)

Bible and theology. Clergy contributed articles establishing both biblical and theological bases for a woman's right to choose an abortion. *Conscience* was sent to over five hundred clergy plus Planned Parenthood affiliates, primarily in the northeastern United States, but, as the years went by, to all parts of the country, including Hawaii (which we deemed the western edge of the Adirondacks).

In 1989 the Adirondack Religious Coalition joined with a pro-choice clergy group from three more counties, Albany, Schenectady, and Rensselaer, which made up the area known locally as the Capital District. In each of those counties we found clergy whose grassroots organization and mobilization skills were indispensable. In Albany County it was the Reverend Kathleen Buckley; in Rensselaer County, the Reverend Betsy Hall and Rabbi Julie Wolkoff; and in Schenectady County, the Reverend Larry Phillips, whose Baptist church was a stalwart supporter of the local Planned Parenthood affiliate. Word of the coalition's activities was spreading and clergy membership passed 100 clergy within a year. In 1991 clergy from Clinton, Franklin, and Essex counties joined us. So our territory now stretched from Albany to the Canadian border. By 1992 ARC had 160 clergy members.[29]

In the area of advocacy, the clergy could see that Planned Parenthood clinics were at the heart of the struggle, where justice would either be given or denied. This is where protesters were always picketing, and throwing scripture at the people working there. The Adirondack Coalition asked the Planned Parenthoods to have an open house for clergy on an occasion when the clinic was not serving patients. One such event in Saratoga Springs welcomed a few right-to-life clergy as well as its clergy supporters. Although it didn't convert the former, it made it clear to them that Planned Parenthood was not a strange place. It was a woman's clinic. Some of the people working there came from congregations just like theirs, and most of the people who went there were church and synagogue members. Those events helped to correct the bizarre picture of Planned Parenthood that was presented at meetings such as those of the Saratoga County Board of Supervisors. The right-to-life clergy who attended the open house could see that those who worked at the clinics were not the Antichrist; they were neighbors, and in many cases, fellow believers.

Over the next few years these Adirondack Religious Coalition clergy made a point of coming to the support of three Planned Parenthood clinics in the area.[30] In Atlanta, Georgia, in the summer of 1988 a new wave of anti-abortion demonstrators arose, known as Operation Rescue. Its forte was blocking access to clinics through massive civil disobedience. These tactics brought enormous media attention and turned a visit to a clinic into a nightmare for hundreds of women. In 1991, when Operation Rescue sent demonstrators to close down Planned Parenthood clinics in the town of Hudson and other cities in the Capital District, the Adirondack Religious Coalition clergy denounced these tactics, drew up petitions of support for clergy to sign, and posted them in the Planned Parenthood clinics to give moral support to the staff working there, to let them know the clergy were with them. A few years later the coalition published an ad in the three principal area newspapers. One hundred fourteen clergy signed the ad, which said: "As clerical leaders of a rich and diverse religious community, we represent a wealth of differing beliefs. But we stand together in our certitude that abortion must remain a personal decision made within a woman's own moral framework. Churches and synagogues, as well as legislatures, should provide compassion and support—not condemnation and barriers—to any woman faced with an unwanted pregnancy."[31]

In one particular area, clergy could be especially useful to the clinics. From time to time, as other abortion providers closed down or retired, a Planned Parenthood affiliate would seek to open abortion services in a county that no longer had inexpensive accessible services. In New York State, such an application involves at least three public meetings before a Health Systems Agency at which anyone can support or oppose the proposed service. Naturally, antiabortion opponents would fill these gatherings and portray the coming of Planned Parenthood as the end of the world. But Adirondack Religious Coalition clergy would speak for the clinics and would hold a press conference or publish an ad to persuade the public that the coming of the abortion service was a good thing, in fact a matter of justice.

In August 1990, Upper Hudson Planned Parenthood (Albany) was petitioning to open services in Rensselaer County (Troy). At a press conference at the First United Presbyterian Church in Troy on August 2, a statement signed by twenty-five local clergy was released to the press. Among other things it said, "We call upon our religious brothers and sisters to recognize that in a free country such as the United States, it is wrong for any people of any one faith perspective to impose their theological doctrines on others."[32]

A far more contentious battle took place in the winter of 1991–92, when Planned Parenthood of Northeastern New York proposed opening abortion services in Glens Falls in Warren County, some fifty miles north of the Capital District. Glens Falls is in the foothills of the Adirondacks, and many

Religious leaders stand up for choice... Will you?

As clerical leaders of a rich and diverse religious community, we represent a wealth of differing beliefs. But we stand together in our certitude that abortion must remain a personal decision made within a woman's own moral framework. Churches and synagogues, as well as legislatures, should provide compassion and support—not condemnation and barriers—to any woman faced with an unwanted pregnancy.

We are pro-choice advocates and call upon people of conscience everywhere to recognize that the principles of separation of church and state and the right to privacy protect us all. It's time to go public for privacy.

The Rev. Larry A. Deyss
The Rev. Dr. Maurice E. Drown
The Rev. Frances H. Duffley
The Rev. Robert E. Eggenschiller
The Rev. John A. Ekman
The Rev. Wendell H. Elmendorf Jr.
The Rev. Leif Erickson
The Rev. Lawrence M. Estey
The Rev. Robert Farmer
The Rev. James A. Farrell
The Rev. Vincent A. Fasano
Rabbi Milton Feierstein
Rabbi Judah L. Fish, D.D.
First Unitarian Society of Schenectady
The Rev. Paul Spear Fraser
The Rev. E.T. Freeborn
Rabbi Baruch Frydman-Kohl
The Rev. Charles N. Geisler
Hope Geisler
The Rev. Dr. Loise L. George
The Rev. Ronald D. Gerber
The Rev. Kathleen Gorman-Coombs
The Rev. Elizabeth S. Hall
The Rev. Andrew C. Hamersley
The Rev. Robert A. Hammond
The Rev. Jane P. Harmes
The Rev. Keith A. Harrington
The Rev. Susan D. Husted
The Rev. Allan Janssen
The Rev. Joan Kahn-Schneider
Rabbi Samuel S. Kieffer

The Rev. J. Larry Phillips
The Rev; Dr. Alvin C. Porteous
The Rev. Lyman G. Potter
The Rev. Robert L. Richardson
The Rev. Stephen C. Robinson
The Rev. Ellen W. Robinson
Rabbi Jonathan Rubenstein
The Rev. Andrew C. Russ
Anne K. Saxton
The Rev. F. Thomas Scholl Jr.
The Rev. Rodney P. Scoville
The Rev. Michael Shafer
The Rev. Marian P. Shearer
The Rev. Charles W. Sheerin Jr.
Rabbi Scott Shpeen
Rabbi Paul B. Silton
Rabbi Martin I. Silverman
The Rev. Stanley E. Skinner Jr.
The Rev. Dr. Charles S. Slap
The Rev. Albert A Smith
Social Responsibility Council of the First Unitarian Society of Albany
The Rev. Dr. Ray R. Stees
The Rev. Donald E. Stroud
The Rev. Christopher V. Taylor
The Rev. Robert B. Thomas
The Rev. James R. Thompson
The Rev. Sylvester Van Oort
The Rev. Cynthia L. Walton
Rabbi Julie Wolkoff
The Rev. Kenneth B. Wonderland
The Rev. Susan Faye Wonderland

Please join us in the campaign to "Keep Abortion Safe and Legal."

____ Please put me on your mailing list for Campaign Advocates and send me information on what I can do to keep abortion safe and legal.

____ I would also like to support Planned Parenthood's Public Affairs efforts with a financial contribution. Enclosed is my tax-deductible contribution in the amount of $ _____.

NAME _____
ADDRESS _____
PHONE NO. _____
(day)   (evening)

Adirondack Religious Coalition for Choice
Albany Presbytery Women's Task Force
Albany United Methodist Society
The Rev. Kathy Jo Blaske
Rabbi Bernard H. Bloom
B'nai B'rith Women, Aviva Chapter #1820
B'nai B'rith Women, Gideon Chapter #150
The Rev. Jane T. Borden
The Rev. Kathleen Buckley
The Rev. Margaret C. Bunnell
The Rev. Duncan C. Cameron
The Rev. Richard Dean Campbell
The Rev. Garry W. Campbell
The Rev. Dana Carroll
Rabbi Donald P. Cashman
Charlton Freehold Presbyterian Church
Congregation Berith Sholom
The Rev. Timothy Coombs
The Rev. George L. Corson
The Rev. Marsha Cutting
The Rev. Dr. John H. Danner
The Rev. Betsy Davis
The Rev. Tom Davis Jr.
The Rev. Roger U. Day

The Rev. George Klohck
The Rev. David R. LaRoe
The Rev. William A. Lasher
The Rev. Mary L. Lautzenhiser
The Rev. Dr. James M. Lavery
The Rev. Robert F. Long
The Rev. M. deForest Lowen
The Rev. Herman E. Luben
Rabbi Beverly W. Magidson
The Rev. Roger J. Martin
The Rev. Ms. Gailey McIntyre
The Rev. Dr. Donna Meinhard
The Rev. John U. Miller
The Rev. James H. Miller
The Rev. Joel B. Miller
The Rev. George F. Miller Jr.
The Rev. J. Phillip Miller-Evans
Rabbi Linda Motzkin
The Rev. Richard W. Neal
The Rev. Hugh Nevin
The Rev. Dr. S. Albert Newman
The Rev. Carrol Newquist
The Rev. Betsy Norton
The Rev. Terrence M. O'Neill
The Rev. Thomas Orr Jr.
The Rev. Thomas F. Parsons
The Rev. G. William Pattison
The Rev. John H. Peatling
The Rev. James M. Perry

Planned Parenthood®
Health Services
of Northeastern New York, Inc.

Administrative Offices
14 Union Street Schenectady, NY 12305

UPPER HUDSON PLANNED PARENTHOOD®

259 LARK STREET
ALBANY, N.Y. 12210

©1990 UHPP Inc. Paid for with private contributions.

Advertisement, "Religious Leaders Stand Up for Choice," March 14, 1990, which appeared in the *Albany Times Union*. (Reprinted courtesy of Upper Hudson Planned Parenthood.)

young women from small Adirondack communities were traveling (often in winter) over mountain roads some distance into Vermont to obtain an abortion. At the Health Systems Agency hearings there was powerful religious opposition to the coming of the service. But the Adirondack Religious Coalition for Choice gathered the signatures of thirty-seven local clergy for a letter of support to be sent to the agency. Then the letter was published in an ad in the *Glens Falls Post Star*. It was titled "Clergy Support Planned Parenthood Plan for Glens Falls Abortion Services." The ad said,

> Planned Parenthood has a demonstrated record of offering a wide variety of health services to the very women who are often unable to afford general medical care. . . . We fully appreciate that many people of good faith will not agree with us. We respect them and we understand their strong beliefs. We also have strong convictions. Many of us have had long experience with this issue. A few of us were ministering in the years when abortion was illegal. We have seen tragedies that persuade us that abortion must be legal, safe, and reasonably available.[33]

We found that statements like this, particularly when signed by local ministers and rabbis who had been there a long time and earned the respect of the town, invariably lowered the temperature of the public debate. It made it much harder to demonize Planned Parenthood.

The Adirondack Religious Coalition for Choice was not alone in its activities. Other parts of the country also saw such clergy organizing. In Kansas City, Missouri, in 1978 Dr. Robert Meneilley, pastor of a large Presbyterian Church, appreciated the intensity of the right-to-life opposition and was instrumental in forming a Religious Affairs Committee for Planned Parenthood of Greater Kansas City. A few years later, that affiliate hired a minister of the Disciples denomination to be its chaplain, one of the first Planned Parenthood chaplains in the country.

Westchester County (New York) Planned Parenthood was also early in the field with clergy organizing. When there was an unrelenting antichoice siege of a woman's clinic in Dobbs Ferry, N.Y., the clergy group was able to come to its defense. On April 2, 1992, they held a special "Day of Theological Reflection: A Conference for Pro-Choice Clergy" to set forth the Protestant, Jewish, and Roman Catholic bases for a woman's right to choose.[34]

Clergy supporting Planned Parenthood were only part of an awakening pro-choice constituency. With the election of another antiabortion president, George H. W. Bush, in 1988, that constituency—with Planned Parenthood

Clergy Support Planned Parenthood Plan for Glens Falls Abortion Services

The following letter was sent to the Health Systems Agency by members of the Adirondack Religious Coalition for Choice

We are a group of clergy from Warren, Washington, Essex and northern Saratoga counties. We are writing in support of the application of Planned Parenthood Health Services of Northeastern New York to provide abortion services in Glens Falls.

We believe such support is justified for at least three reasons:
1. Research indicates that women in the Warren-Washington and Southern Essex area have to travel some distance to find these services. Often they have to go to Vermont where New York medicaid has not been accepted.

2. Planned Parenthood has a demonstrated record of offering a wide variety of health services to the very women who are often unable to afford general medical care. Perhaps its greatest contribution is in the area of education. And women who find it difficult to obtain good, affordable, contraceptive services would go through many more unwanted pregnancies were it not for this agency.

3. Finally, Planned Parenthood has been in Glens Falls for a long time. It has provided help to several generations of Warren and Washington county women and families. It has shown us that it is a responsible agency. Recently, it demonstrated that again when it accepted responsibility for rape crisis services in Glens Falls.

We fully appreciate that many people of good faith will not agree with us. We respect them and we understand their strong beliefs. We also have strong convictions. Many of us have had long experience with this issue. A few of us were ministering in the years when abortion was illegal. We have seen tragedies which persuade us that abortion must be legal, safe and reasonably available. We belong to denominations and religious movements which support a woman's right to choose. For all of these reasons, we support this application.

From Warren County
The Rev. John Barclay
The Rev. Robert Clark
The Rev. Steven Grant
The Rev. Jerome Hevey
The Rev. Linda Hoddy
The Rev. Sheldon Hurst
The Rev. Ralph Marino
The Rev. LaMont Robinson
The Rev. Harold Shippey
Rabbi Richard Sobel
The Rev. Raoul Waters
The Rev. Jack Williams

From Saratoga County
The Rev. Jane Borden

The Rev. Betsy Davis
The Rev. Tom Davis
The Rev. Joyce DeVelder
The Rev. John Ekman
The Rev. Howard Foye
The Rev. Robert Hammond
The Rev. Charles Higgins
The Rev. William Lasher
The Rev. Robert Long
The Rev. DeForest Lowen
Rabbi Linda Motzkin
The Rev. Tom Peterson
The Rev. Lyman Potter
Rabbi Jonathan Rubenstein
The Rev. Rod Scoville
The Rev. Bob Thomas

From Washington County
The Rev. John Chesney
The Rev. Charles Geisler
The Rev. Roger Martin
The Rev. Charles Murn
The Rev. David Parker

Also
The Rev. Janice Palm,
Essex County
The Rev. William Pattison,
Renssealer County
Dr. Arleon Kelly,
NY State Council of Churches

Advertisement, "Clergy Support Planned Parenthood Plan for Glens Falls Abortion Services," April 26, 1992, which appeared in the *Glens Falls Post Star*. (Reprinted courtesy of Planned Parenthood Mohawk Hudson, Inc.)

support—held a major rally in Washington, D.C., on April 9, 1989. Over 400,000 people, including many clergy, turned out for that assembly. Politicians took note. Later that year, when the Supreme Court weakened the *Roe* decision in the *Webster* case by granting the states wider latitude in regulating abortion, the pro-choice community galvanized itself further. This time around, it won some political battles. The governor of Florida called a legislative session to pass a series of antiabortion regulations, but under pro-choice lobbying, including, in particular, the Florida Religious Coalition for Abortion Rights, lawmakers rejected all of them.[35] And in the fall elections for governor of Virginia and New Jersey, right-to-life candidates who were expected to win went down to defeat at the hands of pro-choice candidates who made abortion rights a major issue of their campaigns.[36]

THE RENEWAL OF PLANNED PARENTHOOD

Confronting the radically changed situation of the seventies and eighties, proponents of the Federation would not have been human if they did not mourn the loss of the 1960–1968 period when so many things had gone their way: the pill had been introduced, organized resistance to Planned Parenthood's traditional contraception and sterilization services had been diminishing rapidly, and the addition of many new affiliates had been aided by the new federal government funding. But gone was a future of greater public acceptance, reduced religious opposition, and more improvements in reproductive science and women's health. Instead they were facing greater religious opposition than ever before, an increasingly hostile political climate, and internal organizational consternation over the fact that abortion, such a small part of its services, was fast becoming the only thing that the general public knew about Planned Parenthood.

But perhaps what hampered them most was the awkwardness of having to deal with the *theological* accusations that were being hurled at them. Planned Parenthood is not a religious organization; it is a humane secular service organization that concerns itself with helping women plan and control their reproductive lives. But here staffers were in a situation where their clinics were surrounded by pickets filled with biblical quotes. Moral Majority ministers were denouncing them for not accepting one particular theological position, that life begins at conception, and religious broadcasting stations were suggesting daily that their work was satanic. While they were used to being called immoral, to have church leaders calling them "murderers" was something else entirely.

In its religious intensity, the right-to-life movement was indeed something new in American politics. With the exception of the homosexual issue, most major American political conflicts do not involve religion quite so directly. People who defend the right to keep guns don't quote scripture; they quote the Second Amendment. People on either side of the issues of prison reform, energy independence, the environment, or military defense rarely use theological or religious language. Yet Planned Parenthood was being barraged with it. Their best response in the eighties was to call for separation of church and state. But that argument no longer had the effectiveness that it had in the forties.

America was filling up with religious people who wanted not separation, but greater influence in government. For a long time Protestant fundamentalists had denounced politics and urged their followers to avoid it. Humiliated by their experience in the Scopes "monkey" trial of 1925, where their antievolution views were held up to ridicule by Clarence Darrow and the press, they pulled back from the public scene. In theological terms, they tended to be premillennialists, that is, they believed that the world was in its final days before the second coming of Christ and the last judgment. Accordingly, they viewed the world as a "vale of tears," filled with signs of immorality such as divorce, social dancing, gambling, social conflict, war, and economic depression. Even the church would go astray and be corrupted by the world, but believers who withdrew from worldly ways and tried to live a life of purity would be vindicated in the afterlife.

But the Moral Majority had changed that. Shocked by the Supreme Court decision of 1963 prohibiting prayer in the public schools, and outraged at the legalization of abortion, some born-again Protestants began to believe they should enter the political process and change government programs to reflect *their* values. They did so in great numbers, and as the result of many elections in the eighties, Congress and the state legislatures were becoming dominated by people who opposed much of the work of Planned Parenthood.

Countering these ominous developments was the steady rise of feminism through the seventies and, at a somewhat slower pace, the eighties. The struggle for the equal rights amendment, affirmative action legislation, sexual harassment policies, and programs such as Title 9 were transforming many of the old sexist policies of American culture. Without the feminist movement Planned Parenthood would never have chosen the person they chose as director in 1978. After fumbling around for a few years with a series of leadership changes, the Federation came up with one of the most skilled leaders in late-twentieth-century American social life. In that year, Faye Wattleton, a thirty-four-year-old African-American woman was serving as director of Planned Parenthood of Akron, Ohio. PPFA offered her the top job and she took it. From 1978 to 1991 she re-energized the movement and brought it back to its feminist roots. Despite much of the organization's initial resistance to change, she was propelled forward by the fact that the antichoice character of the presidency of Ronald Reagan frightened so many Americans with pro-choice sentiments that money flowed to Planned Parenthood in impressive quantities.

Faye Wattleton used the funds to go on the offensive and run large bold newspaper ads that took on the religious critics directly. One such ad on sexuality education said "Preaching Hasn't Stopped Unwanted Teen Age Pregnancy. Maybe Teaching Might." Other ads also hammered home the dangers of ignoring the arson and violence being directed toward women's clinics. She took an organization still emerging from a complacent era and woke it up. She represented diversity and she brought a lot of it to an organization that was not ethnically, but temperamentally, still "Waspy." She personified and encouraged a return to female leadership of the organization. She had energy to burn and that was never more obvious than when she entered the media world. She was a TV phenomenon. Appearing on Phil Donohue's show and many of its imitators, she overcame her opponents with hard facts and infectious good humor. By the time she stepped down in 1991, she had, with the help of many feminists, transformed the organization.[37]

But even Faye Wattleton had not done a great deal with supportive clergy. During this period there was no real connection between clergy and Planned Parenthood either as a group within the Federation (as they were in the fifties and sixties) or as a related group doing similar work (such as the Clergy Consultation on Abortion). But that was about to change.

In the early 1990s, Paul Drisgula, director of the Planned Parenthood based in Schenectady, New York, and one of the most respected CEOs in the Federation, told people at the national PPFA office in New York about the work of the Adirondack Religious Coalition for Choice in his area. He encouraged the national office to think seriously about involving the clergy. As a result I was invited to join the national PPFA Board in October 1992. The national board is a diverse body of thirty-six people from all levels of the organization and all parts of the country. The tone of the board was still overwhelmingly secular, but some board members were quite religious. They could see the rationale for clergy support.

Caren Spruch, director of the Office of Special Projects, Planned Parenthood Federation of America. (Reproduced with permission from Planned Parenthood® Federation of America, Inc.© 2004 PPFA. All rights reserved.)

Rachel Strauber, associate director of the Office of Special Projects, Planned Parenthood Federation of America, speaking at the 2001 Annual PPFA Conference in Dallas, Texas. (Reproduced with permission from Planned Parenthood® Federation of America, Inc.© 2004 PPFA. All rights reserved.)

In a short time, the board allowed some clergy work to go forward. Staff support came from the Office of Special Projects, headed by Caren Spruch. Her main tasks had been working with Republicans for Choice and celebrities. Now she had to learn all the arcane mysteries of Protestant denominationalism. She turned out to be a genius at it. By 1994 her office was publishing a newsletter, *Clergy Voices.* She set up a Clergy Advisory Board that began to draw together a coherent movement out of all of the scattered clergy organizations that were found in many of the 164 Planned Parenthood affiliates.[38] Some of the experience gained by the work of the Adirondack Religious Coalition could now be duplicated at the national level. The focus would be the same, theological statements and public advocacy.

In 1998 another natural organizer, Rachel Strauber, took over the clergy work in the Office of Special Projects. It was her idea to set up a prayer breakfast at the annual national PPFA conference. By the year 2000 it was the event that drew the highest approval rating in attendee evaluations.[39] Speakers like Dan Maguire, author of *Sacred Choices,* and the Reverend Paul Wogoman, pastor of Foundry Methodist Church in Washington, D.C., were effective in demonstrating the religious dimensions of what Planned Parenthood was doing. Even the most secular of those at Planned Parenthood began to note the significant number of religious people who gave heartfelt support to the work of the Federation. In effect, after a twenty-year lapse, the National Clergymen's Council (minus the "men's") was back at work.

The Paradox of the Early Post-*Roe* Period: Opposition to Legal Abortion by Churches That Had Ignored Illegal Abortion

From 1973 to 1992, as clergy struggled to understand the power and the extent of the antiabortion movement, certain realities became a part of both political life and clergy consciousness. It was abundantly clear this time that the religious hostility toward Planned Parenthood and other women's clinics was vastly greater than in the earlier struggles over the distribution of contraceptives. During the Sanger era of the thirties and forties, bodies such as the Mormon Church tended to disagree with the practice of birth control, but I could find no evidence of a vigorous Mormon campaign against it. Much the same was true of the Southern Baptists. State-run birth control clinics had been set up in the South in the thirties. Again I could find scant evidence of Baptist displeasure.[40] But in the modern era the addition

of these two denominations plus many smaller fundamentalist denominations to the Roman Catholic forces meant that the religious opposition to
Planned Parenthood was truly enormous

The difficulties experienced in earlier Planned Parenthood clergy victories like the New York Hospital dispute in 1958 (chapter 4) or the Maryland
welfare conflict (chapter 5) now looked almost genteel by comparison. In
the past police had raided Margaret Sanger's Clinical Research Bureau, but
it had not been bombed or besieged by large groups of anti–birth control
picketers. In that earlier time, Planned Parenthood and its supportive clergy
had sought justice by overcoming unjust laws or bureaucratic regulations.
Now the law was on Planned Parenthood's side, but the law itself was under
attack. As clergy sought ways to deal with this new reality, they spent a lot
of time in their theological discussions trying to understand and come to
terms with the exact nature of the religious opposition to abortion and,
specifically, opposition aimed at Planned Parenthood.

There had always been a certain amount of principled opposition to abortion. Dr. Paul Ramsey of Princeton University, a Protestant ethics scholar,
had written extensively on the subject in the fifties and sixties.[41] He opposed
abortion. He carried on a long-running debate about it with Christian
ethicists holding opposing views such as the Reverend Joseph Fletcher, an
Episcopal priest who was the father of "situation ethics." Other prominent
Protestant theologians such as Karl Barth and Dietrich Bonhoeffer had also
condemned it. And to be sure, the right-to-life movement includes many
principled individuals who are deeply troubled by abortion and believe it
should be illegal or at least highly regulated.

But those few ethicists and individual opponents of abortion could not
account for this amazingly powerful right-to-life movement that had been
built by large religious institutions. And there was a strange paradox in this
movement: American society was seeing a torrent of opposition to legal
abortion from these churches when these same institutions appeared to
have made relatively little public effort to stop illegal abortion.

Neither in the literature nor in the actions of the antiabortion churches
could I find signs of any great public effort to prevent illegal abortions in
the pre-1960 period. For example, a survey of the *Catholic Periodical Index*
from 1900 to 1960 reveals that in that entire sixty-year period there were
only 72 articles on abortion, an average of little more than one article
per year. (By comparison, in 1973 there were 257 articles on the subject.)
The older articles were mostly confined to attacks on the small number of
"therapeutic" abortions that were sometimes allowed in hospitals. They

gave relatively little attention to the criminal procedures that made up 90 to 95 percent of the abortions actually being done in that era.[42]

The few articles in Catholic sources that touched on illegal abortions made it abundantly clear that some in the church were aware of the high number of abortions that occurred before abortion was made legal in 1973. In 1934 one Catholic publication suggested that in some places there was one abortion for every two births, a high rate indeed.[43] A 1940 article by a Catholic physician, quoted approvingly in *Theological Studies*, estimated that 500,000 to 1,500,000 abortions were being performed in the United States each year.[44] In 1945 the Very Reverend Edmund M. Burke, chancellor of the Archdiocese of Chicago, told the Catholic Lawyers Guild that their was an "astronomical increase in criminal abortions which easily run into the hundreds of thousands every year."[45] Even the *Catholic Encyclopedia* of 1967 declared that there were more than 15 abortions for every 100 live births in the United States, a percentage that would mean that at least 564,000 illegal abortions were performed each year in the mid-sixties.[46] Adjusting for population increases, that is not qualitatively different from the abortion rate today.

Much the same silence was present in the Southern Baptists in these pre-*Roe* decades. Here too I could find no significant mention of abortion. None in the *Annual Reports of the Southern Baptist Convention* from 1950 to 1970 or in the *Southern Baptist Periodical Index* prior to 1971. Even the editions of the *Southern Baptist Encyclopedia* prior to 1960 make no mention of it. Yet criminal abortion was probably no rarer in the South than in the North in the pre-*Roe* days. Most Baptist preachers were not naïve; they knew what was going on in their cities and towns. While resolutions on alcohol were plentiful at their annual meetings I could locate no resolution condemning abortion during the Depression, World War II, and the first decade of the postwar years. The high rate of criminal abortion before 1960 seemed to produce no concerted sustained public opposition on the part of these churches. It's a curious history for institutions that today see abortion as the gravest of social problems.

Before *Roe v. Wade*, many cities like Portland, Baltimore, Detroit, and Chicago had abortion practitioners who operated more or less openly. Some had offices in downtown buildings.[47] It would not have been hard to find out who they were and what they were doing. Had Roman Catholic or Southern Baptist churches carried out an organized campaign against these illegal abortionists, these practitioners would have been defenseless. Where then were the pickets, the demonstrators, the "Crisis Pregnancy Centers"?

Even when the Clergy Consultation Service on Abortion was formed in 1967, the Diocese of New York City did not make any public criticism. That pattern was. true of almost every city where the Clergy Consultation operated. Churches today that denounce pro-choice clergy were relatively silent in that time. We are left to ask why.

Given this historical disconnect, many pro-choice clergy have come to the conclusion that the "abortion issue" is not ultimately about abortion. It is about the role of women. The churches who complain most bitterly about *Roe v. Wade* are the very denominations that bar women from their ministry and priesthood. It is hard to escape the conclusion that these anti-abortion churches only became truly outraged when women gained the *legal* right to decide on an abortion. Illegal abortion was given mostly verbal condemnation. But when women gained a power they had never had before, then legal abortion was seen as the crime of the century.

As this understanding of the situation became more common among clergy activists on social justice issues, more of them became supportive of Planned Parenthood. Regardless of the complexities of the abortion issue, some clergy saw that this current political struggle was about justice. One could not disconnect the other rights of women from their reproductive rights. The right to control one's own body made all the other rights possible.

Ultimately then, despite all the rhetoric about the "right to life," it remains a question of social justice. What Planned Parenthood clinics faced in the 1980s was different in intensity, but no different in form from the conflicts of the past—it was a struggle against those who would limit the rights of women in the name of natural law, scripture, fetal rights, or God. Past religious discriminations had devastated women's lives. Thousands of women had suffered and died because they were denied effective contraceptives. If the antiabortion movement were to achieve its goals, the consequences for women would be tragic. This awareness gave a special urgency to the involvement of pro-choice clergy. An increasing number of clergy felt that the claim of the sacred for the right-to-life movement should not go unchallenged. Once again it would have to be pro-choice clergy and theologians who challenged such a claim.

The immediate post-*Roe* period gave a new generation of clergy an education in the dangers of excessive religious zeal in our social and political life. But despite all that had happened, no one foresaw that a much worse time was coming.

CHAPTER 9

Deadly Violence and the Renewal of Clergy Support

Christian beware . . .
To vote for Bill Clinton is to sin against God

—(Anonymous election pamphlet, Autumn, 1992)

THOSE REMARKABLE WORDS APPEARED in a flyer distributed widely in the last few weeks of the 1992 presidential campaign. They revealed the influential presence of a part of our society that feels that it can tell us the will of God right down to the question of which candidate to vote for in a national public election. Few things are more dangerous than such absolute certainty, and in 1993 we were about to begin a decade when a few devout but unstable minds would demonstrate the ultimate irony—murder in the name of "life."

President Bill Clinton was the first pro-choice president to be elected to office since President Carter in 1976. He was far more committed to the issue than his Democratic predecessor. In the first few days after his inaugural in January 1993, he signed measures reversing twelve years of presidential antiabortion measures. To many in the right-to-life movement he must have appeared the herald of doom. On January 22, 1993, the twentieth anniversary of the *Roe v. Wade* decision—when the two previous antiabortion presidents would have been giving a telephone pledge of support to the annual antiabortion rally in Washington—this president was entertaining Planned Parenthood and other pro-choice leaders in the White House and signing a series of executive orders that would undo much of what the right-to-life forces had achieved in the previous twenty years. The "gag rule," the Mexico City policy, and other antiabortion policies were either reversed or completely eliminated on that day.[1] Far worse even than these setbacks was the realization that this new president would now appoint

Clergy and other escorts assisting Planned Parenthood of Southeastern Pennsylvania during antiabortion demonstrations in the summer of 2000. (Photo courtesy of Rachel Strauber.)

pro-choice justices to the Supreme Court. For years the antiabortion movement had made steady progress toward their dream of a court that would
reverse *Roe v. Wade*. That original decision had been 7 to 2, but each new
Court appointment had narrowed that majority. Decisions in abortion cases
had been dropping to 6 to 3, then 5 to 4, and, in the 1989 *Webster* case, 5 to
4 against the interests of choice. In the *Casey* decision of June 1992, the
Court had further narrowed *Roe* but upheld it by a 5 to 4 margin. It was
looking as though one more antiabortion justice would someday overturn
it. Or so it seemed to the antiabortion movement. Now that dream was
going to be set back by years. For a dangerous few, these dismal prospects
were finally to bring the unthinkable.

THE BEGINNING OF RELIGIOUS EXECUTIONS

In March 1993, at a women's clinic in Pensacola, Florida, Dr. David Gunn,
the physician who performed abortions at the clinic, was coming in from
his car when a man walked across the parking lot and calmly shot him in
the back. He died instantly. The killer was Michael Griffin, a deeply religious
but very troubled man who seemed to believe he had done something
which God would approve. The previous Sunday at an Assembly of God
church outside Pensacola he had prayed publicly that Dr. Gunn would
accept Jesus as his savior and stop doing abortions.

To much of the press this act seemed to be just an escalation of the
existing pattern of arson, bombings, and harassment. But to many thoughtful people, another line had been crossed. While people might have been
inadvertently killed in any of the bombings and arsons, this was different.
This was premeditated. In biblical terms, Michael Griffin "lay in wait" for
Dr. Gunn.

Seventeen months later, in July 1994, a defrocked minister of the Presbyterian Church in America named Paul Hill went to the same clinic in
Pensacola and with a 12-gauge shotgun fatally shot Dr. John Britton, who
had replaced Dr. Gunn as the clinic physician, and James Barrett, 74, a
retired Air Force lieutenant colonel who was serving as an escort. He also
shot in the arm June Barrett, James's wife. On December 30 of that tragic
year, a young man named John Salvi went into the Planned Parenthood
clinic in Brookline, Massachusetts, and fatally shot Shannon Lowney, a
clinic receptionist. That morning he had already murdered Leanne Nichols
at another women's clinic. By the end of 1998, there would be two other
deaths. An off-duty policeman, Officer Robert Sanderson, was killed when

a bomb destroyed the clinic he was guarding in Birmingham, Alabama, in January 1998. A nurse at the clinic, Emily Lyons, was almost killed. Finally, on a Sabbath evening in October 1998, Dr. Barnett Slepian of Buffalo was shot and killed by a sniper, James Kopp, in front of his family in his kitchen.

Some clergy saw something in these tragedies that secular commentators overlooked. They represented a new phenomenon in American social life, at least something that hadn't been seen since seventeenth-century Salem: these were religious executions. The defendants in Salem were not killed because of *their* religion, but because of the religious beliefs of the people who condemned them and then executed them. They weren't witches, but some people had a religious belief that they were. Such executions demonized women so that society would maintain power and control over them. And similarly in these modern events, the doctors and people working in the clinics were not murderers, but because their assailants believed they were and further believed that killing them was obedience to the will of God, they were executed. Following the murder of Dr. Gunn, twenty-five men issued a statement titled "Defensive Action" in which they defended what Michael Griffin had done. And after John Salvi was arrested in Virginia, a group of his supporters hung out a banner which said, "God bless you, John Salvi."[2]

Secular media are often uncomfortable writing about religion, and so they seemed unable to see that a religious intolerance notorious in history—and easily seen in other parts of the world—was beginning to appear in the United States. It was the awareness of a malignant force. Because of that force clergy were now, for the first time in Planned Parenthood's history, conducting memorial services for women and men who had been killed solely because they were doing the sacred work of providing justice for women.

A MEMORIAL SERVICE AT THE CATHEDRAL OF ST. JOHN THE DIVINE

When the murders occurred at the Brookline Planned Parenthood clinic, Planned Parenthood clergy were ready to respond. Following the earlier shootings in Florida many rabbis and ministers had already led or participated in memorial services for Dr. Gunn, Dr. Britton, and James Barrett. In January 1995, soon after Shannon Lowney and Leanne Nichols were murdered, the dean of the Cathedral of St. John the Divine in New York City, the Very Reverend James Parks Morton, offered to make the cathedral available to Planned Parenthood so that the clergy could hold a service of remembrance for these two women. The Clergy Advisory Board accepted the offer and on the afternoon of January 22, 1995, we held a service that brought together both the religious and the secular pro-choice worlds in the largest cathedral in America.

It is still hard to describe the service and the atmosphere surrounding it. On the one hand there was a certain calm that one felt when one stood in the Cathedral of St. John the Divine. It has always been a powerful symbol of religious reassurance to its neighborhood. Other New York City buildings would come and go, but the massive presence of the cathedral suggested that God was both present and constant. But there was also a terrible violence loose in the country. Four people had been murdered at clinics within the last seven months. Furthermore, it was only a locked door that probably kept John Salvi from killing a large number of people at a clinic in Virginia shortly before his capture. These realities were very much on our minds as the clergy waited to put on our robes for the service while bomb-sniffing dogs checked the room we would use. People were somber, but resolved not only to honor the lives of those who had been killed but also to move people to action.

Coming together to conduct the service that Sunday were some of the leading clergy of the city: the Reverend James Forbes of Riverside Church (the church where the Reverend Harry Emerson Fosdick had championed Planned Parenthood sixty years earlier); Rabbi Balfour Brickner, rabbi emeritus of the Stephen Wise Free Synagogue and a former member of the National Board of Planned Parenthood; national religious leaders such as the Reverend Joan Brown Campbell, general secretary of the National Council of Churches of Christ in the USA; Denise Taft Davidoff, moderator, Unitarian Universalist Association; leading feminists such as Gloria Steinem; and all of the national staff of Planned Parenthood.[3]

The service was opened by the dean of the cathedral, who said, "Organized religion in America is full square solidly in support on this issue." As the next speaker I noted the "seemingly bottomless fear of the change that would be brought about by the coming of full justice for women." The Reverend James Forbes said, "God summons us to responsible partnership, to make choices amid the moral ambiguities of life. . . . God holds before us daily the challenge to choose the best . . . using our best judgment, reflective of the best wisdom available, and the best moral resolve of which we are capable."[4]

And Nicki Nichols Gamble, president of the Planned Parenthood League of Massachusetts (the affiliate that operated the clinic in Brookline where

Shannon Lowney was killed) spoke the words that brought forth the full dimension of this tragedy: "Shannon was a bright shining star whose clarity and dedication gleamed in the midst of her unusually talented and skilled associates. On December 30th, the world lost a young woman who was making it a better place to live. The deaths of Shannon Lowney and Leanne Nichols are a heartbreaking reminder of what happens when fanaticism and terrorism run amok. And surely that evil ought to have been sufficient enough for any day."[5] Remarks by Gloria Steinem, Denise Davidoff, and Joan Brown Campbell followed, and the service was closed by Rabbi Brickner, who said, "We want those who represent us to take out a contract on the outrageous behavior of mad people and restore a covenant of peace with America. Only then will there be peace. And let the voices of the clergy be heard."[6] In the months and years following that service, those voices, the voices of clergy who had been deeply affected by these shootings, were to be heard and heard often.

A Renewed Commitment

In the wake of the murders and with a renewed sense of urgency, Clergy Advisory Board members set to work across the country to reestablish the old tradition of public clergy support for Planned Parenthood and the entire pro-choice movement. Because Planned Parenthood has always had to focus so much on the present, it has tended to neglect its past. Much of the history of clergy support for the Federation had been forgotten. But the clergy organizers believed that this history could be regained and that the effort to do so was worth it, because in that history were resources and traditions that could be immensely helpful in the current struggles. Those clergy chosen to serve on the Advisory Board soon realized that their first task was to persuade the many constituencies of Planned Parenthood—local boards, clinic execs, staff, national officers—that the *religious* nature of its opposition had to be addressed directly. It was not enough to plead longingly for separation of church and state. Planned Parenthood, must, through its national and local clergy supporters, directly challenge and refute the religious claims of its adversaries. In other words, just as their predecessors had in the past, clergy supporters of Planned Parenthood would have to demonstrate the ironic reality that this much criticized organization was usually closer to the sacred work of justice than the religious voices that attacked it.

A number of clergy cohorts were involved in this effort. Though aging, there were still dozens of veterans of the 1967–1973 Clergy Consultation on

Abortion who shared their experience and memory. Others, such as the Reverend James Lawson and Rabbi Brickner, were activists in the civil rights movement and saw the struggle for reproductive freedom as involving the same issues of discrimination that were the focus of that earlier effort. Then there were the younger clergy, now involving large numbers of female ministers and rabbis, who had no memory of past battles but who brought their own personal experience of gender discrimination to their work with Planned Parenthood.

The clergy began to write. Rabbis and ministers restated the solid theological and biblical basis for women's reproductive rights. In an article "Justice, Justice Shall You Pursue" in the *Reconstructionist Journal*, Rabbi Cheryl Jacobs, a vice-president for public affairs at Planned Parenthood Hudson Peconic, detailed the specific Jewish scriptural basis for her presence there, "In truth, what I, as a rabbi, along with the other staff and volunteers at Planned Parenthood, do are the *mitzvoth* (commandments) of *pekuach nefoesh* (preserving life) and *gemilut hasadim* (deeds of lovingkindness). We empower women who feel they are voiceless, and we preserve and improve the quality of life for all of our clients."[7] Rabbi Jacobs was doing for a new generation what the Reverend James Clarke had done in St. Louis many years earlier (see chapter 6), making clear the religious roots of the work of Planned Parenthood.

Other clergy writers critiqued the simplistic and rigid ethics of the antiabortion movement. The Reverend Roger Buchanan used the most traditional biblical images to critique the right-to-life movement's refusal to take responsibility for the consequences of its position and—above all—its lack of concern for the moral agency of women. He said:

> The Biblical tradition also acknowledges that we human beings find it difficult to restrain ourselves from making idols that represent the divine. One of the early stories of conflict in this regard is that of the Golden Calf. . . . I suggest that the sacred fetus is the modern equivalent of the Golden Calf. The sacred fetus has become an absolute around which a host of decisions are made. And these decisions become progressively more destructive. If the fetus is sacred, the mother is subservient, a view that is destructive to women.[8]

The Federation responded positively to the renewed clergy presence. Worship services and prayer breakfasts were instituted at the Federation's annual national conference. As more and more men and women in clergy collars began showing up at meetings, for the first time in a long time the organization began to realize the extent of the clergy presence in all areas of its structure—as board members, chaplains, affiliate CEOs, clinic counselors. Here are some examples of clergy who carry out their ministry within Planned Parenthood.

DIVERSITY OF CLERGY ROLES IN PLANNED PARENTHOOD

Chaplain at Planned Parenthood

In 1995 the Reverend Lynn NewHeart, a minister of the Disciples Church, was serving as chaplain of the Kansas City Planned Parenthood. Most of her work was counseling women who were trying to make a decision about abortion or simply listening to the women who had thought long and hard (the majority) and who had made their decision, but who welcomed the chance to share their feelings with a clergyperson.

Writing in *Clergy Voices*, she spoke of how, in contrast to the hostile pickets, she tried to provide patients a more compassionate view of their situation:

> Whether listening to the radicals outside our building or sitting in the pew of the local religious right church, I am besieged by the images of God and God's will that portray a vindictive, narrow-focused and misogynist deity. Within this theological framework there is no room for discussing the complexity of issues inherent in the decision to have a child or not. Having an ordained chaplain on site is a concrete way of saying that this particular theological viewpoint is not the only viewpoint, and that many mainline segments of the universal church as well as other religious traditions, do not believe in this image of God.[9]

She also spoke of the complex feelings experienced after abortion. For most (as many studies have shown) it was relief, for a few, it was guilt. And for many it was grief, the same grief often felt after a miscarriage. She was privy to some quite difficult situations. "Every so often (too often) there is the 14-year-old who was raped by her stepfather. Or the 33-year-old with four children, no job, and an abusive husband. Or the happily married couple who has been trying for five years to get pregnant and just received horrific results from the amniocentesis. All of these people, in their own way, are wondering about the existence, or the presence, of the justice of God."[10] She concluded her article with a statement of her gratitude at the privilege of being "invited into the deeply intimate and spiritually sacred space where women and men, like Jacob, wrestle with the 'holy.' . . . May God continue to bless my ministry here."[11]

A Clergy Planned Parenthood Board President

In 1994 the Reverend Stephen Mather, pastor of a Presbyterian church in Orange County, California, became the board president of Planned Parenthood of Orange and San Bernadino counties. Suddenly, in the late spring of that year, antiabortion demonstrators gathered outside his church. For the next six months, five to thirty-five pickets appeared each Sunday to protest his serving as a Planned Parenthood board president. They circulated a flyer in the neighborhood asking people to confront him directly and share their outrage that he had accepted such a position. The flyer said that he had disgraced the body of Christ. Members of his congregation were told that they were going to hell, that they and their pastor had blood on their hands. On one occasion a threat seemed serious enough that the police requested that Mather wear a bulletproof vest in the pulpit.

Rejecting the claims of the protesters, the Presbytery of Los Ranchos, an association of the Presbyterian churches of the region, passed a resolution commending the congregation "for its steadfast commitment to its principles and its gracious endurance of an uncomfortable situation."

The experience led Mather to wonder why he was so dangerous. In time he concluded that "to put it simply, I have shattered the illusion that all religious people share the same beliefs."[12] Each Sunday, as he watched the demonstrators insist that he and the Presbyterian Church must obey their demands, his commitment deepened; he became an activist who could see the larger implications of what was happening. He saw that "the issue is not simply reproductive rights, but essential human rights. What's at stake is the right to practice the freedoms guaranteed by the U.S. Constitution."[13] Stephen Mather was scarcely alone in his experience. Churches all across the country which aligned themselves with Planned Parenthood or whose members worked as doctors at Planned Parenthood were visited by the same kind of demonstrators.

Out of his experience, Mather was moved to set down a biblical understanding of why such opposition is a constant reality for Planned Parenthood. He saw the work of the Federation as a movement to create a new alternative reality that would embody more justice for people currently left out. Such a vision is what inspired the prophets and, in modern times, the Reverend Martin Luther King. But such visions always evoke passionate opposition.

[Our opponents] . . . recognize that the Planned Parenthood mission represents an alternative way to promote a new humanity that is, ironically, more consistent with justice models permeating the Bible, than they would care to admit. . . . As Margaret Sanger realized and as those who have been cut down in the course of this ministry make clear, this is a risky business. Today's opponents may be gone tomorrow, but what they represent remains—fear and ignorance that betray a lack of trust in human beings to use their knowledge to build better lives.[14]

Since 1998 Mather has been a member of the national board of Planned Parenthood.

A Southern Baptist Clergy Counselor at Planned Parenthood

In late February 2000 the Virginia legislature was on the verge of passing a law requiring a twenty-four-hour waiting period for women seeking an abortion. The proposed law would also require mandated counseling (which could only be given by a doctor or a nurse) on adoption alternatives, the availability of financial help for needy mothers, "the probable anatomical and physiological characteristics" of a fetus from the time of conception to full term, the possible detrimental psychological effects of abortion, and finally, "any relevant information on the possibility of the fetus' survival."[15]

Everything was in place for the bill's passage until the Reverend Beth McLemore; the coordinator of pastoral education and counseling for Planned Parenthood of the Blue Ridge came before the legislature's Health and Education Committee. Most of McLemore's work involved providing counseling to women seeking abortions. And with her testimony, everything changed.

Beth McLemore grew up in North Roanoke County and her spiritual home was the Green Ridge Baptist Church, where, at age nine, she made public profession that Christ was her savior. When she was sixteen she came to believe that God was calling her to the ministry. She entered Southwestern Baptist Theological Seminary in Fort Worth, Texas, and graduated in 1996 with two master's degrees, one in religious education and the other in marriage and family counseling.

Ordination came when she applied for work at the Pastoral Counseling Center in Roanoke. That facility required its counselors to be ordained. In the Southern Baptist church, it is the local congregation that ordains members into the ministry. On November 16, 1997, she was ordained into the "active ministry."

One year later, David Nova, executive director of Planned Parenthood of the Blue Ridge, was actively looking for an ordained person to talk to women who wanted to examine the spiritual dimensions of their reproductive decisions, especially the decision on abortion. Recognizing that many, if not most, of the patients at Planned Parenthood were Southern Baptists, he felt it was logical to look for a Baptist minister. He heard about Beth McLemore. Soon afterward, he hired her. She began work at the Planned Parenthood affiliate in early January 1999 as coordinator of pastoral education and counseling, an education position that assigned her the mission to reach out and work with churches, Bible study groups, ministers, and youth groups. In working with patients she was not introduced to them as a minister, but when patients expressed concerns about the religious and moral implications of their decision, she made a connection.[16]

In his respect for the religious convictions of the women coming to his clinic, David Nova was operating within the long tradition of close collaboration between Planned Parenthood and religious institutions. He was quoted in the *Roanoke Times* as follows: "There are pregnant women who are deeply conflicted. . . . They feel an abortion is the best decision for them and their family, but that choice contradicts much of what they have heard on Sunday mornings. . . . [At the same time they] are unwilling or unable to approach their pastor regarding a sexual matter or unplanned pregnancy. Beth can reach those women in ways that the rest of our staff cannot."[17]

Beth McLemore offers ample biblical grounds for both her ministry and her special mission. She cites Paul's image in First Corinthians, the attempt to be all things to all people. She also refers to the famous meeting between Jesus and the Samaritan woman at the well in the Gospel of John. In that encounter Jesus was taking his message into a place that was shunned, if not actually cursed. He was also speaking with a woman, something many Jewish leaders of the time would not do. She put it this way, "He was not standing on the sidelines—or on the sidewalks" (referring to the protesters). Finally she uses the question that many Christians use: "I ask myself what would Jesus do? Would he keep his distance? Would he utter hurtful statements? Or would he sit beside these women in their moments of pain and need? Would he accept her? Would he minister to her in any way she needs?"[18]

On February 20, 2000, such views brought her before the Health and Education Committee of the Virginia Senate, where she gave this testimony against a proposed bill that would require a twenty-four-hour waiting period for each woman seeking an abortion:

I am Reverend Bethany McLemore. I am a Southern Baptist minister. . . . I am a professional counselor with a Christian-based clinical practice. I am also the Coordinator of Pastoral Education and Counseling for Planned Parenthood of the Blue Ridge, and on Tuesdays for the past 14 months I have provided pre-abortion counseling to many women seeking abortions. I am here to testify in opposition to House Bill 1482. . . . House Bill 1482 presumes that the legislature somehow needs to protect women from the likes of Planned Parenthood and other abortion providers. Does it surprise the Committee members that a Southern Baptist minister provides counseling in an abortion clinic? Or that there are at least two other ministers in Virginia providing pre-abortion counseling? Does it surprise you that full adoption services are available on site at our clinic or that we provide 30-minute counseling sessions to the partners, friends, and family members who accompany abortion patients to our clinic? If you are surprised, then you do not fully understand the caring and concerned manner in which abortions are provided in Virginia.

Our system for ensuring that all abortion patients have freely given their consent and are fully informed about this procedure reflects the collective wisdom of our staff and our focus on the needs of our patients. I respectfully submit that the honorable members of the Senate will never be able to protect or empower women the way Planned Parenthood does. If you pass this bill you will only harm women in Virginia by disrupting the thoughtful screening programs that exist among clinics throughout the Commonwealth.

Thank you for granting me this opportunity to testify today.[19]

We can't be sure that her experience was the persuasive factor, but in a truly unexpected outcome, the committee voted against the bill 8–7. The victory was short-lived, however. The bill did pass in the 2001 legislative session.

A Clergy Chief Executive

Almost since the earliest days clergy have served as directors of Planned Parenthood clinics. One director estimates that when he joined Planned Parenthood in 1977 about 10 percent of the clinic directors were ministers or rabbis.[20] Today one of the clergy in that role is the Reverend Mark Pawlowski, CEO of Planned Parenthood of South Central Michigan and a member of Planned Parenthood's national Clergy Advisory Board. A graduate of Beloit College and Union Theological Seminary in New York City, he began his ministry at the famous 4,500-member First Community Church of Columbus, Ohio, the very church served by the Reverend Roy Burkhart, a stalwart of the forties Planned Parenthood National Clergyman's Advisory

Council (see chapter 3.) He went on to serve two more churches, First Presbyterian of Greenwich, Connecticut, and the First Presbyterian Church of
Three Rivers, Michigan. Like his many clergy predecessors, he saw no conflict between being a minister and directing a Planned Parenthood affiliate.
Nor has he ever hesitated to bring his biblical and theological knowledge to
the defense of Planned Parenthood.[21]

The affiliate that hired him was Planned Parenthood of South Central
Michigan, an affiliate that knew a lot about enduring through hard times.
On the night of December 1, 1986, four men went up on the roof of the
seven-year-old Planned Parenthood clinic on Michigan Avenue. According
to the police report, they drilled holes through the roof over the administrative center and poured a mixture of kerosene and Coleman fuel into the
offices. After setting it on fire, they fled into the night. The damage was
extensive, but the east wing of the building was protected by a firewall and
it was saved. No one was ever charged with the crime. Within six hours
the affiliate had started to restore some order. Within nine days they were
operating in a different facility. In the next fourteen months they raised
$750,000, and in February 1988, they reopened.[22]

Shortly after Mark Pawlowski went to work for this resolute affiliate he
received a letter from a skeptical young relative who wanted to know why
a "real" minister would direct an organization that provided reproductive
health services that included abortion. He found the words "hard to hear,"
but simply pointed out that he was following the spirit indicated in the words
of Jesus following his baptism: "The Spirit of the Lord is upon me because
he has anointed me to preach good news to the poor, to proclaim release
to the captive, recovery of sight to the blind, to set at liberty those that are
possessed, and to proclaim the acceptable year of the Lord" (Luke 4:18–19).
Furthermore, he confronted the implied criticism with a clear statement of
his theological and biblical conviction, "I believe that God gives life—at first
breath. I think an honest discussion about the Jewish revelation of 'nephesh'
(the Hebrew for 'God's breath of life') and the significance of birth might
help all sides. I prefer this perspective because I do not think I could come
up with a rational theological explanation for the approximately forty percent of all fertilized eggs that are naturally aborted."[23]

Pawlowski's ministry is marked by a number of distinctive traits. First, he
has a comprehensive view of the role of birth control, relating it to problems
of the environment. He believes that "with a population of 6 billion and
still growing in a world that has abused the earth instead of tending it
for the creator, there is much to do. We must commit to living out a more

inclusive moral imperative . . . caring about others, ourselves, and our endangered planet and acting that way."[24]

A second trait of his ministry is his search for common ground with the opposition. He believes that two examples of such areas of agreement are first, supporting a certain role for abstinence in sex education curricula, and second, seeing adoption as a responsible choice. He invites all community organizations "to seek common ground with Planned Parenthood in areas where joining forces will work to enhance the quality of life for people in need."[25] On one occasion he invited the local paper, the *Kalamazoo Gazette*, to bring the two sides together in a conference to seek common ground.[26] On other occasions Pawlowski has used editorials and newspaper "Viewpoints" to remind people that there is no other organization besides Planned

Standing in support of a Planned Parenthood clinic following an arson attempt are Reverend Mark Pawlowski, CEO of Planned Parenthood of South Central Michigan; Reverend David Van Arsdale of the First Presbyterian Church; Reverend John W. Fisher of Sunnyside United Methodist Church; and Reverend Cynthia L. Black of the Parish Church of Christ the King at the Cathedral. Winter 2001. (Photo courtesy of Bob Lohrmann and Planned Parenthood of South Central Michigan.)

Parenthood that does more to provide family planning education to young women and teens and to provide low-cost, high-quality services that reduce unintended pregnancies and hence the need for abortion. "We are particularly heartened by the reported reduction in the rate of teenage pregnancy. Among adolescents 15 to 17, the six year decline was even more dramatic— from 24 to 15 per 1,000, a 39% decrease! When young people have access to reproductive health care services and medically accurate comprehensive sexuality education, they make responsible choices about personal relationships and sexual activity."[27]

But perhaps the most biblical aspect of his calling is his insistence on speaking frankly and powerfully about the needs of poor women. In April 2001 he testified before the House Committee on Children and Family Health of the Michigan state legislature when it was considering an action to de-fund Planned Parenthood. Pawlowski's words, along with other clergy, caught the right-to-life controlled committee off-guard:

> I doubt that you have had a clergy person, let alone a Presbyterian minister in front of you who was also a CEO of a Planned Parenthood. . . . I hope you will ask yourselves why?
>
> I come before you today even though I believe my appearance has about as much [chance of] success as a snowball lasting all day on the 4th of July in Lansing. I'm not politically naïve. But I had to try. And here are my reasons: First I have to try because there are the almost 70,000 innocent victims of this bill who are overwhelmingly poor and have no voice round this table and who are being held hostage to a campaign of hate and intolerance.
>
> My friends, secondly, this is not the way for Right to Life to get even with Planned Parenthood. I can assure you . . . we know how to survive and balance budgets regardless of adversity. In the past 15 years my agency has been successfully burned to the ground by domestic terrorist fire bombings . . . the most recent attempt being Jan 28th [2001].
>
> So I return to the question of who wins and who loses in this political game? Sadly, it will be poor women. Is revenge that sweet?[28]

With many years of youth work and parish experience, Pawlowski has a commitment to partner with clergy and faith communities across the religious spectrum. He believes that one way for churches to renew themselves is to form partnerships with community-based organizations, like Planned Parenthood, that serve the poor. In Kalamazoo he organized a Clergy Advisory Board with more than twenty members. Its expressed purpose is to build a bridge between faith communities and Planned Parenthood's mission in order to provide resources and perspective to a society badly in need of honest and reliable information about sexuality. Activities of the Clergy Advisory Board in his part of Michigan include an annual ecumenical worship service on the anniversary of *Roe v. Wade*, lobbying, and clergy endorsements of such national campaigns as PPFA's "Statement on Comprehensive Sexuality Education."[29]

Clergy "Extraordinaire"

In any movement, or any board, there are sometimes individuals whose contributions stretch over such a long time and are of such a high quality of insight that they can only be called extraordinary. For the Clergy Advisory Board of the Planned Parenthood Federation of America, that person is Rabbi Balfour Brickner. Beginning his career in Washington, D.C., in the early fifties, he founded Temple Sinai, where he served until 1961. Moving to New York he became an executive for the Union of American Hebrew Congregations. Later he became the senior rabbi of the Stephen Wise Free Synagogue in New York City. In both positions he became deeply involved in all of the major struggles for social justice.

As part of the civil rights movement, Balfour Brickner was jailed in a number of southern cities. As part of the antiwar movement he went to Paris to meet secretly with leaders of the Vietcong. He was in Israel during the Yom Kippur War of 1973, where he reported on events as the Israeli troops crossed into Egypt. In 1982 he was in Nicaragua opposing U.S. policies there. As a radio host he won a Peabody Award, and much of his time has been devoted to the Christian-Jewish dialogue. His books and other writings flow from his life.[30]

But perhaps because he has much the same activist instincts as Margaret Sanger, justice for women has always been at the center of his activism. He has served on the national boards of NARAL, the Religious Coalition for Abortion Rights, and Planned Parenthood. But he has a special affection for Planned Parenthood. Relishing tough assignments, he testified in 1974 before the Senate Subcommittee on Constitutional Amendments. Antiabortion legislators were proposing both a human life amendment that would outlaw abortion and a states' rights amendment that would leave it up to each state. Either would, of course, overthrow the *Roe* ruling. Rabbi Brickner pointed out that in Judaism the fetus was not regarded as a person, and that while some ultra-orthodox authorities were strongly opposed to abortion, they did so in opposition to the vast weight of historical Jewish legal opinion.

Congressional questioners pressed him hard on the rights of the fetus but
he would not allow the interests of the mother to be subordinated to the
rights of the fetus.[31]

During all the long years of struggle since 1973, Brickner has lobbied at
both state and national levels, preached many sermons, written innumerable
articles, and attended dozens of gatherings to stand for a form of justice that
includes, not marginalizes, women.

A State Chaplain of Planned Parenthood

In the organizational structure of the United Methodist Church, it is the
bishop who appoints clergy to their positions, even if they are working
for a secular organization. In January 2002, Methodist bishop Elias Galvin
appointed the Reverend Monica Corsaro to a chaplaincy at the Planned
Parenthoods of Washington State. Born in San Francisco but raised in a
rural farming community in Illinois, Corsaro grew up in the Methodist
tradition where she believed, in her words, "she could love life, love God,
and be part of a nurturing community." She knew early on that she was a
feminist and saw no conflict with her faith.

She first encountered the struggle over choice while a student at Illinois
State University. A Christian friend called her to ask if she would be attending the prayer vigil for the unborn that night. Monica, knowing she was pro-
choice, stood there holding the phone, stunned that her friend had made
the assumption that Christian = antichoice. She went to the quad that night,
but was on the other side of the issue. She held candles in a vigil for those
women who had died of illegal abortion.[32]

Since that time Corsaro has been a fervent supporter of choice. While
in seminary at the Iliff School of Theology she drove a vanload of students
from Denver, Colorado, to Washington, D.C., to participate in the 1992
March for Women's Lives sponsored by Planned Parenthood and other
major feminist organizations. In 1994 she took her first church in Spokane,
Washington, and, while serving there, chaired the Clergy Advisory Board
and was a board member of Planned Parenthood of the Inland Northwest.
In 1997 she became the minister of a church in Seattle and in 2000 served
as the director of the Washington State Religious Coalition for Reproductive Choice. In that position she took note that Operation Rescue was planning to come to Wichita, Kansas, to try to close down the long-embattled
clinic of Dr. George Tiller. In 1991 hundreds of demonstrators had failed to
do that and on this tenth anniversary, they would try again.[33] Few places on
earth are hotter than Kansas in the summer. But Corsaro, along with other

pro-choice groups, went to Kansas and organized a national clinic defense during that hot summer of 2001. The protest fizzled out and the clinic stayed open.

As the first state chaplain at Planned Parenthood, Monica Corsaro created a new role for the clergy in the Planned Parenthood movement. It is likely that other state affiliates will seek clergy like her. In her thirties, she represents the latest generation in this long alliance.

Church Partnerships

Finally, there is one more creative "return to the past" that is relinking Planned Parenthood to the world of religion—church partnerships. In chapter 5 we saw, for example, how Planned Parenthood of Maryland set up auxiliary clinics in churches around Baltimore in the sixties. This pattern went on for decades, especially in New England states with anticontraception statutes, as clergy and church members drove Planned Parenthood clients into neighboring states to obtain prescriptions and birth control materials. In that era the Episcopal Church seemed to have a special affection for the work of the Federation. One Episcopal priest in Binghamton, New York told me that his congregation would have asked him to leave if he had not supported the Planned Parenthood clinic in the church.[34]

In 1992 Planned Parenthood resumed its old practice of forming partnerships with congregations. As the Baltimore, St. Louis, and many other affiliates had done in the forties, fifties, and sixties, Planned Parenthood of Metropolitan Washington in 1992 formed a warm relationship with the Mt. Airy Baptist Church in northwest Washington, D.C. They began with classes for parents on how to talk with their teens about sexuality. This initial contact developed into the Planned Parenthood Metropolitan Washington (PPMW) Church Partnership Teen Pregnancy Prevention Program.[35] Famous in its field, the program provides comprehensive sexuality education plus an appreciation of biblical values. Today PPMW has partnership programs that include health fairs and workshops as well as weekly meetings under church auspices, with groups of teens and one group of fourth- to sixth-graders. Now twelve churches are involved. Perhaps the jewel of the program is the Mt. Airy Baptist Church/Sursum Corda outreach program. This is a life skills education program for teens from the Sursum Corda public housing project in Washington, D.C. Directed by a Planned Parenthood outreach educator, this program seeks to give students the skills and the information to make responsible choices in life. Children may enter as young as nine and stay until they are eighteen.[36]

In 1997 Planned Parenthood of Georgia began to develop such religious connections. They reached out to two organizations, the Interdenominational Theological Center (a consortium of six seminaries) and the Concerned Black Clergy, a group of local clergy and activists that met weekly to consider the political issues of the day. Clergy were shy at first, but the Reverend Timothy McDonald, a politically savvy minister, supported the idea and the other clergy joined in. Today that program is flourishing. Planned Parenthood of Georgia has relationships with twenty-five churches involving six denominations—Baptist, Methodist, Pentecostal, Episcopal, Presbyterian, and Church of God in Christ. Planned Parenthood staffs go to the churches, make announcements about current programs, and ask for volunteers.[37]

In 2000 the national office of Planned Parenthood—through its Clergy Project and the special skills and experience of Planned Parenthood of Metropolitan Washington—organized a training for seven affiliates whose CEOs had expressed a strong interest in making the commitment necessary to undertake partnerships with religious institutions in their cities. These affiliates had already established a connection with at least one religious organization and several had programs already under way. In the training sessions, representatives from the affiliates heard from teens who were being served and from the Reverend Larry Greenfield, a consultant helping Planned Parenthood/Chicago Area work with churches in underserved areas in an effort to train parents to become sexuality educators for their own children.

These church partnerships are different in some ways, yet basically similar to the work Planned Parenthood did with so many congregations in earlier decades. Through such linkages, Planned Parenthood is able to reach the women who need its services while congregations find an additional way to give concrete practical form to their mission of compassion.[38]

CONCLUSION: CLASH OF THEOLOGIES

Ultimately the conflict between the opponents of Planned Parenthood and its clergy defenders is a theological one. In contrast to most of the critics, who proceed on the basis of a different theology, clergy supporters of Planned Parenthood, in both their activities and their writings, demonstrate what might loosely be called a form of humane theology. Though these clergy come from different backgrounds and even different religions, their various theologies converge around three specific values: knowledge, experience, and responsibility. Humane theology values knowledge and opposes the suppression of knowledge. The hallmark of the religious opponents from

Cover of the pamphlet advertising the Church Partnership Program of Planned Parenthood of Metropolitan Washington. (Reprinted with permission of Planned Parenthood of
Metropolitan Washington, D.C., and Peter Ferko.)

Sanger's day to the present has generally been to keep women ignorant of knowledge that would give them vastly greater control over their lives and, in some situations, even save their lives. The Comstock laws epitomized this.

Today policies such as the gag rule and abstinence-only sex education withhold knowledge that women and teens desperately need. Although such policies are being put forward with considerable public relations skill, ultimately the proposals of modern opponents are little different from those of Anthony Comstock, who felt he had a perfect right to withhold information on contraception from an entire nation. And while modern religious opponents can't directly outlaw the information, they do try to de-fund any program that does provide it. So it is necessary for clergy like Beth McLemore and Mark Pawlowski to testify to state legislative committees so that Planned Parenthood affiliates can keep giving women the facts they need.

Clergy supporters of the Federation have a great appreciation for the role of human experience in the forming of a humane theology. While respecting scripture as the original source of any authentic Christian or Jewish theology, they believe it must be supplemented by the truth God reveals in the experience of living a human life. Unfortunately religion has its share of sterile theologies, which, by ignoring experience, allow clergy to hover comfortably in the air like a helicopter suspended over the confusing world of cultural change and scientific development. Up there in the air it is easy to make pronouncements about what is and isn't against natural law and what is God's decision about how women are to live. But if that helicopter sets down into the specifics of human lives, into the political turmoil, it is not so easy to pontificate: it is far more important to listen. When, from the thirties to the seventies, clergy started listening to Margaret Sanger, to Planned Parenthood, and to women who spoke about their situations, they stopped telling them how to live and instead offered support. Rabbis and ministers involved in the Clergy Consultation Service on Abortion discovered a whole world of desperate need that altered profoundly both their ministries and their lives. And today, the clergy who work with the clinics as volunteers, escorts, or board members go to the clinics, listen to the staff, and hear about the actual conditions of many women's lives. These clergy acknowledge that the sacred is more often revealed not in abstract pronouncements, but in the experience of human beings trying to deal with the inequities and tragedies of human life.

Finally, Planned Parenthood clergy believe in a theology of responsibility. Religion can, and does, come up with theologies that seem not to consider the consequences of their pronouncements. Protestants who wanted prohibition gave no weight to the fact that they were spawning a criminal empire that corrupted much of the body politic. The same mind-set seems to be true of much of the right-to-life movement. De-funding birth control programs inevitably leads to more unwanted pregnancies (which means more abortions), but no weight is given to that reality. Abstinence-only sex-ed programs ignore the reality that ill-informed and ill-prepared teens may abandon abstinence, become sexually active, and risk pregnancy. Since such a policy is seen as moral and "right," it doesn't matter if it works.

In sharpest contrast, clergy supporting Planned Parenthood believe it is irresponsible to keep information from teens that would help them avoid an unwanted pregnancy; irresponsible to refuse to let a pregnant woman know where she can get an abortion; irresponsible and sexist to let insurers deny coverage for birth control pills while they cover the costs of Viagra; irresponsible to try to ban the abortion pill RU 486; irresponsible for pharmacies to refuse to stock emergency contraception; and profoundly irresponsible for a hospital emergency room to deny emergency contraception to a woman who has been raped. Clergy supportive of Planned Parenthood argue that to do such things is ultimately to prefer a fantasy world to the real world. These clergy believe that a theology of knowledge, experience, and responsibility is a theology of justice that helps real women in the real world. It is such knowledge, experience, and responsibility that are more likely to focus on the effective compassion that all religions proclaim.

Some of these clergy are sustained by what they believe to be realistic hope. In justification of such an attitude they point to the simple truth that the religious opponents of Planned Parenthood have lost battle after battle for the last seventy years. The anti's could not keep the Comstock laws from being declared unconstitutional. They couldn't prevent Planned Parenthood and other birth control clinics from opening offices. They couldn't stop government funding of contraception and—in some states—abortions for poor women. They couldn't keep Planned Parenthood out of the Yellow Pages, out of the public hospitals, out of the state and city welfare offices, out of the welfare councils, and, above all, out of the affections and respect of millions of Americans.

None of this guarantees that the future may not turn against the Federation. Above all else, clergy should be realists. A good seminary education teaches one that history can turn in incredibly destructive directions. Nevertheless, decades of involvement in the sacred work of justice have built a long tradition of support for the work of Planned Parenthood. And thousands of clergy are comfortable in that tradition.

CHAPTER 10

The Future of the Alliance

IN THE SPRING OF 2004 the Planned Parenthood Federation of America announced that it was hiring a national chaplain. The Reverend Ignacio Castuera, a Methodist minister from Los Angeles, was the first person to occupy the position. This step represented an advance over the relationships with the previous clergy advisory boards, because it was a far more visible embodiment of the fact that Planned Parenthood enjoys extensive religious support. Furthermore, when religious attacks occur, the chaplain will be in a unique position to respond to them. The hiring is the latest development in this alliance which has lasted through depression, war, postwar prosperity, the turbulent sixties, and the seemingly endless battles over abortion. Will this alliance continue? At the beginning of a new century, what are the issues that are likely to strain it or strengthen it?

Ironically, some current issues are largely the same old conflicts in modern dress. Instead of the Comstock law, we have the gag rule, but both arise out of the same idea—withholding important health information in order to control women's choices. Can the state silence doctors and laypeople who seek to give women proper medical alternatives? It is the same battle over freedom of speech that led clergy to fight to get contraception into the New York City hospitals (see chapter 4). Where Margaret Sanger's opposition glorified abstinence as the only permissible way for married couples to practice birth control, today's opponents want abstinence-only sex education to be the only sex education American teens can obtain. Where Roman Catholic hospitals used to dismiss doctors who worked with Planned Parenthood, today they merge with secular hospitals and cut off contraceptive, sterilization, and abortion services for women. Where conservatives in

Congress once opposed all government funding for contraceptives, now they seek to cut off Title X, the main form of government aid for birth control, and to stop all government aid for international family planning organizations. The breadth of their activities expresses a determination to chip away at every facet of the structure that embodies women's reproductive rights.

But these visible battles may not be as significant as some subtle long-term cultural shifts. The dominance of market values, changes in the perception of marriage and family, and developments in reproductive technology are three issues that are likely to transform much of what today seems familiar and permanent.

MARKET VALUES AND AMERICAN CULTURE

An insightful description of current society can be found in the book *Wealth and Democracy*, where the longtime economic and political critic Kevin Phillips makes a persuasive case that in modern America we are back in the world of 1902.[1] As in that era, the corporations are riding high, the wealthiest among us increase their wealth astonishingly, and the middle classes find it increasingly hard to do the things that were much easier (send children to college, have one breadwinner per family) in the 1930 to 1980 period.[2] Market values increasingly dominate our cultural discourse. College departments of business that were almost moribund in the sixties now attract droves of students. A national newspaper devotes one of its four sections to "Money." The language of business—brokers, instruments of investment, portfolios, online trading, and mutual funds—dominates our television screens, our daily conversations, and even begins to invade the artistic, political, and religious worlds. Neither Planned Parenthood nor the clergy are unaffected by these trends.

In the nineties, as government subsidies began to shrink and as the health care industry began to change rapidly and unpredictably, Planned Parenthood sought, out of financial necessity, to develop as a business. It looked for ways to market products—condoms, books—under the Planned Parenthood trademark. At the highest level, the national board was willing to hear a venture capitalist outline a marketing proposal to sell such products. At the local level Planned Parenthood affiliates changed the title of their main employee from director to chief executive officer. In 1994–1995 Planned Parenthood briefly considered a reorganization that would have taken it far closer to becoming a chain of health clinics rather than an agency of social change. The change did not take place because many of its staff and its funders, big and small, demanded that it not downgrade its historic function as an advocate for women.

Clergy too have had to keep their balance in the heady atmosphere of what one scholar has called "ecstatic capitalism."[3] The business culture has even affected the terminology of church life. For the purposes of the annual drive to raise funds a traditional term like families has morphed into "pledging units." A church building becomes known as "the plant." The situation is not helped by the fact that mainline Protestantism, the chief source of Planned Parenthood's clergy supporters, has been notoriously uncritical of capitalism's individualism. Both Roman Catholicism and Judaism have been much more responsible in their willingness to criticize the excesses of wealth. But when wealthy parishioners may donate much-needed funds to a church, there is a temptation to avoid the radical causes that could cause controversy in the congregation. It becomes more difficult for clergy to stress that justice—not just philanthropy—is the purpose of the gospel. For people of a religious temperament, the modern glorification of wealth is reminiscent of the scene in *Pilgrim's Progress* where the allegorical hero, Christian, and his companion, Faithful, come to a place called Vanity Fair, the symbolic home of inhuman unlimited materialism, "a Fair, wherein should be sold all Sorts of Vanity." In this frenzied locale everything is for sale, "houses, lands, trades, honors, preferments, titles . . . pleasures . . . gold, pearls, precious stones, . . . wives, husbands, children . . . lives, blood, bodies, souls."[4]

All of this has implications for the future of reproductive rights, because market values are for the most part unfriendly to feminism and humanism. In a workplace where women as well as men are viewed either as a commodity (labor) or as consumers, economic growth tends to trump the values of social justice. In such a climate women sometimes have to struggle to hold on to rights they have won in the past. Business and corporations have an interest in shrinking state and federal governments and the social services they offer: they want to reduce their taxes. Alternatively, they want to shift government programs to the private sector. As government shrinks its commitment to women's reproductive services, conservative religionists have persuaded many that such matters are best handled by a certain part of the private sector—religious institutions.

"Soft" Cultural Change

In September 2003 the Web site of the Religious Coalition for Reproductive Choice reported that "the President privately told leaders of catholic charities that his proposed massive new faith-based initiative will help them promote opposition to a woman's right to choose. Bush also promised the group he would act immediately to oppose abortion rights through 'legislative initiatives' . . . Beyond that, he said, 'There's a larger calling' which he described as 'changing the culture of the country.'"[5]

A few years back, we heard that the goal of the antiabortion movement was to make abortion illegal in twenty-five years. It was the first warning of a more patient, more dangerous threat to women's reproductive rights—cultural change. Cultural change can come in two forms—hard and soft. Since the 1930s Planned Parenthood and its clergy supporters have been accustomed to battling the immediate, direct threats to choice that constitute hard cultural change—coercive governmental actions to impose parental consent laws, cutting off Medicaid funding of abortion, criminalizing late-term abortions, abolishing Title X funding for family planning. But what if these proposals prove to be not as dangerous as soft cultural change, the subtle erosion of the social ground that undergirds support for a woman's right to choose?

From the views of President George W. Bush reported by the RCRC Web site, we can see that faith-based initiatives, despite disclaimers, are a type of cultural change targeted directly at women's rights. And these initiatives are not alone. Planned Parenthood and its supportive clergy are operating in a situation where religious conservatism is stronger than it has been in decades. Its representatives move from conservative foundations to government posts. Its power is impressive. And nothing is clearer than the fact that its main goal is to limit the reproductive freedom of women to the greatest extent that the culture will sanction. Religious conservatives generate and support any cultural change that will enhance this prospect. So what are the chances that they will succeed?

The kind of cultural shift that is damaging to women seems to ride on two distorted images of the society that are promoted by conservative religionists as well as by others: first, a fear that society is in an advanced form of moral decline, and second, a conviction that traditional institutions such as marriage and the family must be strengthened even at the cost of great injustice to individuals. Concerning the first, the society is awash in books proclaiming that we have become Sodom and Gomorrah.[6] This myth of a lost golden age is used by religious radio stations and legions of cable pundits to denigrate modern social conditions, often implying that feminism and the changed conditions of women's lives are largely responsible for our plight.

Current signs of cultural change that are troubling include the "marriage movement," a well-publicized effort by many center and right-wing groups and individuals to promote marriage. The Bush administration is proposing to spend one and one-half billion dollars on the effort. On the surface the overall goal seems unexceptional. Who could object to helping couples form a good marriage? Its adherents speak earnestly of the importance of equality in marriage, and they support divorce when there is abuse or addiction. But the movement is too uncritical of religion's long history of subordinating women, and it underestimates the continuing sexism of the institution of marriage in American society. In addition, any concerted campaign to promote marriage cannot help but lead to an increase in teen marriage as a way to deal with unwanted teen pregnancy. The tragedy of a teen birth will be no less if the couple is married, but society will be able to believe that it is. Yes, marriage is important. But that's not the only issue: there are other realities that are being neglected—decent housing, jobs, education—that are even more important than marriage.[7]

Another concerning sign is the growing sentimentality about the family. In many discussions and publications one can discern a nostalgia for a family pattern of the 1950s in which there was almost always a parent at home. There isn't much doubt as to which parent that should be. The proponents of "family values" seldom acknowledge that many of those traditional families operated on the unspoken premise that the mother would put aside her dreams of career or profession in order to give her time and energy to her family. Feminism has done much to remedy that injustice. It is also ironic that when legislation such as government-permitted family leave, a program that clearly helps families, is proposed, conservatives oppose it on the ground that it would demand too much of business.

But a family has no inherent value per se. It has value when it provides love and justice to its members. Many traditional families—father, mother, and two or three children—fail badly in that task. Almost 50 percent of such marriages end in divorce.[8] Furthermore, alcoholism, drug addiction, and domestic violence are widespread in traditional families, and many children have to be taken from their parents. Conversely there are many untraditional families, single-parent families, families formed by gay men, lesbians, and transsexuals, that do provide love and justice to their children, but are not acknowledged by the marriage movement, and are condemned by the religious defenders of the romanticized families of the past.[9]

But clergy are forced to deal with families as they really are, both those that are effective and caring in their parenting and those that are destructive to their members. At their best, clergy do not get sentimental about either marriage or families. Planned Parenthood clinics also have to deal with people as they are, with all their problems, not as we might wish they were. A good clinic, like a good rabbi or minister, will have a long list of agencies to which troubled families can be referred. Regardless of cultural change, the real goal, whether seen in religious or in secular terms, is the same, to seek the greatest measure of help and justice in each situation.

Even progressive religious groups have been "slowed" by these subtle cultural changes. In their programs and social action, other values increasingly take precedence over women's issues. The Interfaith Alliance is a coalition of moderate and liberal clergy, churches, and synagogues formed to combat the agenda of the religious right. But because their membership includes prominent Roman Catholic clergy, the group will not speak out on pro-choice issues. In this case it is the value of unity that is more important than women's reproductive concerns. Progressive Evangelicals is a group that has shown great courage and determination in opposing government policies that harm the poor, but they are silent on abortion. Economic justice is taken seriously, but women's reproductive issues are not prominent among their concerns. In November 2003 yet another liberal religious group, the Clergy Leadership Network, came into existence to combat the policies of the Bush administration. But it too has said that it will be silent on issues such as abortion and gay marriage. Even the many hundreds of local councils of churches and clergy associations that were the strongest religious supporters of Planned Parenthood in the forties, fifties, and early sixties no longer speak out on issues of choice, because they now have Roman Catholic members they don't wish to offend. Today such groups most often speak out only when they have consensus. No one can predict the ultimate effect of these soft cultural changes, but they would seem to justify a measure of concern by people worried about the future of women's reproductive freedom.

BIOETHICS AND THE REVOLUTION IN REPRODUCTIVE TECHNOLOGY

Perhaps the most unpredictable element that could affect the future of both Planned Parenthood and the clergy is the phenomenal development in genetics and genetic research. When in vitro fertilization was developed in the early 1980s we had something that had never existed before, a living human embryo outside of a woman's body. The Roman Catholic Church stated its opposition to IVF on religious grounds, and others feared that children born this way would be stigmatized. When the United States government refused to support or fund such research, other nations forged ahead of us. The first "test-tube" baby was born in England. The fear of children being stigmatized proved to be groundless and today over eighty thousand children have been born by in vitro fertilization.

But basic IVF has now been supplemented by many new reproductive techniques to get around infertility. Hormones can be used to induce ovulation. Men who cannot produce sperm nevertheless often have spermatacids, an earlier form of sperm. With new techniques these can be used to initiate fertilization. If egg and sperm will not fuse, a specialist can now select a single sperm and inject it into the egg.[10]

Scientists have developed radical new genetic technologies that are generating far more controversy than IVF. For some time scientists have been able to study the evolution of human cells. They watched them develop, age, and die. They knew that the human body began with stem cells that had the potential to differentiate into various bodily tissues and organs. The great breakthrough came in 1998, when researchers were able to grow human stem cells from embryonic and fetal tissues. They learned how to keep the cells from differentiating into specific tissues. Instead the stem cells proliferated like rabbits in their petri dishes, creating a "line" of stem cells. When injected into a diseased organ these stem cells are potentially capable of repairing damaged human organs such as the pancreas, liver, and brain. Theoretically they could bring about effective treatments for ailments such as diabetes, spinal cord injuries, Alzheimer's, and Parkinson's disease. A researcher at the Geron Institute described them as "magic."[11]

These stem cells were gathered primarily from two sources, from fetal tissue donated by women who had had an abortion and who wanted to help this research, and from tiny embryos (about the size of a period on this page) created by infertile couples in their attempt to conceive. Since many more embryos are created than will ever be used, the remaining embryos are frozen and stored. By May of 2003 fertility clinics in the United States had 396,526 embryos in their freezers.[12]

But the technology is caught up in controversy over the moral status of the embryo. Major religious bodies such as the Roman Catholic Church and the Southern Baptist Church regard these embryos as fully human persons. One opponent of the research called them "our tiniest human beings."[13] Therefore those churches oppose stem-cell research and instead urge the use of stem cells taken from adult tissues. The difficulty is that many leading scientists in the field do not believe that such cells have as much potential as the embryonic stem cells.[14] Perhaps the real difficulty is the fact that theological considerations are being allowed to block scientific research.

But while some religious groups believe it is immoral to go on with the research, other religious groups and clergy believe it is immoral not to. Despite some attempts to promote adoption of unwanted embryos, the truth is that virtually none of the frozen embryos will ever be implanted in a woman and almost all will eventually be destroyed. Religious supporters of the research point to the ocean of human suffering that might be relieved through it. They note that each year that the research is delayed, 51,000 people will get Parkinson's, 360,000 will contract Alzheimer's, and 798,000 will become diabetic in the United States alone.[15] Mainline clergy are acutely aware that these are the very diseases that are most threatening to their aging congregations. Parents of juvenile diabetics also plead for this research, and prominent figures such as Nancy Reagan, Michael Fox, and Christopher Reeve have lobbied hard to have the government support it.

Interestingly, the controversy has broken down the usual lines between antiabortion and pro-choice forces. A prominent Mormon senator, Orrin Hatch of Utah, a stalwart opponent of abortion, is in favor of stem-cell research. And some usually liberal environmental groups are suspicious of it.[16] Many mainline churches have not taken a definitive position on it, but one has. In its General Synod meeting of the whole church in the summer of 2001, the United Church of Christ adopted this statement:

> WHEREAS, Jesus set an example, by his ministry of healing and caring for the sick and disabled, challenging us to follow his example by supporting the healing and caring ministry in our own day, and
>
> WHEREAS, human embryonic stem cells can form virtually any type of human cell and thus have the potential to form tissues for any part of the body, and
>
> WHEREAS, many scientists agree that research on embryonic stem cells is more promising than that of adult stem cells that have only a limited capacity to form certain cell types, and
>
> WHEREAS, many scientists believe that embryonic stem cell research could relieve suffering and possibly cure patients with a variety of disorders such as Alzheimer's and Parkinson's disease, juvenile diabetes. . . .
>
> THEREFORE BE IT RESOLVED that the Twenty-Third General Synod of the United Church of Christ supports federally-funded embryonic stem cell research within ethically sound guidelines.[17]

While mainline churches and clergy are interested in the healing possibilities of stem-cell research, Planned Parenthood is interested because stem-cell research and related technologies such as cloning and germ line modification are already revolutionizing human reproduction.[18] Parenthood is happening in new ways. Planned Parenthood is looking ahead to the year 2025 and setting goals for that era. Goal 8 of its "Vision for 2025" plan for the future is "to be an authoritative voice on bio-ethical standards related to reproductive health and sexuality."[19] In pursuit of that goal, on July 23–25, 2003, the group called together thirty of the leading national and international experts in this field to a three-day colloquium, "Beyond Abortion: Critical Bioethical Issues in Reproductive Health for the 21st Century," in Snowbird, Utah. The conference was cosponsored by the Federation's Clergy Advisory Board. Virtually every aspect of this complex subject and its ethical implications were analyzed by scientists, historians, social workers, and clergy. The four panel discussions, covering sixteen hours, were videotaped for distribution to interested affiliates.

As the various areas of Planned Parenthood discuss and debate these issues over the next few years, the Federation will ultimately issue informed statements on the values and dangers of this research. To the affiliate CEOs who were at the colloquium, it was already clear that this is an area where Planned parenthood and clergy will be drawn together as each struggles with the healing and the reproductive potential of this complex technology. Both Planned Parenthood and the clergy have a stake in seeing that with adequate safeguards such research goes forward. As they work together, their efforts will be reminiscent of their cooperation in the 1930s, when society also feared the social consequences of a new reproductive technology, the diaphragm.

HARD THEOLOGICAL REALITIES

Whatever the shifts in cultural emphases and political agendas, when it comes to human sexuality, the theological face of the opposition is exactly the same as in the past, a belief that all sexual intercourse must occur within heterosexual marriage and an iron conviction that life begins at conception. All human sexual relationships are forced to lie on the Procrustean bed of these tenets, and most, of course, are found wanting. This movement has a plethora of cohorts. There are the sentimentalists who adhere passionately to romantic ideas of the past, an imaginary golden age when Americans supposedly did not have abortions and did not have much sex before marriage.

There are the fundamentalists who interpret the Bible selectively to foster their sexist convictions. And there are those Roman Catholics—a distinct minority of Catholics—who believe with the pope that all artificial birth control is wrong. Through it all and beneath it all is fear of a world in which women can control their own reproductive lives.

And if we seek to understand that fear, we are brought back to the place where we began—the tension between the two conflicting strains in religion. On the one hand we have the divine imperative for righteousness or justice, and on the other the subordination of that demand to the strictures of religious sexism. For a tragic truth lies at the base of the long struggle for reproductive justice for women. That truth is that much of the religion in the world has never been able to transcend its fear of women. From the Taliban down to the smallest fundamentalist sect, that fear leads inevitably to an insistence on controlling women's lives, at the same time blind to the justice due them.

It is a startling phenomenon. When it comes to racism most religions can see the injustices clearly. All world religions—at their best—preach doctrines that transcend race and nationality. If an American church, mosque, or synagogue refused to allow African Americans to become clergy because of their race, it would be seen as racism. In recent times the Southern Baptist denomination formally apologized to the African-American community for its past participation in the racist policies of segregation. Into modern times the Mormon Church would not allow African Americans to become priests, but the policy was notoriously racist and they dropped the restriction in 1979. But when these same denominations (along with the Roman Catholic Church and Orthodox Judaism) bar women from serving as clergy, it is not seen as discrimination. Instead it is called "tradition."

Why is it so easy to see the injustice in one case and not in the other? The underlying fear is that if women are accorded real equality in the religion, then those institutions would change and change drastically: the world of male control would be gone or greatly diminished. To resist that, the religions that discriminate against women throw up sexist scriptures, sexist traditions, and try to accord these distortions the full majesty of the sacred. Since religion plays such an influential and integral role in American life, this curious religious blindness to gender discrimination can not help but have a powerful effect on the most serious political issues. It is therefore no surprise that a 1999 study done by the Center for Gender Equality, an organization founded by former Planned Parenthood president Faye Wattleton, revealed that in the 1990s more women were moving into conservative religion, and the more religious they were the more willing they became to support limits on women's reproductive freedom.[20] What is occurring is a subtle process of cultural change that may undercut some hard-won rights.

This understanding of religion's suspicion and fear of women makes it easier to see why women have had such a difficult time securing basic rights. Even in the United States it took over one hundred years for women just to obtain the right to vote, and organized religion did little or nothing to help. In most cases it opposed women's suffrage. When Margaret Sanger came along and wanted to place in women's hands the ability to determine how many children they would have, it was a red flag to religious institutions that wanted no change in women's status. It therefore makes sense that Planned Parenthood would be seen by conservative religious leaders as an evil organization and that its decades-long development would be resisted at every stage, for Planned Parenthood is, above all, a woman's movement.

But justice is a seamless garment, to borrow the late Cardinal Joseph Bernadin's felicitous phrase. To leave one group outside the charmed circle of advocacy rends the garment. It helps to legitimate a certain marginalizing of women's concerns. Politicians are quick to sense when support for one group is softer than for others. No serious politicians in America will espouse a racist position, but they have no comparable fear of taking a position that discriminates against women. Yet no prophetic faith can leave a group behind. It is, in fact, the essence of prophetic religion to seek justice for the very group that is left out.

Ultimately the rigid theologies that oppose women's reproductive rights and seek to prevent embryonic stem-cell research are theologies that yield too much to fear. Such a theological stance dries up the soul and closes the door to the future.

CONCLUSION

America has come a long way in the seventy-plus years since the first major American religious body—the Federal Council of Churches—publicly endorsed a woman's right to have control over her reproductive life. In that endorsement was the implicit recognition that spirituality and sexuality cannot be separated. It was the beginning of the churches' awakening from a twisted Victorian notion that sex could be walled off from our deepest spiritual longings. It was a recognition that our sexuality is an essential part of both our spirituality and our humanity. It was the beginning of a spiritual alliance between Planned Parenthood and clergy.

Plato said that what is honored in a country is cultivated there. It is a sad truth that this country has often not honored women's lives. Clergy and other people of faith hear from their own congregants—or know from their own experience—the stories of teens cast out by their families, or women abandoned by their boyfriends, who found little or no support through public agencies and sometimes not even from religious agencies, but who were helped by Planned Parenthood. From the desperate immigrant women Margaret Sanger helped down to the lost teens and battered women of modern America, this imperfect "cursed" human organization has carried out sacred work to the people that scripture calls "widows, orphans, and the stranger in your midst" (Exodus 22:21–22). Those clergy who tried to keep themselves attuned—however imperfectly—to the same imperative often found themselves drawn to Planned Parenthood's work. Those ministers and rabbis who were open to learning more and becoming more active in support found that a bond was formed between them and the people of Planned Parenthood.

An expression of this bond, which has endured for seventy years, can be found in a prayer written by the Reverend G. Anthony Hoeltzel, an Episcopal priest from Westchester County, and read at the January 1995 memorial service for Shannon Lowney and Leanne Nichols. Its simple words express perfectly the convictions of Planned Parenthood clergy.

O God,
You are known by many names
and your people hear your will spoken in many different ways—
but most clearly you are known by the
names of Justice, Freedom, and Peace.
    You are the source of our hope,
You are our only cause for courage.
    You have blessed your people with freedom.
You have given us the gifts of memory, reason, and skill;
    You have given some among us the special gifts of healing—physicians,
nurses, and aides; clinic staff and volunteers.
Yet some would deny these Your servants the right to exercise their gifts as
they and You have determined best for us.
    Some would deny it by intimidation, some by obstruction,
and some, Lord, by terror, violence or even death.
    We ask your special blessing this day, O God, upon those whose commitment to providing your children all the choices you have given us has placed

them under attack, and who labor daily under the most difficult and terrify-
ing circumstances to deliver quality health care.

Bless them, Lord God, and be with them, with their families and friends.
Give them courage, give them hope, and give them especially

a right awareness of Your love.[21]

Timeline

1914—Margaret Sanger edits and publishes *The Woman Rebel.*

1916—Sanger arrested and convicted for operating a birth control clinic in Brownsville, New York. She serves a thirty-day jail sentence.

1917—Sanger begins to publish the *Birth Control Review*, which helps to keep the various birth control leagues around the country in touch with one another.

1921—Using the staff of the *Birth Control Review* as a nucleus and with the addition of wealthy financial backers, Sanger organizes the American Birth Control League on November 11. This is the organization that in 1942 will evolve into Planned Parenthood Federation of America. It is organized on the eve of the first birth control conference in New York City. The closing meeting of the conference is raided by police.

1923—Sanger establishes the Birth Control Clinical Research Bureau in an office adjacent to the offices of the American Birth Control League in New York City. She uses this clinic to gather data that document the value of birth control in women's lives.

1931—The Committee on Marriage and the Home of the Federal Council of Churches of Christ in America (forerunner of the National Council of Churches of Christ in America) issues a report that supports birth control to relieve poverty and improve the health of women and children. A number of American churches criticize the report.

1934—The American Episcopal Church endorses birth control.

1942—The American Birth Control League becomes Planned Parenthood Federation of America.

1943—The first supportive clergy committee, the National Clergymen's Advisory Council of Planned Parenthood, is formed through the efforts of Margaret Sanger and Kenneth Rose, then executive director of Planned Parenthood.

1944–1945—The National Clergymen's Advisory Council of the Planned Parenthood Federation of America publishes "Ministerial Counseling and Planned Parenthood" by the Reverend Roy Burkhart. He is pastor of the First Community Church (United Church of Christ) in Columbus, Ohio. This counseling guidebook was one of the first of its kind. It was an early recognition that, in order to be responsible, clergy needed to offer realistic advice about sexuality to couples planning to be married. It was distributed to Protestant clergy.

1946—The National Clergymen's Advisory Council arranges the Twenty-fifth Anniversary Celebration of Planned Parenthood at the Waldorf Astoria in New York City.

1952—Seven non-Catholic physicians in Poughkeepsie, New York, are told by St. Francis Hospital, a Roman Catholic institution, that they must stop working with the Planned Parenthood League of Poughkeepsie or lose their hospital privileges. This action is taken because the hospital disagrees with the contraceptive programs of the Planned Parenthood League of Poughkeepsie. Clergy and physician protests against the expulsion of the doctors affect public opinion. By 1953 St. Francis Hospital retracts its demand and the doctors resume their privileges.

1955—Planned Parenthood sponsors the first major conference on the issue of abortion.

1958—Planned Parenthood, the Protestant Council of New York, and the New York Board of Rabbis protest the refusal of the New York City hospitals to provide birth control services because of a fear of offending the Roman Catholic dioceses of Manhattan and Brooklyn. After several months of public controversy, the Hospital Board changes the policy and contraception becomes available to married New Yorkers who use the city hospitals.

1960—A second clergy group, the Clergymen's National Advisory Council, is formed by Planned Parenthood. This one is led by the Reverend James Pike, dean of the Cathedral of St. John the Divine in New York City and later bishop of California.

1962—Planned Parenthood of Maryland asks its Clergymen's Advisory Board to help it change the policies of the Maryland State Board of Welfare, which will not provide birth control to welfare clients, even if they ask for it. The board is persuaded to change its policies.

1965—Planned Parenthood of Maryland's Clergymen's Advisory Board argues that the Maryland State Department of Welfare should extend the provision of contraceptives to unmarried women. Their arguments prevail and the policy is changed.

1962–1968—The Roman Catholic Church undergoes a sea change in doctrine and structure through the work of Vatican II (1962–1965). In this same period Dr. John Rock, a practicing Catholic, develops a new form of contraception, the birth control pill. Planned Parenthood, often in conjunction with the new federal government antipoverty programs, is able to help bring birth control services into hospitals and public health programs all across the country. Planned Parenthood and Roman Catholic clergy hold amicable meetings in many areas. A new era of cooperation appears to be beginning.

1967—The Clergy Consultation Service on Abortion begins in New York City. Over the next five years, nearly two thousand ministers and rabbis join this network, which helps women find safe abortions.

1967—California makes modest reforms to its abortion laws. The bill is signed into law by Governor Ronald Reagan.

1968—Pope Paul VI issues an encyclical, *Humanae Vitae*, reaffirming the Catholic Church's traditional opposition to all "artificial" birth control, including the birth control pill.

1970—New York State repeals its old abortion laws. Abortion is now legal in New York State for the first twenty-eight weeks of pregnancy.

1970—Planned Parenthood creates a third religious advisory group, this time called the Religious Affairs Committee. For the first time, women are members. It lasts until 1974.

1973—The sweeping Supreme Court decision *Roe v. Wade* makes abortion legal in every state. The right-to-life movement begins, and once again Planned Parenthood finds itself at odds with both the Roman Catholic Church and many Protestant fundamentalist churches.

1973—Increasing numbers of Planned Parenthood affiliates begin to offer abortion services.

1986—Increasing attacks on Planned Parenthood and other women's clinics awaken clergy concerns in various parts of the country. A pro-choice clergy group, the

Adirondack Religious Coalition, is formed in eastern upstate New York and begins to work with regional Planned Parenthoods. In Kansas City, Missouri, local clergy form a committee to support the local Planned Parenthood. This leads to the hiring of a member of the clergy to serve as chaplain for the clinic. In several other areas of the country Planned Parenthoods experience increased clergy support.

1994—The fourth, and current, Planned Parenthood of America Clergy Advisory Board is formed. It begins to organize clergy across the country in support of the work of Planned Parenthood. It publishes a newsletter, *Clergy Voices.* More than its predecessors, this clergy board focuses on theological critiques of the antiabortion movement and a theological defense of the work of Planned Parenthood.

January 1993—President Bill Clinton is inaugurated. He reverses the gag rule and other antiabortion regulations of the outgoing Bush administration.

1993—The first murder of a doctor who performs abortions occurs in Pensacola, Florida, when Michael Griffin shoots and kills Dr. David Gunn as he is entering a women's clinic.

1994—Dr. John Britton and James Barrett, his escort, are shot and killed at the same Pensacola clinic as Dr. Gunn. June Barrett, the wife of James Barrett, is wounded. The shooter is Paul Hill, a defrocked Presbyterian minister.

December 1994—John Salvi enters the Preterm Health Services Clinic in Brookline, Massachusetts, and kills a receptionist, Leanne Nichols. He then goes to Planned Parenthood of Brookline, enters, and kills another receptionist, Shannon Lowney. Five other people are wounded.

January 22, 1995—The PPFA Clergy Advisory Board holds a memorial service for Shannon Lowney and Leanne Nichols at the Cathedral of St. John the Divine in New York City. Attendees include Gloria Steinem, the Reverend James Forbes of Riverside Church, the Reverend Joan Brown Campbell (general secretary of the National Council of Churches), Rabbi Balfour Brickner (rabbi emeritus of the Stephen Wise Free Synagogue), and Denise Taft Davidoff of the Unitarian Universalist Association.

1998—Officer Robert Sanderson, an off-duty policeman, is killed in a bombing at a woman's clinic in Birmingham, Alabama.

1998—Dr. Barnett Slepian, a doctor at a woman's clinic in Buffalo, New York, is shot to death in his home by a sniper.

2000—The Clergy Advisory Board initiates prayer breakfasts at the annual conference of PPFA. They become the most popular events at the conference.

2001—The Planned Parenthood Federation adopts a twenty-five year plan, "Vision for 2025."

2003—The Clergy Advisory Board cosponsors a conference, "Beyond Abortion: Critical Bioethical Issues in Reproductive Health for the 21st Century," in Snowbird, Utah. It brings together thirty leading experts in the related fields together with Planned Parenthood staff.

2004—Planned Parenthood Federation announces that for the first time in its history it will have a national chaplain. The Reverend Ignacio Castuera, a Methodist minister from California and editor of *Dreams on Fire, Embers of Hope: From the Pulpits of Los Angeles after the Riots*, is appointed to the post. It is the latest form of the alliance between Planned Parenthood and its clergy supporters.

Notes

CHAPTER 1. THE CONCEPT OF SACRED WORK

1. Mircea Eliade, *The Sacred and the Profane* (New York: Harcourt Brace and Jovanovich, 1959), 11–12.

2. Judith Plaskow, *Standing Again at Sinai* (New York: Harper & Row, 1990), 174–175. Plaskow details the extent to which women were disqualified from participation in the sacred.

3. Phyllis Trible, "Eve, the Theologian" (article printed by the Task Force on Women of the United Church of Christ, New York, 1973), 2.

4. Ibid., 3–4.

5. Cited in Rosemary Ruether, *Religion and Sexism* (New York: Simon and Schuster, 1974), 105.

6. Linda Gordon notes that with the exception of the hormone-suppressing birth control pill, all current birth control methods were practiced in the ancient world. *Woman's Body, Woman's Right* (New York: Grossman Publishers, 1976), 28.

7. Roland Bainton, *Here I Stand* (Nashville: Abingdon Press, 1950), 224–225.

8. *Annual Report, 2001–2002*, Planned Parenthood Federation of America, New York, 2003, 6.

9. A thorough discussion of this point is found in Carole R. McCann, *Birth Control Politics in the United States, 1916–1945* (Ithaca, N.Y.: Cornell University Press, 1994), 196–197.

10. *Annual Report, 2001–2002*, 3.

11. In the total American population, 22 percent of women say they are Catholic, but 27 percent of abortion patients identify themselves as Roman Catholic. Thirteen percent of patients describe themselves as born-again or evangelical Christians. (Alan Guttmacher Institute, "Facts in Brief—Induced Abortion, 2003," www.agi-usa.org/pubs/fb_induced _abortion.html.)

12. David R. Zimmerman, "Abortion Clinics' Toughest Cases," *Medical World*

News, March 9, 1987. This was a study of eight abortion clinics in five midwestern states. Because of medical confidentiality and lack of resources, clinics have not systematically studied this matter. Much of the information is anecdotal, but most clinic workers have encountered at least one such case.

13. *Little Red Songbook*, Industrial Workers of the World, (London, 1917).

14. Walter Bruggemann, *Hope within History* (Louisville, Ky.: John Knox Press, 1987), 86–87.

15. Edward Levinson, *Labor on the March* (Ithaca, N.Y.: ILR Press, 1938), 169.

16. Philip Taft, *Organized Labor in American History* (New York: Harper & Row, 1964), 528.

17. Robert Zangrando, "About Lynching," excerpted from a larger article in *The Reader's Companion to American History*, edited by Eric Fonen and John A. Garrity (New York: Houghton Mifflin, 1991).

18. Alan Graebner, "Birth Control and the Lutherans," *Journal of Social History* 2 (Summer 1969): 305–306.

19. See especially Leslie J. Reagan, *When Abortion Was a Crime* (Berkeley: University of California Press, 1997), 11–14. Dr. Storer felt that women used abortion to avoid their maternal duties. Cf. John D'Emilio and Estelle B. Freedman, *Intimate Matters* (New York: Harper & Row, 1988), 146–147.

20. Janet Farrell Brodie, *Contraception and Abortion in Nineteenth-Century America* (Ithaca, N.Y.: Cornell University Press, 1994), 281, notes that women in Chicago in the early 1960s knew less about their bodies and about birth control than did women a century earlier.

21. Reagan, *When Abortion Was a Crime*, 23–24.

22. Perhaps the most impressive evidence for this statement is the thousands of letters received by Margaret Sanger describing the abundance of unwanted pregnancies. Margaret Sanger, *Motherhood in Bondage* (Columbus: Ohio State University Press, 2000).

23. Graebner, "Birth Control and the Lutherans," 329–330.

CHAPTER 2. MARGARET SANGER RECRUITS THE CLERGY

1. Stephen B. Oates, *Let the Trumpet Sound: A Life of Martin Luther King* (New York: HarperCollins Press, 1982), 56.

2. Anthony Comstock once boasted that he had convicted enough people to fill a "sixty-car passenger train." Ellen W. Chesler, *Woman of Valor* (NewYork: Simon and Schuster, 1992), 66. See also Andrea Tone, *Devices and Desires: A History of Contraceptives in America* (New York: Hill and Wang, 2001), 7, 26, who notes that Comstock made hundreds of arrests.

3. Janet F. Brodie, *Contraception and Abortion in Nineteenth-Century America* (Ithaca, N.Y.: Cornell University Press, 1994), 280.

4. Margaret Sanger, *My Fight for Birth Control* (Elmsford, N.Y.: Maxwell Reprint Company, 1931), 58.

5. Lawrence Lader, *The Margaret Sanger Story* (Westport, Conn.: Greenwood Press, 1955), 102–103.

6. Ibid., 134.

7. The Reverend John Ryan, "Family Limitation," *Ecclesiastical Review* (January–June 1916): 684.

8. Ibid., 690.

9. Ibid., 687.

10. Quoted in John Noonan Jr., *Contraception* (Cambridge: Harvard University Press, 1986), 423.

11. Chesler, *Woman*, 200.

12. Lader, *Sanger*, 174.

13. Chesler, *Woman*, 203.

14. David M. Kennedy, *Birth Control in America: The Career of Margaret Sanger* (New Haven: Yale University Press, 1970), 97.

15. This was not the first or the last time that political figures tried to silence Margaret Sanger. In 1929 she was to speak in Boston at the Ford Forum. Under the administration of Mayor James Curley, Boston authorities threatened to prevent her from speaking. As with the Town Hall incident, she turned the occasion to her favor. She stood on the stage with a gag over her mouth while Arthur Schlesinger, Sr., read her speech. *A Tradition of Choice* (New York: Planned Parenthood Federation of America, 1991), 18.

16. Margaret Sanger, *Margaret Sanger: An Autobiography* (New York: W. W. Norton and Co., 1938), 299–300.

17. Carole R. McCann, *Birth Control Politics in the United States, 1916–1945* (Ithaca, N.Y.: Cornell University Press, 1994), 102n10.

18. See especially Linda Gordon, *Woman's Body, Woman's Right* (New York: Grossman Publishers, 1976), 281–282, 330–333. McCann, *Birth*, 99–173, takes a more nuanced view. See also Charles Valenza, "Was Margaret Sanger a Racist?" *Family Planning Perspectives* (January–February 1985): 44–46.

19. Margaret Sanger, "Birth Control and Racial Betterment," *Birth Control Review*, (February 1919): 11–12.

20. Chesler, *Woman*, 215.

21. By 1938 the Clinical Research Bureau had served 65,000 women. McCann, *Birth*, 192n56.

22. Chesler, *Woman*, 254.

23. Margaret Sanger, *Motherhood in Bondage* (1928; Columbus: Ohio State University Press, 2000), xlvii.

24. Letter from the Reverend James Oesterling, Superintendant of the Inner Mission Society of the Evangelical Lutheran Church of Baltimore City and Vicinity Inc. to Margaret Sanger, January 23, 1932. Papers of Margaret Sanger, container number 109, microfilm reel 72, Library of Congress: Manuscript Division, Washington, D.C. Hereafter MS-LC.

25. Kennedy, *Birth Control*, 19.

26. Lader, *Sanger*, 124.

27. Madeline Gray, *Margaret Sanger* (New York: Richard Marek Publishers, 1979), 175.

28. Margaret Sanger inveighed against the feminists of her time who focused on general social reforms rather than on women's issues such as birth control. Chesler, *Woman*, 517n8. Modern reformers such as Ralph Nader also tend to see women's issues as merely a function of larger issues such as reform of corporate power.

29. Sanger was not collegial. She did not like to share power and could be petty in her relationships with potential rivals like Mary Ware Dennett, president of the rival National Birth Control League, and Eleanor Jones, chair of the American Birth Control League. Whenever possible Sanger wanted to make the decisions herself. Chesler, *Woman*, 238–239.

30. Sanger, *Motherhood*, 145.

31. Ibid., 368–369.

32. Ibid., 306.

33. McCann, *Birth*, 217.

34. Central Conference of American Rabbis, "Message of Social Justice," September 1930. MS-LC.

35. Letter from Margaret Sanger to Rabbi Edward Israel, December 13, 1932. MS-LC.

36. Lader, *Sanger*, 266.

37. Kennedy, *Birth Control*, 169.

38. Quoted in ibid., 162.

39. Ibid., 164.

40. *Commonweal*, April 1, 1931, 589.

41. Kennedy, *Birth Control*, 154.

42. *Washington D.C. News*, May 25, 1933. MS-LC.

43. Chesler, *Woman*, 319.

44. *Omaha Bee*, February 6, 1936. MS-LC.

45. *New York Times*, November 30, 1936.

46. Kennedy, *Birth Control*, 167.

47. Letter from Margaret Sanger to Guy Shipler, June 4, 1934. MS-LC.

48. "Presbyterian Board Approves Birth Control," *New York Herald Tribune*, April 27, 1931.

49. Excerpted from remarks delivered at a gathering at the Park Center Hall, November 19, 1921. *Stenographic Record of the Proceedings, First American Birth Control Conference, November 11–13, 1921*, American Birth Control League, New York. Papers of Margaret Sanger and Planned Parenthood Federation of America, box 18, folder 1. Sophia Smith Collection, Smith College, Northampton, Mass. Hereafter SSC.

50. Linda Gordon, *The Moral Property of Women* (Urbana: University of Illinois Press, 2002), 280, 289.

CHAPTER 3. BUILDING PUBLIC ACCEPTANCE, 1935–1957

1. John Cogley and Roger Van Allen, *Catholic America*, expanded and updated (Kansas City, Mo.: Sheed and Ward, 1986), 8.

2. Charles R. Morris, *American Catholic* (New York: Random House, 1997), 54–63.

3. Ibid., 73.

4. Ibid., 160–161.

5. Chester Gillis, *Roman Catholicism* (New York: Columbia University Press, 1999), 215.

6. "Syllabus of Errors," 1864.

7. Paul Blanshard, *American Freedom and Catholic Power* (Boston: Beacon Press, 1948).

8. *New York Times,* October 22, 1947, 18:5.

9. Howard M. Sachar, *A History of the Jews in America* (New York: Alfred A. Knopf, 1992), 392–393.

10. "No woman is required to build the world by destroying herself." A famous saying by Rabbi Moshe Sofer, a leading Talmudist of the nineteenth century who lived in Pressburg, Hungary.

11. *New York Times,* December 9, 1935, 5:1.

12. Ibid.

13. Ibid.

14. From the reply of the clergy to Cardinal Hayes, "The Ethics of Birth Control," 3, Katherine Dexter McCormick Library of the Planned Parenthood Federation of America, New York. Hereafter KDM-PPFA.

15. Madeline Gray, *Margaret Sanger* (New York: Richard Marek Publishers, 1979), 383.

16. Ibid.

17. Excerpted from "Report" of March 5 meeting at Hotel Weylin, March 18, 1941. SSC.

18. Minutes of the National Clergy Committee, February 17, 1943. SSC.

19. "Suggested Policy on the Catholic Church," Statement of the Executive Committee of the Planned Parenthood Board, April 6, 1943. SSC.

20. "Proposed Functions and Powers of the National Clergymen's Advisory Council . . . as Defined by the Executive Committee of the Planned Parenthood Federation of America," June 6, 1944. SSC.

21. "Statement by Religious Leaders on the Responsibilities of Parenthood" 1943. SSC.

22. "Resolution," Public Statement by the National Clergymen's Advisory Council of the Planned Parenthood Federation of America. Signed by 3,200 Protestant and Jewish Clergy, November 1946. Planned Parenthood Association Records: 1930–1975. Western Historical Manuscripts Collection at the University of Missouri at St. Louis. Hereafter WHMC-UMSL.

23. Ibid.

24. Unsigned and unidentified letter found in SSC.

25. Randall Balmer and Laura F. Winner, *Protestantism in America* (New York: Columbia University Press, 2002), 66.

26. One of the most complete treatments of the subject is found in James Hudnut-Beumler, *Looking for God in the Suburbs: The Religion of the American Dream and Its Critics, 1945–1965* (New Brunswick, N.J.: Rutgers University Press,

1994). On the question of numbers he notes that membership in churches and synagogues increased by 30 percent at a time when the population increase was only 19 percent (31).

27. Ibid., 33.

28. PPFA *News Exchange*, February 1946, 2. KDM-PPFA.

29. Ibid.

30. From the memo "Cooperation with Religious Leaders," December 8, 1947, 1. SSC.

31. PPFA *News Exchange*, May 1947, 3. KDM-PPFA.

32. *Poughkeepsie New Yorker*, January 30, 1952, 1.

33. Ibid.

34. Ibid., January 31, 1952, 1.

35. Ibid.

36. Ibid.

37. Ibid.

38. *New York Herald Tribune*, February 1, 1952, 1.

39. *New York Times*, February 4, 1952, 15:1.

40. *New York Telegram and Sun*, February 1, 1952, 1.

41. Ibid.

42. *New York Herald Tribune*, February 1, 1952, 1.

43. *New York Times*, February 3, 1952, 1.

44. *The Compass*, February 3, 1952. Clipping found in archives of Planned Parenthood of the Mid-Hudson, Poughkeepsie, New York, 1.

45. *New York Times*, January, 22, 1953, 1:4.

46. *Poughkeepsie New Yorker*, January 21, 1953, 1.

47. In this 1936 judicial decision with the curious name "One Package of Japanese Pessaries" (diaphragms) the United States Appeals Court ruled that doctors could prescribe devices that saved the life of the patient or helped the patient's wellbeing. This meant that contraception was no longer limited to the issue of the prevention of disease. Carole R. McCann, *Birth Control Politics in the United States, 1916–1945* (Ithaca, N.Y.: Cornell University Press, 1994), 75.

48. The main group supporting such mergers is the National Conference of Catholic Bishops and the New York State Catholic Conference. Opposing groups include the American Civil Liberties Union, Catholics for a Free Choice, Planned Parenthood, and the Family Planning Advocates of New York State. Family Planning Advocates created the Mergerwatch Project, which has published extensively on such mergers. See especially their study *No Strings Attached: Public Funding of Religiously-Sponsored Hospitals in the United States,* by Lois Uttley and Ronnie Pawelko, a publication of the Education Fund of Family Planning Advocates of NYS, Albany, N.Y., 2002.

49. While the term is broad, conservative Protestant churches are most easily grouped together as those churches which (a) disagreed with the social and theological views of liberal Protestantism and (b) refused to join the National Council of Churches. This includes denominations such as the Church of Christ, the Southern

Baptist Church, the Church of the Nazarene, the Church of God, Pentacostal bodies, and many more. Their reluctance to support birth control seemed to stem from at least two sources, a fear that it was a threat to the family, and a belief that it violated scripture.

CHAPTER 4. THE 1958 BATTLE OVER THE NEW YORK CITY HOSPITALS

1. See especially Chapter 6, "Raids and Rules" in Reagan, *When Abortion Was a Crime* (Berekley: University of California, 1997), 160–173. See also Carole Joffe, *Doctors of Conscience* (Boston: Beacon Press, 1995).

2. At the California Hospital in Los Angeles, the number of therapeutic procedures dropped from an average of fifteen a year to six. Chicago's Mt.Sinai Hospital started a committee in 1956, and its annual rate went from fifteen to three. Reagan, *When Abortion*, 178–179.

3. Joffe, *Doctors of Conscience,* 75, is the most detailed account of the practice of illegal and therapeutic abortion in this period.

4. There was also a racial agenda in the politics of sterilization. While white women could not get sterilizations, black women were often sterilized without their consent. See Johanna Schoen, "Fighting for Child Health: Race, Birth Control, and the State in the Jim Crow South," *Social Politics* 4 (Spring 1997) 90–113, and "Between Choice and Coercion: Women and the Politics of Sterilization in North Carolina, 1929–1975," *Journal of Women's History* 13:1 (2001): 132–157.

5. Reagan, *When Abortion*, 200.

6. *New York Times*, April 2, 1958, 26:4.

7. Annual Report, Department of Hospitals, City of New York, 1958, 1. I could find no breakdown on the socioeconomic status of hospital patients, but it is widely assumed that poorer people usually used the city hospitals.

8. "Anatomy of a Victory," ms., Planned Parenthood Federation of America files, 1958, 3.

9. Ibid., 2–3. As this statement suggests, even some private hospitals were reluctant to offer contraceptive services. That reluctance and the secretiveness it promoted makes it difficult to know how available birth control was in these facilities in New York City in 1958.

10. Ibid., 11.

11. Joe Kahn, "Birth Control: New York's Untold Story," *New York Post,* [Spring] 1957, article I.

12. Ibid, article II.

13. Ibid.

14. "Anatomy of a Victory," 12.

15. *New York Times*, March 3, 1958, 21:5.

16. Ibid.

17. Ibid.

18. *New York Times*, May 22, 1958, 33: 4.

19. *New York Times*, May 23, 1958, 46:8.

20. *New York Times*, May 26, 1958, 32:4.

21. "Anatomy of a Victory," 8.

22. *New York Times*, July 17, 1958, 29:8.

23. Ibid.

24. Planned Parenthood Federation of America, *Planned Parenthood News*, Fall, 1958, 2. KDM-PPFA.

25. Ibid.

26. Ibid.

27. Editorial, "In the City's Hospitals," *New York Times*, July 18, 20:2.

28. *New York Times*, July 23, 1958, 17:1.

29. *New York Times*, July 24, 1958, 27:8.

30. *New York Times*, July 25, 1958, 20:3.

31. *New York Times*, July 28, 1958, 26:1.

32. *Planned Parenthood News*, Fall 1958, 4. KDM-PPFA.

33. *New York Times*, August 4, 1958, 23:1.

34. *New York Times*, August 20, 1958, 25:3.

35. *Commonweal*, September 12, 1958, 586.

36. Cited in *Planned Parenthood News*, Fall 1958, 3. KDM-PPFA.

37. *Planned Parenthood News*, Fall 1958, 2. KDM-PPFA.

38. *Planned Parenthood News*, Fall 1958, 1. KDM-PPFA.

39. *New York Times*, September 18, 1958, 12:5.

40. Ibid.

41. Ibid.

42. *Planned Parenthood News*, Fall 1958, 3. KDM-PPFA.

43. "Anatomy of a Victory," 13.

CHAPTER 5. SACRED WORK IN BALTIMORE, 1961–1965

1. "The Ethics of Family Planning," statement adopted by the Clergymen's National Advisory Council of the Planned Parenthood of America, April 1960, 2. SSC.

2. Quoted in William T. Russell, *Maryland: The Land of Sanctuary* (Baltimore: J. H. Furst Company, 1907), 203–204.

3. Pat Romero, untitled ms. from the files of the Baltimore Planned Parenthood, 2. Planned Parenthood of Maryland. Hereafter PPM.

4. Ibid., 4.

5. Ibid., 2.

6. Laurie Zabin, unpublished remarks at a Planned Parenthood Symposium, October 1, 1962, 109. Archives of PPM.

7. Lenore Guttmacher, "Notes on Her Years with Planned Parenthood," 1977, unpublished from the files of the Baltimore Affiliate, 2. PPM.

8. Lara Marks, *Sexual Chemistry* (New Haven: Yale University Press, 2002). See chapter 2, "Divisive Device: The Pill and the Catholic Church," 216–234.

9. *New York Times*, March 10, 1948, 20:2.

10. Quoted in David Garrow, *Liberty and Sexuality* (New York: Macmillan Publishing Company, 1994), 217.

11. Romero, untitled ms., 8.

12. Ibid., 8.

13. Zabin, unpublished remarks, 110.

14. Ibid., 111.

15. Ibid., 118.

16. Notes from Laurie Zabin included in a letter to Tom Davis from Nana Henderson, August 21, 2003.

17. PPFA *News Exchange,* December 1946, no. 21, 1. KDM-PPFA.

18. From a letter to Anne Huppman, executive director of Planned Parenthood from the Reverend E. Rudolph Obey, minister of the Cherry Hill Community Church, March 22, 1961. From archives of PPM.

19. Linda Gordon, *The Moral Property of Women* (Urbana: University of Illinois Press, 2002), 322.

20. Minutes of Clergymen's Advisory Board meeting, January 10, 1963, 4. PPM.

21. Ibid., 2.

22. Caroline S. Cochran, chair of the Welfare Committee of the grand jury, in a December, 4, 1964, letter to Purl E. Ansel, foreman of the September 1964 grand jury, 1. PPM.

23. Minutes of the Clergymen's Advisory Board meeting, January 10, 1963, 3. PPM.

24. Helen Henry, "Maryland Unit Is U.S. Model," *Baltimore Sun,* April 24, 1966.

25. Ibid.

26. A. Lieberman "Overview of Experiences at Planned Parenthood," report prepared for the fiftieth anniversary television show, April 25, 1977. PPM.

Chapter 6. Victories in the Sixties

Epigraph: From Planned Parenthood Association records 1930–1975. Western Historical Manuscripts Collection, University of Missouri-St. Louis (hereafter cited as WHMC-UMSL).

1. St. Louis, Denver, and San Francisco were selected primarily because of geographical diversity. Dozens of other cities and small towns went through much the same conflicts as they did.

2. *Planned Parenthood Beginnings,* Affiliate histories compiled by Lenore Guttmacher for the Margaret Sanger Centennial Celebration, 1979 PPFA Annual Meeting, Houston, Texas. November 15, 1979, 25. KDM-PPFA.

3. "The Anatomy of a Victory II: Denver's Big Push," Planned Parenthood Federation of America, 1961, 4. KDM-PPFA. (Hereafter "Anatomy II.")

4. Esther W. Shoemaker, "Denver's Big Push," in "Anatomy II," 1961, 1. KDM-PPFA.

5. Clergy Committee Statement to the Board of Health and Hospitals of the City and County of Denver, October 1, 1960. "Anatomy II," 9.

6. Letter from Board of Directors, "Anatomy II," 5.

7. "Anatomy II," 7.

8. "Anatomy II," 2.

9. Editorial in *Denver Post*, "Let Planned Parenthood Be Heard," October 8, 1961.

10. Madeline Gray, *Margaret Sanger* (New York: Richard Marek Publishers, 1983), 122.

11. Lader, *The Margaret Sanger Story* (Westport, Conn.: Greenwood Press, 1955), 101.

12. Statement of the Metropolitan Church Federation unanimously adopted May 16, 1946. From Planned Parenthood Association records 1930–1975. WHMC-UMSL.

13. Ibid.

14. The Reverend James Clarke, minister of the Second Presbyterian Church, "The Ethics of Planned Parenthood," radio broadcast, February 1949, 3. Planned Parenthood Association records. WHMC-UMSL.

15. Ibid., 4.

16. *St. Louis Globe Democrat*, February 22, 1964.

17. *St. Louis Globe Democrat*, April 8, 1964.

18. Deborah R. McFarlane and Kenneth J. Meier, *The Politics of Fertility Control* (New York: Chatham House Publisher, 2001), 41–42.

19. Donald T. Critchlow, *Intended Consequences: Birth Control, Abortion and the Federal Government in Modern America* (NewYork: Oxford University Press, 1999), 54.

20. Lara Marks, *Sexual Chemistry* (New Haven: Yale University Press, 2001), 216–232.

21. John Leo, "American Cardinals in Perspective," *Christianity and Crisis*, May 11, 1964, 86–89.

22. Dorothy Roudebush Papers, 1959–1982. WHMC-UMSL.

23. *St. Louis Post Dispatch*, February 10, 1964.

24. Letter from the Metropolitan Church Federation to Mrs. Dorothy Roudebush, June 15, 1964. Roudebush Papers. WHMC-UMSL

25. "The St. Louis Story—Its Broad Outlines," January 14, 1969. Roudebush Papers. WHMC-UMSL.

26. In 1965–1966, as poverty money began to flow, the National Conference of Catholic Bishops could not agree on whether or not to fight the funding of family planning services. Cardinal Ritter and Cardinal Shehan of Baltimore persuaded the bishop's conference to issue no statement and each bishop was left to decide what to do in his area. With the exception of a few cities such as Milwaukee, Philadelphia, and Trenton where bishops publicly opposed the coming of birth control services funded by the War on Poverty, most bishops ignored the issue. Critchlow, *Intended*, 124–128.

27. I am indebted to Tom N. Saunders, author of *Planned Parenthood Alameda/San Francisco, 1929–1994*. As a longtime supporter of the affiliate, he compiled this history in the mid-1990s. He was most generous in sharing his writing and his thoughts with me.

28. Ibid., 17.

29. Ibid., 42.

30. Ibid., 45.

31. Ibid., 44.

32. The Reverend John Courtney Murray, S.J., "American's Four Conspiracies," in *Religion in America*, edited by John Cogley (Cleveland: Meridian Books, 1958), 12–41.

33. *Planned Parenthood News*, November 1966, 3.

34. Critchlow, *Intended*, 62.

35. *Planned Parenthood News*, November 1966, 3.

36. Lara Marks *Sexual Chemistry*, 216–227, argues that *Humanae Vitae* was a point-by-point refutation of Rock's published cause for contraception.

37. Personal communication.

Chapter 7. PLANNED PARENTHOOD AND THE CLERGY CONSULTATION SERVICE ON ABORTION, 1967–1973

1. Quoted in Carole Joffe, *Doctors of Conscience* (Boston: Beacon Press, 1995), 25.

2. Gerald Gardner, *The Censorship Papers* (New York: Dodd, Mead & Company, 1987), 207–212.

3. Leslie Reagan, *When Abortion Was a Crime* (Berkeley: University of California Press, 1997), 209.

4. Ibid., 211.

5. Eugene Quay, "Justifiable Abortion—Medical and Legal Foundations," *Georgetown Law Journal* 49 (Winter 1960): 233–234, 397–399.

6. David Garrow, *Liberty and Sexuality* (New York: Macmillan Publishing Company, 1994), 282.

7. Lawrence Tribe, *Abortion* (New York: W. W. Norton & Company, 1990), 37.

8. Garrow, *Liberty*, 285–289.

9. Rickie Solinger, *Abortion Wars* (Berkeley: University of California Press, 1998), xi.

10. Cynthia Gorney, *Articles of Faith* (New York: Simon and Schuster, 1998, 2000), 76–78.

11. Ibid., 74–75.

12. Laurence Lader, *Abortion II* (Boston: Beacon Press, 1973), 75–76.

13. Howard Moody and Arlene Carmen, *Abortion Counseling* (New York: Judson Press, 1973). Used by permission of the publishers.

14. Reprinted from Moody and Carmen, *Abortion Counseling*, copyright 1973 by Judson Press. Used by permission of Judson Press, 800-4-JUDSON,www.judsonpress.com 30–31. Emphasis in original.

15. Joshua D. Wolff, "Ministers of a Higher Law: The Story of the Clergy Consultation on Abortion," senior thesis, Amherst College, April 1998, 62.

16. Ibid., 59.

17. The Clergy Consultation Service did not keep records of the numbers of clergy involved, so these numbers represent the highest and lowest estimate. The higher number comes from the *National Clergy Consultation Service Newsletter*, vol. 2, no. 1, July 1971.

18. Lader, *Abortion II*, 76–78.

19. Ibid., 77.

20. Reagan, *When Abortion*, 242.

21. Moody and Carmen, *Abortion*, 36.

22. The American Lutheran Church, the New York City Protestant Council of Churches the Episcopal Diocese of New York, and the New York State Council of Churches all came out for the reform of the abortion law.

23. Thirty-six abortions were performed on the day the clinic opened its doors. In that first month the clinic did seven hundred. Every one was referred by the Clergy Consultation. Wolff, "Ministers," 13.

24. Moody and Carmen, *Abortion*, 75.

25. Joffe, *Doctors*, 132.

26. Gorney, *Articles*, 96–97.

27. Joffe, *Doctors*, 138.

28. Reagan, *When Abortion*, 158–159, 187–188.

29. Mary Calderone, M.D., ed., *Abortion in the United States* (New York: Harper Brothers, 1958), 118.

30. Ibid., 113.

31. Garrow, *Liberty*, 295.

32. The Reverend Howard Moody, Closing Address at PPFA Religious Affairs Conference, "Sexism, Religion and Family Planning" at Yale Divinity School, November 1973, 2. SSC.

33. *New York Times*, April 10, 1970, 42:7.

34. "First Trimester—Abortion Services," May 21, 1987. KDM-PPFA.

35. Gorney, *Articles*, 218.

36. Memo to Dr. Alan Guttmacher from Dr. Langmyhr, May 15, 1967. KDM-PPFA.

37. Ibid.

38. Lelia V. Hall, *A Brief History of PP-WP's Religious Affairs Committee.* Undated, probably mid-1973. SSC.

39. "Abortion, Birth Control, and the Ethics of Limiting Reproduction in the Framework of Religious Thought," Planned Parenthood Federation, 1972.

40. Moody, "Closing Address," 2.

Chapter 8. The Post-*Roe* Era, 1973–1992

1. Perso. conversation with the Reverend Betsy Davis, November 4, 1998.

2. Virgil C. Blum, "Public Policy Making: Why the Churches Strike Out," *America*, March 6, 1971, 224–228. This was a prophetic article acknowledging that the pro-choice movement had been astonishingly effective and urging Roman Catholic bishops to realize that they had to change their strategy and organize a grassroots movement. Everything Blum recommended was done within a few years.

3. *New York Times*, February 1, 1973, 22:1.

4. *New York Times*, August 14, 1973, 67:3.

5. *New York Times*, March 8, 1974, 40:4.

6. *New York Times*, November 21, 1975, 19:2.

7. "To Those in Support of the Right to Choose," Mary Ellen Haines, director of the Family Planning and Abortion Program, in a letter from the United Church Board of Homeland Ministries, May 1, 1973, 1. Author's files.

8. Ibid., 2.

9. The organization changed its name to the Religious Coalition for Reproductive Choice in 1993.

10. See chapter 9.

11. A sample would include "Is the Fetus a Person? The Bible's View," by Dr. Roy Bowen Ward; "Religious Liberty: A Heritage at Stake," by Dr. Paul Simmons, formerly of the Southern Seminary (Southern Baptist) in Louisville; and "How Good Women Make Wise Choices," by the Reverend Nancy Rockwell. Published by the Religious Coalition for Reproductive Choice.

12. See especially their 1996 pamphlet "Black Ministers Support Your Right to Choose." The National Sexuality summits have been held at Howard University every summer since 1997. Under the leadership of the current director, the Reverend Carlton Veazey, RCRC has obtained grants to work in the Union of South Africa. Their most recent effort is work with churches there.

13. Frances Kissling, "Women's Freedom and Reproductive Rights: The Core Fear of Patriarchy," in *Encyclopedia of Women and Religion in North America,* ed. Rosemary Ruether and Rosemary Keller (forthcoming).

14. An example would be their citation of a poll by the National Opinion Research Center that said that only 11 percent of Catholics disapproved of abortion in all circumstances. See their ad, "A Diversity of Opinions Regarding Abortion Exists among Committee Catholics," *New York Times,* October 7, 1984, E7.

15. *New York Times,* October 7, E7.

16. Lawrence Tribe, *Abortion* (New York: W. W. Norton and Company, 1990), 172.

17. "America's Abortion Dilemma," *Newsweek,* January 14, 1985, 23.

18. *The Saratogian,* November 19, 3A.

19. Ibid., November 21, 1984, 1A.

20. Ibid., November 21, 1984, 8A.

21. Ibid., November 23, 1984, 7A.

22. Ibid., November 15, 1985, 3A.

23. Ibid., November 24, 1985, 8A.

24. Ibid.

25. Ibid.

26. Ellen Warren, "If You Can't Beat 'Em, Pray That God Strikes 'Em Dead," *Albany Times Union,* June 8, 1986.

27. Minutes of the Adirondack Religious Coalition for Choice, November 25, 1986.

28. *The Saratogian,* July 23, 1987, 1.

29. Internal records of the Adirondack Religious Coalition for Choice, 1993.

30. The three affiliates were Planned Parenthood of Northeastern New York, (Schenectady), Upper Hudson Planned Parenthood (Albany), and Planned Parenthood of Northern New York (Plattsburgh), 140 miles north of Albany.

31. *Albany Times Union, Schenectady Gazette, The Saratogian,* March 14, 1990.

32. *Troy Record,* August 2, 1990. 1.

33. *Glens Falls Post Star,* April 26, 1992, 8.

34. "Day of Theological Reflection: Summary of Proceedings," Wainright House, Rye, New York. Planned Parenthood of Westchester/Rockland, 1992.

35. *New York Times,* October 11, 1989, I, 1:6.

36. In an analysis, R. W. Apple suggested that the abortion issue was hurting the Republicans, because poll data indicated that opposition to abortion was part of the reason the Republican candidates for governor in New Jersey and Virginia went down to defeat in the 1989 fall elections. *New York Times,* November 9, II, 14:5.

37. Marcia Ann Gillespie, "Repro Woman," noted how Wattleton had returned Planned Parenthood to the kind of militancy the movement had in the early days under Sanger. *Ms.,* October, 1989, 50–53.

38. Records of the Office of Special Projects, Planned Parenthood Federation of America.

39. Ibid.

40. One study of the period in question is Kathleen A. Tobin, *The American Religious Debate over Birth Control, 1907–1937* (Jefferson, N.C.: McFarland & Company, 2001), 59, 101–102.

41. See especially Paul Ramsey, *The Ethics of Fetal Research* (1975); *Ethics at the Edges of Life* (1978); *Basic Christian Ethics* (1977); and *Deeds and Rules in Christian Ethics* (1983).

42. Estimates of illegal abortions in the period between 1920 and 1955 cover a wide range. Perhaps the most reasonable was the one from PPFA's Conference on Abortion in 1955, which estimated that there were anywhere from 200,000 to 1,000,000 abortions a year. Although we have the number of therapeutic abortions performed at a number of hospitals, we have no total for the nation. But we can make a rough estimate by noting that New York City averaged 600 therapeutic abortions per year in the 1947–1950 period. New York City had about 5 percent of the population in the United States at that time. If we multiplied 600 by 20, we might get a very rough estimate of 12,000 therapeutic abortions per year. Even if we doubled that number to 24,000, it is still a small percentage of the 200,000 to 1,000,000 estimated abortions. Most abortions in America were being done illegally in that pre-*Roe* period.

43. J. A. McHugh, O.P., "Casus Moralis: Abortion and the Natural Law," *Homiletic and Pastoral Review* (December 1933): 302.

44. "Statistics," *Theological Studies* (December 1940): 427–428. The article is citing the remarks of Dr. Frank Rice from "A Catholic Physician's View on Family Limitation," *Ecclesiastical Review* (July 1940).

45. "Home Front Sabotage," *Ave Maria,* February 17, 1945, 99.

46. *Catholic Encyclopedia* (New York: McGraw-Hill, 1967), vol. 1, 28.

47. See especially Leslie Reagan, *When Abortion Was a Crime* (Berkeley: University of California Press, 1997), 148–159, who describes the more or less open practice of abortion by Dr. Gabler in Chicago, Dr. Keener in Detroit, and Dr. Timanus in Baltimore.

CHAPTER 9. DEADLY VIOLENCE AND THE RENEWAL OF CLERGY SUPPORT

1. The "gag rule" was a policy that said that any family planning clinic that received government grants could not inform a woman who was pregnant that abortion was one of her options. After a long struggle in the courts, the policy was upheld by the Supreme Court (5–4) in *Rust v. Sullivan* during the spring of 1991. Clinton canceled the policy on January 22, 1993.

American law states that the United State Agency for International Development (USAID) funds cannot be spent on abortions. In 1984, at the International Conference on Population in Mexico City, President Reagan extended the policy by terminating such financial aid to any organization (but not governments) that provided abortions with its own money. This became known as the "Mexico City policy," or the "global gag rule." On January22, 1993, President Clinton repealed the Mexico City restrictions.

2. *New York Times*, January 2, 1995, 10 (in caption).

3. The Reverend Tom Davis, "At the Cathedral: A Response to Murder," *Clergy Voices*, April 1995, 1.

4. Ibid., 2.

5. Ibid., 3.

6. Ibid., 3.

7. Rabbi Cheryl Jacobs, "Justice, Justice, Shall You Pursue," *Reconstructionist Journal* (Winter 2001–2002).

8. The Reverend Roger Buchanan, "The Modern Golden Calf," *Clergy Voices*, June 1996, 5.

9. The Reverend Lynn NewHeart, "A Chaplain at Planned Parenthood," *Clergy Voices*, December 1994, 3.

10. Ibid., 4.

11. Ibid., 4.

12. The Reverend Stephen Mather, "Resisting Intimidation from the Religious Right," *Clergy Voices*, December 1994, 4.

13. Ibid.

14. The Reverend Stephen Mather, "A Vision for Planned Parenthood for the 21st Century," *Clergy Voices*, October 2000, 2.

15. *Roanoke Times*, February 25, 2000, B1–B4.

16. *Roanoke Times*, May 25, 1999, 6.

17. Cody Lowe, "All Things to All People," *Roanoke Times*, May 25, 1999, 1.

18. Ibid., 6.

19. From remarks before the Virginia Senate Health and Education Committee February 20, 2000.

20. Statement made by Jim LeFevre, chief strategic officer of PPFA, May 1999.

21. In a "Guest Viewpoint" column in the *Kalamazoo Gazette* he identifies himself as a "Calvinist" and defends his choice to speak out as a clergyperson. September 15, 1998.

22. Based on remarks delivered by Bob Lohrmann at the Thirtieth Anniversary Celebration of Planned Parenthood of South Central Michigan, October 29, 1996.

23. The Reverend Mark Pawlowski, "Why a 'Real' Minister Works for Planned Parenthood," *Clergy Voices*, September 1999, 3.

24. The Reverend Mark Pawlowski, "At the Political Conventions," *Clergy Voices*, October 2000.

25. The Reverend Mark Pawlowski, "Celebrating the Significance of *Roe v. Wade*: A Year of Providing Choices," remarks on the anniversary of *Roe v. Wade*, Planned Parenthood of South Central Michigan, Kalamazoo, Michigan, January 1998.

26. The Reverend Mark Pawlowski, "Who Really Should Define Competent Medical Care?" *Kalamazoo Gazette*, August 4, 1998.

27. The Reverend Mark Pawlowski, "Guttmacher Report: National Abortion Rate Declines," *Kalamazoo Gazette*, October, 2002.

28. The Reverend Mark Pawlowski, testimony before the Michigan State House Committee on Children and Family Health, in re HB 4655, April 2001.

29. *Clergy Voices*, May 2003, 4–5; *Clergy Voices*, October 2001, 5.

30. Brickner has written extensively. Among his books are *Searching the Prophets for Values* and *Finding God in the Garden*. He also has written numerous articles for the *New York Times*, the *Saturday Review*, the *Washington Post*, *Newsday*, the *Christian Century*, and *Newsweek*.

31. Samuel A. Mills, "Abortion and Religious Freedom: The Religious Coalition for Abortion Rights (RCAR) and the Pro-Choice Movement, 1973–1989," *Journal of Church and State* (Summer, 1991): 573–574.

32. From a letter from Monica Corsaro to the author, October 9, 2003.

33. *New York Times*, July 13, 2001, A17:1.

34. Conversation in Binghamton, New York, October 5, 1988.

35. Stacey Little-Pyfrom and Kimberly Buck, "The Church Partnership Program," Planned Parenthood of Metropolitan Washington, D.C., Inc., April, 2001. The program was pioneered by Brenda Rhodes Miller, director, DC Campaign to Prevent Teen Pregnancy; the Reverend Dr. A. Knighton Stanley; and the Reverend Leon G. Lipscombe, Sr.

36. Ibid., 10.

37. Ibid., 39.

38. *The Church Partnership Program*, 40.

CHAPTER 10. THE FUTURE OF THE ALLIANCE

1. Kevin Phillips, *Wealth and Democracy* (New York: Broadway Books, 2002), See especially chapter 8, "Wealth, Money-Culture Ethics and Corruption," 317–346.

2. Ibid., 68–83.

3. Kay Hymowitz, "Ecstatic Capitalism's Brave New Work Ethic," *City Journal* 11 (Winter 2001),

4. John Bunyan, *Pilgrim's Progress* (London: London Anniversary Society, 1928), 98.

5. Religious Coalition for Reproductive Choices, home page www.rcrc.org. Accessed September 20, 2003.

6. A representative sample would include Robert Bork, *Slouching toward America: Modern Liberalism and American Decline*; Michael Medved, *Saving Childhood: Protecting Our Children from the National Assault on Innocence*; Gertrude Himmelfarb, *On Looking into the Abyss: Untimely Thoughts on Culture and Society*, and *One Nation, Two Cultures*.

7. Editorial, "Heartless Marriage Plans," *New York Times*, January 17, 2004.

8. Stephanie Coontz, *The Way We Never Were* (New York: Basic Books, 1992), 182.

9. See especially *Love Makes a Family: Portraits of Lesbian, Gay, Bisexual, and Transgendered Parents and Their Families*, ed. Peggy Gillespie (Amherst: University of Massachusetts Press, 1999).

10. Lee Silver, *Remaking Eden: Cloning and Beyond in a Brave New World*, (New York: Avon Books, 1997), 72–77.

11. Laurie Zoloth, "Jordan's Banks, a View from the First Years of Human Embryonic Cell Research," *American Journal of Bioethics* 2 (Winter 2000): 3–4.

12. *New York Times*, May 9, 2003, A24: 5–6.

13. Richard Land is president of the Ethics and Religious Liberty Commission of the Southern Baptist Convention. The remark appeared in an article "He Held the Line," on Beliefnet in August of 2001. http:www.beliefnet.com/story/86/story_8603_1.html.

14. The Commission on Christian Action of the Reformed Church of America has produced a comprehensive and balanced view of this technology. That report notes that some day researchers might be able to "trick" adult stem cells into the full potential of the embryonic stem cells, but as yet they have not succeeded. Report of the Commission on Christian Action, General Synod 2002, www.rca.org/synod; minutes.2002/action.html, 3–4.

15. For Alzheimer's: American Health Assistance Foundation, 2004, Clarksburg, Maryland, http://www.ahaf.org/alzdis/about/adabout_body.htm. For Parkinsons: National Institute of Neurological Disorders and Stroke, http://www.ninds.nih.gov/health_and_medical/pubs/Parkinson's_disease_backgrounder.htm. For diabetes: National Diabetes Information Clearinghouse (NDIC), http://diabetes.niddk.nih.gov/dm/pubs/statistics/index.htm. All sites accessed April 17, 2004.

16. Environmentalists are concerned about genetic engineering. See especially Bill McKibben, *Enough: Staying Human in an Engineered Age* (New York: Henry Holt, 2003), and Francis Fukuyama, Our *Posthuman Future: Consequences of the Biotechnology Revolution* (New York: Farrar, Straus and Giroux, 2002).

17. General Synod XXIII Resolutions: Support for Federally Funded Research on Embryonic Stem Cells, September 30, http:www.ucc.org/synod/resolutions/res30.htm 2.

18. There are many articles on the new reproductive technologies. One of the best collections is *Beyond Cloning*, edited by Ronald Cole-Turner (Harrisburg, Pa.: Trinity Press International, 2001).

19. "Vision for 2025," Planned Parenthood Federation of America, New York, New York, 2001, 8–12.

20. "The Impact of Religious Organizations on Gender Equality: A Report of Findings from a National Survey Conducted for the Center for Gender Equality by Princeton Survey Research Associates." January 1999. http://www.coaauw.og/boulder-oldsite/aauwb_center_for_equality.html.

21. Prayer delivered at the Cathedral of St. John the Divine, New York City, January, 22, 1995.

Bibliography

"Abortion." *The Catholic Encyclopedia.* Vol. 1. New York: McGraw-Hill, 1967.

"The Anatomy of a Victory." Manuscript. Planned Parenthood Federation of America files, 1958.

"The Anatomy of a Victory II: Denver's Big Push." Manuscript. Planned Parenthood Federation of America files, 1961.

Annual Report, Department of Hospitals, City of New York, 1958.

Annual Report, 2001-2002. Planned Parenthood Federation of America, New York, 2003.

Bainton, Roland. *Here I Stand.* Nashville: Abingdon Press, 1950.

Baumer, Randall, and Laura F. Winner. *Protestantism in America.* New York: Columbia University Press, 2002.

Blanshard, Paul. *American Freedom and Catholic Power.* Boston: Beacon Press, 1948.

Blum, Virgil C. "Public Policy Making: Why the Churches Strike Out." *America,* March 6, 1971, 224–228.

Brickner, Balfour. *Finding God in the Garden.* Boston. Little Brown & Co., 2002.

Brodie, Janet Farrell. *Contraception and Abortion in Nineteenth-Century America.* Ithaca, N.Y.: Cornell University Press, 1994.

Bruggemann, Walter. *Hope within History.* Louisville, Ky.: John Knox Press, 1987.

Buchanan, Roger. "The Modern Golden Calf." *Clergy Voices,* June 1996.

Buck, Kimberly, and Stacey Lyttle-Pyfrom. "The Church Partnership Program." Planned Parenthood of Metropolitan Washington, D.C. April 2001.

Bunyan, John. *Pilgrim's Progress.* London: London Anniversary Society, 1928.

Calderone, Mary, ed. *Abortion in the United States.* New York: Harper Brothers, 1958.

Chesler, Ellen. *Woman of Valor.* New York: Simon and Schuster, 1992.

Cogley, John, ed. *Religion in America.* Cleveland: Meridian Books, 1958.

Cogley, John, and Roger Van Allen. *Catholic America:* Expanded and updated. Kansas City, Mo.: Sheed and Ward, 1986.

Cole-Turner, Ronald, ed. *Beyond Cloning*. Harrisburg, Pa.: Trinity Press, 2001.

Coontz, Stephanie. *The Way We Never Were*. New York: Basic Books, 1992.

"Cooperation with Religious Leaders," December 8, 1947, 1. Sophia Smith Collection, Smith College.

Critchlow, Donald T. *Intended Consequences: Birth Control, Abortion, and the Federal Government in Modern America*. New York: Oxford University Press, 1999.

Davis, Tom. "At the Cathedral: A Response to Murder." *Clergy Voices*, April 1995.

D'Emilio, John, and Estelle B. Freedman. *Intimate Matters: A History of Sexuality in America*. New York: Harper & Row, 1988.

Douglas, Emily Taft. *Margaret Sanger: Pioneer of the Future*. Garrett Park, Md.: Garrett Park Press, 1975.

Editorial: "Heartless Marriage Plans." *New York Times*, January 17, 2004.

Editorial: "In the City's Hospitals." *New York Times*, July 18, 1958.

Editorial: "Let Planned Parenthood Be Heard." *Denver Post*, October 8, 1961.

Eliade, Mircea. *The Sacred and the Profane*. New York: Harcourt Brace and Jovanovich, 1959.

"The Ethics of Birth Control." Reply of the Clergy to Cardinal Hayes of New York City, 1935. Katherine Dexter McCormick Library, Planned Parenthood Federation of America.

"The Ethics of Family Planning." Statement adopted by the National Clergymen's Advisory Council of Planned Parenthood of America, April 1960. Sophia Smith Collection, Smith College.

Feldt, Gloria. *Behind Every Choice Is a Story*. Denton: University of North Texas Press, 2002.

Fukuyama, Francis. *Our Posthuman Future: Consequences of the Biotechnology Revolution*. New York: Farrar, Straus and Giroux, 2002.

Gardner, Gerald. *The Censorship Papers*. New York: Dodd, Mead & Company, 1987.

Garrow, David. *Liberty and Sexuality: The Right to Privacy and the Making of Roe v. Wade*. New York: Macmillan Publishing Company, 1994.

Gillespie, Peggy, ed. *Love Makes a Family: Portraits of Lesbian, Gay, Bisexual, and Transgendered Parents and Their Families*. Amherst: University of Massachusetts Press, 1999.

Gillis, Chester. *Roman Catholicism*. New York: Columbia University Press, 1999.

Gordon, Linda. *The Moral Property of Women*. Urbana: University of Illinois Press, 2002.

———. *Woman's Body, Woman's Right*. New York: Grossman Publishers, 1976.

Gorney, Cynthia. *Articles of Faith*. New York: Simon and Schuster, 1998, 2000.

Graebner, Alan. "Birth Control and the Lutherans." *Journal of Social History* (Summer 1969): 303–317.

Gray, Madeline. *Margaret Sanger*. New York: Richard Marek Publishers, 1979.

Guttmacher, Lenore. "Notes on Her Years with Planned Parenthood." Baltimore. 1977. Planned Parenthood of Maryland.

Guttmacher Institute. "Facts in Brief—Induced Abortion, 2003." http:www.agi-usa.org/pubs/fb_induced_abortion.html.

Henry, Helen. "Maryland Unit Is U.S. Model." *Baltimore Sun,* April 24, 1966.

"Home Front Sabotage." *Ave Maria,* February 17, 1945.

Hudnut-Beumler, James. *Looking for God in the Suburbs: The Religion of the American Dream and Its Critics, 1946–1965.* New Brunswick, N.J.: Rutgers University Press, 1994.

Hymnowitz, Kay. "Ecstatic Capitalism's Brave New Work Ethic." *City Journal* 11 (Winter 2001).

Jacobs, Cheryl. "Justice, Justice, Shall You Pursue." *Clergy Voices,* Winter 2001–2002.

Joffe, Carole. *Doctors of Conscience: The Struggle to Provide Abortions before and after Roe v. Wade.* Boston: Beacon Press, 1995.

Kahn, Joe. "Birth Control: New York's Untold Story." *New York Post,* [Spring] 1957.

Kennedy, David M. *Birth Control in America: The Career of Margaret Sanger.* New Haven: Yale University Press, 1970.

King, Martin Luther. "Family Planning: A Special and Urgent Concern." Planned Parenthood Federation of America, 1966.

Kissling, Frances. "Women's Freedom and Reproductive Rights: The Core Fear of Patriarchy," in *Encyclopedia of Women and Religion in North America,* edited by Rosemary Ruether and Rosemary Keller. Forthcoming.

Lader, Larry. *Abortion II.* Boston: Beacon Press, 1973.

_____. *The Margaret Sanger Story.* Westport, Conn.: Greenwood Press, 1955.

Land, Richard. "He Held the Line." August 2001. *Beliefnet.* http:www.beliefnet.com/story/86/story_8603_1.html.

Leo, John. "American Cardinals in Perspective." *Christianity and Crisis,* May 11, 1964.

Levinson, Edward. *Labor on the March.* Ithaca, N.Y.: ILR Press, 1938.

Lieberman, A. "Overview of Experiences at Planned Parenthood," Report prepared for the fiftieth anniversary television show on Planned Parenthood of Maryland, April 25, 1977.

Lowe, Cody. "All Things to All People." *Roanoke Times,* May 25, 1999.

Maguire, Daniel C. *Sacred Choices: The Right to Contraception and Abortion* in *Ten World Religions.* Minneapolis: Fortress Press, 2001.

Marks, Lara. *Sexual Chemistry.* New Haven: Yale University Press, 2002.

Mather, Stephen. "Resisting Intimidation from the Religious Right." *Clergy Voices,* December 1994.

_____. "A Vision for Planned Parenthood for the Twenty-First Century." *Clergy Voices,* October 2000.

McCann, Carole R. *Birth Control Politics in the United States, 1916–1945.* Ithaca, N.Y.: Cornell University Press, 1994.

McFarlane, Deborah R., and Meier, Kenneth J. *The Politics of Fertility Control: Family Planning and Abortion Policies in the American States.* New York: Chatham House Publishers, 2001.

McHugh, J. A., O.P. "Casus Moralis: Abortion and the Natural Law." *Homiletic and Pastoral Review* (December 1933): 302.

McKibben, Bill. *Enough: Staying Human in an Engineered Age.* New York: Henry Holt, 2003.

Miller, Patricia. *The Worst of Times.* New York: Harper Perennial, 1994.

Moody, Howard, and Arlene Carmen. *Abortion Counseling and Social Change.* Valley Forge, Pa.: Judson Press, 1973.

Moore, Gloria, and Ronald Moore. *Margaret Sanger and the Birth Control Movement: A Bibliography, 1911–1984.* Metuchen, N.J.: Scarecrow Press, 1986.

Morris, Charles R. *American Catholic.* New York: Random House, 1997.

Murray, John Courtney, S.J. "America's Four Conspiracies," in *Religion in America*, edited by John Cogley. Cleveland: Meridian Books, 1958.

NewHeart, Lynn. "A Chaplain at Planned Parenthood." *Clergy Voices*, December 1994.

Noonan, John, Jr. *Contraception.* Cambridge: Harvard University Press, 1986.

Oates, Stephen B. *Let the Trumpet Sound: A Life of Martin Luther King.* New York: HarperCollins Press, 1982.

Pawlowski, Mark. "At the Political Conventions." *Clergy Voices*, October 2000.

———. "Celebrating the Significance of *Roe v. Wade*: A Year of Providing Choice." Remarks on the anniversary of *Roe v. Wade*. Planned Parenthood of South Central Michigan, Kalamazoo, Mich. January 1998.

———. "Guttmacher Report: National Abortion Rate Declines." *Kalamazoo Gazette*, October, 2002.

———. "Who Really Should Define Competent Medical Care?" *Kalamazoo Gazette*, August 4, 1998.

———. "Why a 'Real' Minister Works for Planned Parenthood." *Clergy Voices*, September, 1999.

Phillips, Kevin. *Wealth and Democracy.* New York. Broadway Books, 2002.

Plaskow, Judith. *Standing Again at Sinai.* New York: Harper & Row, 1990.

"Presbyterian Board Approves Birth Control." *New York Herald Tribune*, April 27, 1931.

Quay, Eugene. "Justifiable Abortion—Medical and Legal Foundations." *Georgetown Law Journal* 49 (Winter 1960): 233–234, 397–399.

Reagan, Leslie. *When Abortion Was a Crime: Women, Medicine, and Law in the United States, 1867–1973.* Berkeley: University of California Press, 1997.

Reed, James. *From Private Vice to Public Virtue: The Birth Control Movement and American Society since 1930.* New York: Basic Books, 1978.

Report of the Commission on Christian Action. General Synod of the Reformed Church in America 2002. http.www.rca.org/synod: minutes. 2002/action.html.

Report on Support for Federally Funded Research on Embryonic Stem Cells. General Synod XXIII Resolutions. September 2001. http.www.ucc.org/synod/resolutions/res30.htm.

Ruether, Rosemary. *Religion and Sexism.* New York: Simon and Schuster, 1974.

Russell, William T. *Maryland: The Land of Sanctuary.* Baltimore: J. H. Furst Company, 1907.

Ryan, John. "Family Limitation." *Ecclesiastical Review.* 54 (January–June 1916) 684–696.

Sachar, Howard M. *A History of the Jews in America.* New York: Alfred A. Knopf, 1992.

Sanger, Margaret. "Birth Control and Racial Betterment." *Birth Control Review* (February 1919): 11.

―――. *Margaret Sanger: An Autobiography.* New York: W. W. Norton and Co., 1938.

―――. *Motherhood in Bondage.* 1928. Columbus: Ohio State University Press, 2000.

―――. *My Fight for Birth Control.* Elmsford, N.Y.: Maxwell Reprint Company, 1931.

Saunders, Tom. *Planned Parenthood Alameda/San Francisco, 1929–1994.* San Francisco: privately printed, 1996.

Schoen, Johanna. "Fighting for Child Health: Race, Birth Control, and the State in the Jim Crow South." *Social Politics* 4 (Spring 1997): 90–113.

Silver, Lee. *Remaking Eden: Cloning and Beyond in a Brave New World.* New York: Avon Books, 1997.

Solinger, Rickie, ed. *Abortion Wars: A Half Century of Struggle, 1950–2000.* Berkeley: University of California Press, 1998.

"Statistics." *Theological Studies* (December 1940).

"Suggested Policy on the Catholic Church." Statement of the Executive Committee of the Planned Parenthood Board, April 6, 1943.

Taft, Phillip. *Organized Labor in American History.* New York: Harper & Row, 1964.

Tobin, Kathleen A. *The American Religious Debate over Birth Control, 1907–1937.* Jefferson, N.C.: McFarland and Company, 2001.

Tone, Andrea. *Devices and Desires: A History of Contraceptives in America.* New York: Hill & Wang, 2001.

A Tradition of Choice: Planned Parenthood at 75. New York: Planned Parenthood Federation of America, 1991.

Tribe, Lawrence. *Abortion: The Clash of Absolutes.* New York: W. W. Norton and Company, 1990.

Trible, Phyllis. "Eve, the Theologian." Task Force on Women of the United Church of Christ. New York. 1974.

Uttley, Lois, and Pawelko, Ronnie. *No Strings Attached: Public Funding of Religiously-Sponsored Hospitals in the United States.* Education Fund of Family Planning Advocates of NYS, Albany, N.Y., 2002.

Valenza, Charles. "Was Margaret Sanger a Racist?" *Family Planning Perspectives* (January–February 1985): 44–46.

Warren, Ellen. "If You Can't Beat 'Em, Pray That God Strikes 'Em Dead." *Albany Times Union*, June 8, 1986.

Watkins, Elizabeth Siegel. *On the Pill: A Social History of Oral Contraceptives 1950–1970.* Baltimore: Johns Hopkins University Press, 1998.

Wolff, Joshua. "Ministers of a Higher Law: The Story of the Clergy Consultation on Abortion." Senior thesis, Amherst College. April 1998.

Zangrando, Robert. "About Lynching." *The Reader's Companion to American History*, edited by Eric Fonen and John A. Garrity. Boston: Houghton Mifflin, 1991.

Zimmerman, David R. "Abortion Clinics' Toughest Cases." *Medical World News*, March 9, 1987.

Zoloth, Laurie. "Jordan's Banks: A View from the First Years of Human Embryonic Cell Research." *American Journal of Bioethics.* 2 (Winter 2000).

Index

abortion: change in public attitude toward, 124–126; Comstock law censorship and, 28; cost of, 134; doctor's campaign against, 24; laws against, 24, 123, 131 (*See also* abortion law reform); as social justice issue, 169; spiritual aspect to, 135, 177–178; therapeutic, 73–74, 122–123, 124, 224n42. *See also* clergy, abortion issue and; Planned Parenthood Federation of America (PPFA), abortion and; Pro-choice movement; Pro-life movement

abortion, illegal: through Clergy Consultation Service, 126–133, 134; complications from, 24, 72, 123; estimated numbers, 124, 133, 168, 224n42; prosecutions for, 74, 131–133; public silence about, 167–169; unprosecuted, 73, 127, 131

abortion law reform: American Law Institute proposals, 123; in California, 133, 137; Clergy Consultation Service and, 129–130, 133; gag rule and, 69, 170, 225n1; Medicaid funding and, 143–144; in New York State, 133–135, 137, 138, 142; Planned Parenthood

and, 135–138; *Roe v. Wade*, 2, 47, 132, 135, 138; threat to overturn *Roe v. Wade*, 142–143, 145, 172, 185–186, 195; waiting period and, 180–181

abstinence, 32, 192

abstinence-only sex education programs, 190, 191

Adams, Hampton, 81

Adirondack Religious Coalition for Choice, 151–160, 164, 166

adoption, 153

African Americans, in pro-choice movement, 145, 146

African American, The, 97

Albany Times Union, 158, 159

American Association of University Women, 115

American Birth Control League, 3, 5, 18, 25, 32, 34, 36, 51, 115

American Civil Liberties Union, 33

American Conference of Catholic Bishops, 70

American Freedom and Catholic Power (Blanchard), 50

American Jewish Congress, 84

American Law Institute (ALI), abortion law reform proposals of, 123

American Medical Association (AMA), 36, 83
Amos (prophet), 8–9
Anti-abortion movement. *See* Pro-life movement
anti-Catholicism, 48–49
anti-Semitism, 50
Apha, Arthur, 81
Augustine, bishop of Hippo, 12

Baehr, George, 83
Baltimore, welfare system contraceptive services controversy in, 89–90, 91–92, 94–98
Baltimore Council of Churches, 94
Baptist churches, 16, 42, 144, 155, 168, 201
Baptist Ministers' Conference, 81–82
Baptist Youth Conference, 42–43
Barrett, James, 172, 173
Barrett, June, 172
Barth, Karl, 167
Bennett, John, 89
Bennett, William, 64
Bernardin, Joseph, 202
biblical morality, 7–10, 45, 52–54, 176, 180
bioethics, 197–200
birth control. *See* birth control movement; contraception
Birth Control Clinical Research Bureau, 34, 36
Birth Control Federation of America, 54
birth control movement, 3, 18, 25; clergy in (*See* clergy in birth control movement; Clergy-Planned Parenthood partnership); conflicts with Roman Catholic Church, 31–34, 40–41, 53–54; conflicts within, 34–35; early advocates, 28; eugenics movement and, 18, 34–36; founded by Sanger, 29–31; Martin Luther King on, 27; medical professions' attitude

toward, 34, 36; police raid on, 32–34. *See also* contraception campaigns; Planned Parenthood Federation of America (PPFA); Sanger, Margaret
birth control pill, 85, 92, 98, 112, 113, 119
Birth Control Review, 32
Blanshard, Paul, 50
Bonhoeffer, Dietrich, 167
Borden, Jane, 152
Brahman (Hinduism), 6
Brasile, Victor, 63
Brennan, William, 152
Brickner, Balfour, 145, 174, 175, 176, 185–186
Bridges, Harry, 22
Britton, John, 172, 173
Brown v. Board of Education, 23
Bruggemann, Walter, 21
Buchanan, Roger, 176
Buckley, Kathleen, 157
Buck v. Bell, 35
Burkhart, Roy, 61
Bush, George H.W., 160, 194–195, 196

Calderone, Mary, 135
California, abortion law reform in, 133, 137
Calvin, John, 13
Campbell, Joan Brown, 174, 175
Candlin, Francis, 105, 108
Carmen, Arlene, 128
Carter, Jimmy, 144
Casey decision, 172
Castuera, Ignacio, 155, 192
Cathedral of St. John the Divine, 88, 117, 173–175
Catholic Church. *See* Roman Catholic Church
Catholic Encyclopedia, 168
Catholic Messenger, 83
Catholic Physicians Guild, 81
Catholics for a Free Choice, 146–147
celibacy, clerical, 12, 13
Center for Gender Equality, 201–202

Central Conference of American Rabbis, 41, 51

Chicago Board of Rabbis, 132

Christian Realism, 59

church attendance, 57, 59

Churchill, Winston, 32

Churchman, The, 43, 55

church partnerships, 187–188, 189

civil rights movement, 22–23

Clarke, James, 110, 176

clergy: celibacy of, 12, 13; homosexual, 16; market culture and, 194; marriage counseling responsibilities of, 57, 61; Niebuhr's followers, 59; personal experience of contraception, 24–25; Planned Parenthood and (*See* Clergy-Planned Parenthood partnership); popular image of, 14; religious revival and, 57, 59; vulnerable position of, 14–15; women, 13–14, 15

clergy, abortion issue and, 121; Clergy Consultation Service on abortion, 126–136, 154, 169, 175–176; counseling on abortion decision, 177–178, 179–181; defense of clinics, 151–162, 186–187; memorial services for murder victims, 173–175, 203–204; pro-life clergy, 153–154, 167; religious response to pro-life movement, 175–177, 180, 182; social justice concerns in, 169, 184–185

clergy in birth control movement, 3, 4, 5, 36–37; in Baltimore, 93–94, 102–103; Clergymen's Advisory Council proclamation, 55–56, 98; endorsements by mainline Protestant denominations, 41–43, 58; endorsements by rabbis, 41, 50–51; influence on public opinion, 45–46; justice arguments of, 103, 106–107; organization of local clergy, 60–61; organization of national network, 54–55; political effectiveness of, 86; religious response to Catholic

arguments, 52–53, 60, 71; in St. Louis, 109–110; sanction of sacred, 44, 47; in San Francisco, 116; Sanger's influence on, 37, 41; at twenty-fifth anniversary of Planned Parenthood, 60. *See also* Clergy-Planned Parenthood partnership

Clergy Consultation Service on Abortion, 2, 3, 126–136, 154, 169, 175–176

Clergy Leadership Network, 197

Clergymen's Advisory Council, 54, 55–56, 60–61, 98

Clergymen's National Advisory Council, 88–89, 117

Clergy-Planned Parenthood partnership, 202–203; Baltimore welfare system contraceptive services conflict, 94–98; Catholic hospital doctor dismissal conflict, 61–70, 86; church partnerships, 187–188, 189; Denver hospital contraceptive services conflict, 105–108; diversity of roles, 177–188; humane theology and, 188, 190–191; national chaplain, 192; New York City hospital contraceptive services conflict, 78–87, 103; renewal of, 164–166, 175–177; St. Louis public health agency contraceptive services conflict, 113–114; San Francisco hospital contraceptive services conflict, 116–118; unmarried women policy and, 98–102. *See also* clergy, abortion issue and

Clergy Voices, 166, 177

Cleveland Plain Dealer, 132

Clinton, Bill, 170

cloning, 200

coalition strategy, 85–86

Cody, Cardinal John, 143

Cogley, John, 48

Committee of 100, 62

Commonweal, 42, 82–83, 85

Compass, The, 66

Comstock, Anthony, 29
Comstock laws, 23–24, 29, 54, 57, 69, 90
Concerned Black Clergy, 188
Congregational Church, 43, 53, 61, 65, 81
Congress of Industrial Organizations
    (CIO), 22
Conscience, 155–156, 157
Constitutional amendment to ban
    abortion, 143, 144, 145
contraception: diaphragms, 29, 36;
    distribution of, 68, 85; in France,
    29; information about, 23, 29, 57,
    61; laws against, 23–24, 28, 54, 57,
    69; oral contraceptives, 85, 92, 98,
    112, 113, 119; public acceptance of, 85;
    as religious obligation, 96, 98;
    Roman Catholic Church position
    on, 32, 119. *See also* birth control
    movement
contraception campaigns: for hospital
    services in Denver, 105–108; for
    hospital services in New York City,
    75–87; for hospital services in San
    Francisco, 116–118; for public health
    services in St. Louis, 110–111, 113–114;
    for unmarried women in Baltimore,
    98–102; for welfare system services
    in Baltimore, 89–90, 91–92, 94–98;
    for welfare system services in St.
    Louis, 114
Conway, J.D., 83
Cook County Hospital, Chicago, 123
Corsaro, Monica, 186–187
counseling on abortion decision:
    clergy's role in, 177–178, 179–181;
    mandatory, 144, 179
Cox, Harold, 33
Cuomo, Mario, 146
Cushing, Cardinal Richard, 93

Dalton, John, 111
Darrow, Clarence, 163
Davidoff, Denise Taft, 174, 175
Davies, A. Powell, 56

Davis, Betsy, 142, 151
Delafield, Lewis, 33
Dennett, Mary Ware, 28, 214n29
Denver: birth control movement in,
    104–105; hospital contraceptive
    services controversy in, 105–108
Denver Post, 108
DeVelder, Joyce, 152
Dewey, John, 59
diaphragms, 29, 36
doctors: attitude to birth control
    movement, 34, 36; murders of abor-
    tion providers, 172–173; therapeutic
    abortion and, 127, *See also* abortion,
    illegal; hospitals
Donohue, Captain, 33
Dorsch, Monsignor, 95, 96
Dreiser, Theodore, 32
Drisgula, Paul, 164
DuBois, W.E.B., 23

Ecclesiastical Review, 31
Edwards, Edward, 66
Eisendrath, Maurice, 89
Eisenhower, Dwight, 45–46
Eliade, Mircea, 6
embryo, moral status of, 198–199
Episcopal Church, 16, 41–42, 43, 155
ethics: biblical, 7–10, 55, 176, 180;
    bioethics, 197–200; of Niebuhr, 59
eugenics movement, 18, 34–36
Evans, J. Claude, 131

Fairfield County Medical Association, 62
faith-based initiative, of Bush admin-
    istration, 195
family, sentimentality about, 196–197
Farber, Robert, 100
Federal Council of Churches in
    America, 42, 59, 65, 202
Feminist movement, 163
Ferraro, Barbara, 147
Ferraro, Geraldine, 146
Fewer and Better Babies (Robinson), 28

Finkbine, Sherri, 124, 125
Finn, James, 82–83
Fletcher, Joseph, 167
Florida Religious Coalition for Abortion Rights, 162
Flynn, Timothy J., 77, 78
Forbes, James, 174
Ford, Gerald, 144
Fosdick, Harry Emerson, 37, 52, 89, 174
Fox, Michael, 199
freedom of speech, 69

gag rule, 69, 170, 190, 192, 225n1
Galvin, Elias, 186
Gamble, Nicki Nichols, 174–175
Garden of Eden, 7, 11
gender inequality. *See* sexism
genetic research, 197–199
Georgetown Law Review, 123
germ line modification, 200
Glasner, Samuel, 93
Glen Falls Post Star, 160
Goldman, Emma, 28
Goldstein, Lewis, 83
Goldstein, Sidney, 55, 56
Gollance, Harvey, 79
Gordon, Charles A., 83
Gottdiener, Florence, 63, 64, 65–66
Greenfield, Larry, 188
Griffin, Michael, 172, 173
Griswold decision, 47, 93, 140
Gunn, David, 172, 173
Gurner, Rowena, 125
Guttmacher, Alan, 75–76, 80, 92, 136, 138, 139, 141
Guttmacher, Lenore, 92
Guttmacher (Alan) Institute, 16–17

Hall, Betsy, 157
Hare, Robert, 131–132
Harriman, Joan, 146
Harrington, Donald, 89
Harrison, Beverly, 155

Harvey, Hale, 134
Hatch, Orrin, 199
Hayes, Patrick J. Cardinal, 51–53
Hellman, Louis, 72, 73, 77, 79, 85, 87
Heyman, David M., 83
Hill, Paul, 172
History of the Jews in America, A (Zachar), 51
Hoeltzel, G. Anthony, 203–204
Holmes, John Haynes, 37, 38, 52
Holmes, Oliver Wendell, 36
homosexuals, ordination of, 16
Hope within History (Bruggemann), 21
Hopkins, Harry, 45
hospitals: abortion services in, 155; Catholic, doctor dismissal cases, 61–70; contraceptive services in Denver case, 105–108; contraceptive services in New York City case, 75–77; contraceptive services in San Francisco case, 116–118; mergers of Catholic/secular hospitals, 70; sterilization committees in, 74–75; therapeutic abortions committees in, 74, 122–123
Humanae Vitae, 119
humane theology, 188, 190–191
Huppman, Anne, 99
Hyde, Henry, 133
Hyde Amendment, 143–144, 146

immigration restriction, 35
infertility, genetic technology and, 197–198, 200
Ingersoll, Robert, 28
Interdenominational Ministers' Alliance, 82
Interdenominational Theological Center, 188
Interfaith Alliance, 197
International Council of Religious Education, 56
International Workers of the World (Wobblies), 20–21

in vitro fertilization, 197–198
Israel, Edward, 41

Jacobs, Cheryl, 176
Jacobs, Morris, 77, 78, 79, 80, 81, 82, 83,
    84, 86, 87
Jerome, 12
Jesus, 9–10, 182
Jews: anti-Semitism and, 50; ordination
    of women, 13; in pro-choice
    movement, 145, *See also* Rabbis
Johnson, Lyndon, 111
John XXIII, Pope, 85, 92, 111, 118
Jones, Eleanor, 214n.28
Judson Church, 127, 134

Kahn, Joe, 76
Kennedy, Anne, 32, 33
Kennedy, Ted, 146
King, Martin Luther, 21, 23, 27, 152,
    178
King's County Hospital, New York City,
    72, 77, 79
Kinsey, Alfred, 124, 135
Kirchoff, Virginia, 93
Kissling, Frances, 147, 155
Klein, Edward E., 89
Kopp, James, 173
Krol, Cardinal John, 143
Kruse, H.D., 77
Kurtz, Ron, 154

labor movement, 22, 38
Lambeth Conference, Anglican Bishops
    of, 41–42
Lasher, Bill, 154
Lasker, Mary, 83
Lawrence Textile workers strike, 38
Lawson, James, 176
Leverick, Ida, 114–115
Leviticus, Holiness Code of, 7–8, 9
Lewis, John L., 22
Lewis, Sinclair, 57
Lowney, Shannon, 172, 173–174, 175, 203

Luther, Martin, 13
Lutheran churches, 16, 23, 42, 58, 81,
    109, 110, 155
Lynch, John J., 83
lynching, 22–23
Lyons, Emily, 173

MacKenzie, E. Gordon, 64
McDonald, Miles F., 72, 74
McDonald, Timothy, 188
McLemore, Beth, 179–181, 190
McQuillan, Patricia Fogarty, 146
Maginnis, Patricia, 125
Maguire, Dan, 166
Manley, Herbert Waldo, 81
Manning, Cardinal Timothy, 143
marriage counseling, 57, 61
marriage promotion campaign, 196
Marshall, Robert, 132
Maryland: clergy support for birth
    control, 93–94, 102–103; contra-
    ceptive services for unmarried
    women, 98–102; formation of
    Planned Parenthood in, 90–91;
    religious freedom tradition in, 89;
    Roman Catholicism in, 92–93;
    welfare system contraceptive
    services (Baltimore) controversy,
    89–90, 91–92, 94–98
Mather, Stephen, 178–179
Matthew, 9
May, Joseph, 82
Meager, David, 151
Medeiros, Cardinal Humberto, 143
Medicaid, 143
Melish, John Howard, 37, 52
Mencken, H.L., 57
Meneilley, Robert, 160
Mergerwatch Project, 216n48
Methodist churches, 16, 43, 55, 145, 154,
    155, 186
Metropolitan Church Federation, 109
Meyer, Adolph, 90
Meyer, William, 65

Miller, Jim, 154
Mollenkott, Virginia Ramey, 155
Mondale, Walter, 146
Moody, Howard, 2, 127–128, 131, 132,
    136–137, 140–141, 155
Moral Majority, 144, 162–163
Moral Man and Immoral Society
    (Niebuhr), 59
Morgenthau, Henry, 33
Morton, James Parks, 173
Moscowitz, Henry, 23
Moses, Bessie, 19, 90–91, 115
Motherhood in Bondage, 39, 43
Mother's Milk Fund, 115
Motzkin, Linda, 152
Mt. Airy Baptist Church/Sursum Corda
    outreach program, 187
Mulcahy, Meta, 146
Murphy, Howard, 97
Murray, John Courtney, 118
Murray, Peter Marshall, 83
Murray, Philip, 22

NAACP, 23
National Association for the Repeal of
    Abortion Laws (NARAL), 133, 142
National Catholic Welfare Conference,
    111
National Conference of Catholic
    Bishops, 216n48, 220n26
National Council of Catholic Men, 81
National Council of Catholic Women,
    81
National Council of Churches, 3, 42
National Council of Jewish Women, 72
National Family Week, 55–56
National Labor Relations Law, 22
National Sexuality Summit, 146
New Hampshire, abortion law in, 123
NewHeart, Lynn, 177–178
New Testament, 9–10, 11–12, 180, 182
New York Board of Rabbis, 80, 86
New York City, hospital contraceptive
    services controversy in, 75–87, 103

New York City Welfare and Health
    Council, 76
New York Post, 76, 80
New York State: abortion law reform
    in, 133–135, 137, 138, 142; abortion
    referral service in, 137–138; Adiron-
    dack Religious Coalition for Choice,
    151–160, 164, 166; Catholic hospital
    doctor dismissal case, 63–70, 86;
    pro-life attack on Planned Parent-
    hood funding, 149–151
New York State Religious Coalition for
    Abortion Rights, 154
New York Times, 2, 33, 52, 63, 78, 79–80,
    137, 146–147
New York World Telegram, 65, 80
Nichols, Leanne, 172, 173–174, 175,
    203–204
Niebuhr, Reinhold, 10, 42, 59
Nirvana (Buddhism), 6
Noonan, John T., Jr., 119
Notre Dame University, 119
Nova, David, 180

O'Brien, John A., 118
O'Connor, John Cardinal, 146
Oesterling, James, 37
Office of Economic Opportunity
    (OEO), 111
Ohio, abortion law in, 132
Old Testament, 7–9, 11, 52–53
Omri, King, 8
Operation Rescue, 157–158, 186
oral contraceptives, 85, 92, 98, 112, 113,
    119
Orcutt, Elgin, 116
ordination: of homosexuals, 16; of
    women, 13–14, 15
Orthodox Rabbinical Alliance of
    America, 81
O'Shea, Michael P., 63, 64, 65, 66, 70
Otto, Rudolph, 6
Ovington, Mary White, 23
Oxnam, G. Bromley, 55, 60, 89

parental consent laws, 144
Parsons, E. Spencer, 131, 132–133
Pasteur Guild, 81
Pattison, Bill, 152, 155
Paul (apostle), 11
Paul VI, Pope, 112, 119
Pawlowski, Mark, 181–185, 190
Peale, Norman Vincent, 89
Phelan, Lana, 125
Phillips, Kevin, 193
Phillips, Larry, 157
Pike, James, 88–89, 117, 118
Pilpel, Harriet, 137
Pius IX, Pope, 49–50
Pius XI, Pope, 81
Pius XII, Pope, 118
Planned Parenthood Federation of
    America (PPFA): avoidance of
    religious controversy, 55, 85; beliefs
    of, 17–18; Catholic rapprochement,
    112–113, 114, 118–119; clergy support-
    ers of (See clergy in birth control
    movement; Clergy-Planned Parent-
    hood partnership); coalition strategy
    of, 85–86; conflicts within, 19;
    cultural change and, 194–197; under
    Faye Wattleton's leadership, 164;
    genetic research and, 197–200;
    historical phases of, 17; marital
    status policy of, 99–100, 139; market
    values in, 193–194; mission of, 19–20,
    25–26; philanthropic backers of,
    18–19, 115; public acceptance of, 118;
    religious hostility toward, 3, 162–163,
    164, 166–167; secular culture of, 3, 4,
    6; structure of, 16–17, 19; "Vision
    for 2025" plan, 200. See also
    contraception campaigns
Planned Parenthood Federation of
    America (PPFA), abortion and:
    clergy support for clinics, 139–141,
    151–162, 186–187; clinic services, 138,
    147; commitment to abortion rights,
    147–148; division of opinion, 136–137;

murders of abortion providers,
    172–175; pro-life attack on state
    grants for, 149–151; pro-life demon-
    strations against, 148, 157–158, 186;
    pro-life violence against, 148, 172,
    182; public conference on abortion,
    135–136; referral service, 137–138;
    unmarried women policy, 139
Planned Parenthood Metropolitan
    Washington (PPMW) Church
    Partnership Teen Pregnancy
    Prevention Program, 187, 189
Plato, 203
police raid, 32–34
Poteat, E. McNeill, 37
Potter, Dan, 78–79, 81
Poughkeepsie hospital controversy,
    63–70, 86
Powell, Adam Clayton, Jr., 56
prayer breakfast, 166
Presbyterian churches, 16, 42, 43, 82,
    132, 154, 155, 178
pro-choice movement, 144–145;
    Catholics for a free choice, 146–147;
    clergy recruitment to, 151–162; clergy
    response to religious claims, 175–177;
    Clinton administration and, 171–
    172; Planned Parenthood and, 147;
    Religious Coalition for Reproductive
    Choice, 145–146
Progressive Evangelicals, 197
pro-life movement, 142–143; consti-
    tutional amendments of, 144, 145;
    demonstrations at clinics, 148, 178,
    186; Hyde Amendment, 143–144, 146;
    murders of abortion providers,
    172–175; Planned Parenthood
    funding attacked by, 149–151; in
    presidential elections, 144; religious
    institutions in, 143, 144, 162–163, 167;
    reversal of Roe v. Wade and, 172, 195;
    silence in pre-Roe V. Wade period,
    2–3, 167–168; violent tactics of, 148,
    172, 182

Protestant Council of the City of New
    York, 78, 81, 83, 84, 86
Pyle, Barbara, 134

Quay, Eugene, 123

Rabbis: in birth control movement,
    41, 50–51; in Clergy Consultation
    on Abortion, 132; in pro-choice
    movement, 152, 174, 175, 176, 185–186;
    support for hospital contraceptive
    services, 80, 86. *See also* clergy in
    birth control movement; Clergy-
    Planned Parenthood partnership
racism, 12, 18, 201; eugenics movement
    and, 35–36
Ramsey, Paul, 167
Rappeleye, Willard C., 83
Reagan, Nancy, 199
Reagan, Ronald, 133, 144
Reconstructionist Journal, 176
Reeve, Christopher, 199
Reformed Church of America,
    227n14
religion: conservative denominations,
    216–217n49; cultural change and,
    197–198; fundamentalism, 162–163;
    gender inequality in, 12–14, 201–202;
    humane theology, 188, 190–191;
    market culture of, 194; revival of,
    57, 59
Religious Coalition for Reproductive
    Choice, 145–146, 194–195
Republican Party, antiabortion stance
    of, 144
Reuther, Walter, 22
rhythm method, 32, 52, 112, 118
right-to-life movement. *See* pro-life
    movement
Rishell, Paul W., 81
Ritter, Joseph Cardinal, 112–113
Riverside Church, 15, 37, 52
Robinson, James, 60
Robinson, William, 28

Rock, John, 85, 92, 112, 113, 136
Rockefeller, Nelson, 142
Roe v. Wade, 2, 47, 132, 135, 138; threat
    to overturn, 142–143, 145, 172,
    185–186, 195
Rogers, John F., 63, 64, 67
Roman Catholic Church: abortion
    opposition, 119–120, 123, 143, 144;
    anti-Catholicism and, 48–49;
    anti-modernism of, 50; on in vitro
    fertilization, 197–198; in Maryland,
    92–93; pressure on Protestant
    churches, 53–54; Protestant distrust
    and fear of, 49–50; separate insti-
    tutions of, 49; Vatican II Council,
    85, 92, 111–112, 118
Roman Catholic Church, birth control
    and: in Baltimore welfare system
    contraceptive services case, 90, 94–
    95, 96–97; campaign against repeal
    of Comstock law, 54; Catholic hos-
    pital system doctor dismissal cases,
    61–70; challenge from Protestant
    clergy, 54–55, 60, 71; *Commonweal*
    criticism of Church policy, 82, 85;
    on Episcopal endorsement, 42; in
    New York City hospital contracep-
    tive services case, 75–77, 78, 81,
    84–85; papal encyclical on, 119;
    Planned Parenthood rapproche-
    ment, 112–113, 114, 118–120; position
    on, 31–34, 40–41, 51–54, 119
Roosevelt, Theodore, 109
Roos, Lawrence K., 111
Rose, Kenneth, 54, 55
Rosenberg, Albert A., 64, 67
Rosenberg, Anna, 83
Roudebush, Dorothy S., 111, 112–113
Rusk, Howard A., 83
Ryan, John, 31–32

sacred work: birth control movement,
    23–26; civil rights movement,
    22–23; clergy and, 14–16; defined,

sacred work (*continued*)
  6–7; ethical commandments for,
  7–10; labor movement, 22; ritual
  dimension of, 7; secular leadership
  of, 20–22; sexism and, 10–14
St. Francis Hospital, Poughkeepsie,
  63–70
St. Louis: abortion services in, 138;
  clergy support for Planned Parenthood, 109–110; contraceptive services
  through public health agencies
  controversy, 110–111, 113–114; contraceptive services through welfare
  system controversy, 114; Planned
  Parenthood-Catholic Church
  cooperation in, 112–113, 114; Sanger
  in, 108–109
St. Louis Globe Democrat, 109, 111
St. Louis Post Dispatch, 108, 109
Salvi, John, 172, 173
Sanderson, Robert, 172–173
San Francisco: clergy supporters of
  birth control, 116, 117; contraceptive
  services through hospitals controversy, 116–118; formation of Planned
  Parenthood in, 114–115; Roman
  Catholic Church opposition to
  birth control movement, 115–116;
  wealthy backers of birth control
  movement, 115
Sanger, Ethel, 30, 38
Sanger, Margaret: background of,
  28–29; Bessie Moses and, 90; clerical
  supporters of, 37, 41, 43, 45–46, 47,
  54; Clinical Research Bureau of, 34,
  36; on compulsory sterilization,
  35–36; confrontational strategy of,
  55, 116; contribution of, 37, 44–46;
  disagreements with ABCL leadership, 34; economic reform and,
  38–39; eugenics movement and,
  34–35; feminists and, 214n28; founding of birth control movement,
  29–31; on immigration restriction,

  35; lectures and speeches of, 53–54,
  104–105, 108–109, 125; Martin Luther
  King on, 27; in police raid, 32–33;
  secular views of, 6, 25; at textile
  workers strike, 38; trial of, 30;
  wealthy backers of, 25, 115; on
  women's reproductive freedom, 38;
  women's response to, 39–40
Saratoga Hospital, 155
Saratogian, The, 149, 150, 155, 156
Saunders, Tom, 116
Scopes "monkey" trial, 163
separation of church and state
  argument, 163
Sewell, William, 150
sex education, 61, 100–101, 164;
  abstinence-only programs, 190, 191
sexism: biblical foundation for, 10–12;
  in opposition to reproductive rights,
  4, 140; religious inequality and,
  12–14, 201–202
Sexual Behavior of the Human Female
  (Kinsey), 124
Shaw, Abraham, 93, 101–102
Shelley, John F., 116
Shipler, Guy, 43, 55
Shoemaker, Esther, 106, 107
Shriver, Sargent, 111
Simmons, Paul, 155
Sister M. Ann Roberta, 63, 64, 65, 66
Slepian, Barnett, 173
Smith, Al, 49
Social Gospel ideology, 51
social justice work. *See* sacred work
social purity movement, 28
Society for Humane Abortion,
  125–126
Southern Adirondack Planned
  Parenthood, 149–151
Spellman, Francis Cardinal, 66, 77
Springfield, Oliver L., 62, 63
Spruch, Caren, 165, 166
Starratt, Alfred B., 88, 93
Stein, Francine, 137

About the Author

Tom Davis was ordained into the ministry of the United Church of Christ in July 1960 after graduating from Union Theological Seminary in New York City. Following a brief stint as a campus chaplain at the University of North Carolina at Chapel Hill, he received his doctorate from the Graduate School of Religion at Duke University. A native of Scranton, Pennsylvania, he spent most of his ministry as chaplain and associate professor of religion at Skidmore College in Saratoga Springs. He and his late wife, the Reverend Betsy Davis, also worked in the alcoholism treatment field in the state of New York, where he chaired the first New York State Alcoholism Counselor Credentials Board. Both were members of the Clergy Consultation on Abortion in the late 1960s. From 1992 to 1998 he served on the national board of Planned Parenthood. Currently he is a member of the Religion and Culture Task Force of the National Campaign to Prevent Teen Pregnancy and the national board of the Religious Coalition for Reproductive Choice. He and his wife, Linda Davis, live in Saratoga Springs, New York.

Steinberg, Milton, 52
Steinem, Gloria, 174, 175
stem-cell research, 198–200
sterilization: for birth control, 74–75; compulsory, 35–36
Stone, Hannah, 36
Stone, Robert J., 81
Storer, Horatio, 24
Strauber, Rachel, 165, 166
Swartz, Philip Allen, 65, 69
"Syllabus of Errors", 49–50

Taylor, Gardiner C., 81
Tertullian, 12
textile workers strike, 38
Textile Workers' Union, 53–54
thalidomide, birth defects from, 124
Theological Studies, 168
therapeutic abortion, 73–74, 122–123, 124, 224n42
Thomas, Barbara, 150
Thomas, John L., 118–119
Thorpe, Herbert, 29
Ticktin, Max, 132
Tiller, George, 186
Timanus, L. Cottrell, 136
Time Has Come, The (Rock), 112
Time magazine, 66
Town Hall raid, 32–34
Tribe, Lawrence, 148
Trible, Phyllis, 11
Tucker, Raymond R., 111

Union Theological Seminary, 10, 11, 59
Unitarian churches, 16, 29, 37, 38, 155
United Church of Christ, 16, 145, 154, 155, 199–200
University of Chicago, 132, 133

unmarried women: abortion services for, 139; contraceptive services for, 98–102
unwed mothers, 100–102

Vatican II Council, 85, 92, 111–112, 118
Villiard, Oswald Garrison, 23
Vogt, William, 66, 78

Wagner, Robert, 76, 80, 82, 84, 86
waiting period, 180–181
Walling, William English, 23
Warburg, Paul, 33
Ward, Edgar, 93
War on Poverty, 111
Warren, Earl, 115, 152
Washington Post, 5
Wasson, Carson, 81
Wattleton, Faye, 164, 201
Wealth and Democracy (Phillips), 193
Webster decision, 162, 172
welfare system: Catholic, 49; contraceptive services through, 89–90, 91–92, 94–98, 110–111, 114; unwed mothers and, 100
Wells-Barnett, Ida, 23
Whitridge, John, 96
Wise, Stephen, 41
Wogoman, Paul, 166
Wolkoff, Julie, 157
Woman Rebel, The, 29
women, ordination of, 13–14, 15
Women's Services clinic, 134–135
World Council of Churches, 98

Young Men's Christian Association, 28
Young, N. Louise, 90

Zachar, Howard, 51